Attached at the Heart:

Eight Proven Parenting Principles for Raising Connected and Compassionate Children

(From Preconception to Five Years)

By
Barbara Nicholson and Lysa Parker

D0188384

iUniverse Star
New York   Bloomington

Attached at the Heart

Eight Proven Parenting Principles for Raising

Connected and Compassionate Children

iUniverse Star
an iUniverse, Inc. imprint

iUniverse books may be ordered through booksellers or by contacting:

iUniverse
1663 Liberty Drive
Bloomington, IN 47403
www.iuniverse.com
1-800-Authors (1-800-288-4677)

ISBN: 978-1-935-27886-3 (sc)
ISBN: 978-1-935-27887-0 (ebook)

Library of Congress Control Number: 2009910390

Printed in the United States of America

iUniverse rev. date: 9/29/2009

Endorsements

"Trust me. This is the only baby book you'll ever need! It's amazing, heartwarming, and completely user-friendly. Just add your heart!"

Christiane Northrup, MD,
author of *Mother-Daughter Wisdom*,
The Wisdom of Menopause and
Women's Bodies, Women's Wisdom

"Attachment parenting has worked so well for our family and I'm thrilled that more and more people are becoming familiar with the idea. *Attached at the Heart* will help acquaint parents with principles to ensure connected, confident children and provide them with tools they can use in every relationship or endeavor in their adult lives. I have seen the benefits with my own children and I hope you will find some words of wisdom and useful techniques in this wonderful book."

Melora Hardin
Actress
Plays "Jan" in the hit NBC show, *The Office*

No two babies are born the same—they come with no instructions and no guarantee, and yet parents are expected to raise perfect children every time! Parents have to rely on their instincts, but human instincts are intensely colored by our own childhood experiences of being raised—for better or for worse.

To make raising children even more confusing, there is a bewildering array of conflicting information for parents, the media feeds off stories of family drama and distress, and cultural change during the past thirty years has been so extensive that many family values are often seen as being old-fashioned or outdated. So how do parents cope with the greatest challenge of their lives? How do parents raise children to flourish in the world that they will inherit?

Raising healthy children to become healthy adults requires parents to give babies, toddlers, and small children a prodigious amount of time and appropriate attention. Attachment parenting is not a soft option—yes, it can bring lasting joy, strong family bonds, and immense satisfaction, but, like any worthwhile undertaking, it requires knowledge, commitment, and support to achieve a positive result. Attachment parenting is in many ways the practical application of my father's theory.

In *Attached at the Heart*, Barbara Nicholson and Lysa Parker have gathered from around the world an astonishing array of carefully selected information about parenting babies and toddlers. This thought-provoking anthology has been intelligently organized into "eight principles" that guide readers on a journey of discovery—sometimes reassuring and sometimes a reality check! The authors have managed to précis academic research findings with a light touch and merge them with years of personal experience and of helping countless parents through Attachment Parenting International (API). The depth of knowledge presented in *Attached at the Heart* allows readers to draw their own conclusions about how best to apply the information to their own personal circumstances.

Sir Richard Bowlby, Bt
Son of Dr. John Bowlby

"This is a wise and nurturing book for parents, helping them nurture their children according to their emotional and developmental needs. A much needed guide to attuned parenting. I highly recommend it."

Harville Hendrix, PhD,
Coauthor with Helen LaKelly Hunt
Giving the Love that Heals: A Guide for Parents

Attached at the Heart is the first book to present attachment theory in an accessible and contemporary way. Its 8 Principles are critical guideposts by which parents can light their way to a healthy relationship with their children.

Peggy O'Mara
Editor and Publisher
Mothering magazine

"*Attached at the Heart* is a breathtaking wake-up call for parents and children everywhere. With stunning acuity, scientific insight, and a rare passion, authors Barbara Nicholson and Lysa Parker unlock the keys to creating compassionate, connected families. The result is that there is truly no other parenting book that covers as much crucial ground as deeply, accessibly, and comprehensively as this one. The gift is that they have succeeded in writing a revolutionary book that offers a shining light for parents, and a huge impetus for positive, lasting change."

Lu Hanessian,
Author of acclaimed memoir
*Let the Baby Drive: Navigating
the Road of New Motherhood*
Former NBC anchor, syndicated columnist,
and parent educator

"Here's the book that not only answers your questions about attachment parenting but includes the research that backs it up. *Attached at the Heart* is a gift for all of us looking for practical information on how to strengthen the emotional connections in our families, a powerful and undeniable influence towards achieving a compassionate world."

Marian Tompson,
Cofounder, La Leche League International
Founder and president
AnotherLook at breastfeeding and HIV/AIDS

"Simple changes in the way you parent can make a huge difference in your child's confidence, resilience and ability to love. *Attached at the Heart* is thoroughly loving, compelling and supportive-packed with practical, good-sense advice to help you to strengthen and deepen your child's humanity...every single day."

Harvey Karp, MD, FAAP
Creator of the book/DVD,
The Happiest Baby on the Block

"This is really quite a remarkable book. It's a veritable encyclopedia of attachment parenting. Hard to think of any area not covered, and hard to find any reference that's missing. The style is clear and from beginning to end suffused with the warmth and gentleness of the authors. *Attached at the Heart* will serve as a comprehensive reference resource for attachment parenting parents who want to support their choices with the wide-ranging research that's out there, but hard to find in one place."

Elliott Barker, MD,
Forensic Psychiatrist
Founder, Canadian Society
For the Prevention of Cruelty to Children (CSPCC)

"*Attached at the Heart* communicates an enormous spectrum of information that is valuable and inspirational to parents and professionals. It defines Attachment Parenting in the most comprehensive and profound way. *Attached at the Heart* is an indispensable primer for any new parent."

Isabelle Fox, PhD,
Author
Being There: The Benefits of a Stay-at-Home Parent

"Sometimes, we parents lose sight of just how important we are. *Attached at the Heart* is a loving reminder of how crucial mothers and fathers are to children--and to the human story. Nicholson and Parker have put together an accessible, to-the-point, and inspiring manual that offers practical ways to foster a sense of the sacred in the work of raising children."

Enola Aird,
Director, The Motherhood Project
Visiting Scholar, Judge Baker Children's Center, Boston, MA

"We need to give birth to a new vision of parenting. This vision would be based on what we know about the special bond between parent and child, through which even ordinary communication is a sacrament. It would be based on reverence for what our children can bring to us, as well as what we can bring to them. By their light, we see what is hurt and hidden in ourselves, and we open creatively to new ways of responding to problems. Through them, we understand that parenting is a spiritual process in which we get back tenfold the love we give."

Harville Hendrix, PhD, and Helen Hunt, PhD
Giving the Love that Heals: A Guide for Parents

We dedicate this book to our beloved husbands and children,
for the encouragement and sacrifices they made to help make API and
this book possible:
Gary Nicholson and Jim Parker
Nathan, Travis, Adam, and Luke Nicholson
Jesse and Jamison Parker

You taught us the power of love.

In Loving Memory of
Max Ellendorff and Betty Lowery

Contents

Parents' Call to Arms

The Big Picture: How Parenting Affects Society
Hope for the Future
Why Attachment Parenting?

Charting a New Course: Breaking the Ties that Bind

You Can't Give What You Don't Have
Ghosts from the Past
When "Normal" Childrearing Crosses the Line
Understanding Bonding and Attachment
Nature and Nurture
The Legacy of John Bowlby and Mary Ainsworth
The "Strange Situation"
Attachment: An Idea Whose Time Had Come
Changing Course
API's Eight Principles of Parenting
Appendix to Chapter One: Additional Research and Resource
Recommendations

Principle 1 Prepare Yourself for Pregnancy, Birth, and Parenting: What Every Parent Needs to Know

Planning For Baby—Preparing Your Body, Mind, and Spirit
What Kind of Birth Experience Do I Want?
Ten Steps of the Mother-Friendly Childbirth Initiative for Mother-
Friendly Hospitals, Birth Centers, and Home Birth Services

The "Fussy" Baby
Responding at Night
When Baby's Cries Overwhelm You
Why Do Babies Cry?
Toddlers and Beyond
Responding to Toddler Tantrums and Strong Emotions
Helping Children Learn to Express Feelings
Just for Dads
What about Boys?
How to Be Responsive in Spite of Life's Challenges
Appendix to Chapter Four: Additional Research and Resource
Recommendations

Principle 4 Use Nurturing Touch:
The Healing Power of Physical Closeness

Touch: A Matter of Life and Death
Human Babies—Cache or Carry?
Why Is Touch So Important?
Kangaroo Care
How You Can Provide Nurturing Touch
Infant Massage
"Babywearing"
Nurturing Touch and the Older Child
Appendix to Chapter Five: Additional Research and Resource
Recommendations

Principle 5 Ensure Safe Sleep-Physically and Emotionally: The
Critical Importance of Nighttime Needs

Understanding Infant Sleep Patterns
What Exactly is Cosleeping?
The Benefits of Cosleeping
Are There Dangers with Bedsharing?
America's Anti-cosleeping Campaign
What about Cosleeping with Nonbiological Parents?
Sharing Sleep with Multiples
Establishing Nighttime Routines

The Magic of Lullabies
Developing Healthy Sleep Habits for the Older Child
Transitioning out of the Family Bed
Communicating with Your Partner
Night Waking
Gentle Ways to Get Your Baby to Sleep
The Problem with Sleep Training
Appendix to Chapter Six: Additional Research and Resource
Recommendations

Principle 6 Provide Consistent, Loving Care:
Keeping Your Attachment with Baby Secure

How Stress Affects a Baby's Brain
Studies on Childcare
Working and Alternate Caregivers
Making the Transition to Work
Separations due to Shared Custody
Short-term Childcare Choices
Practical Tips for Short Separations
Appendix to Chapter Seven: Additional Research and Resource
Recommendations

Principle 7 Practice Positive Discipline:
Be the Change You Wish to See

A New Way of Seeing Children
Becoming a Conscious Parent
What is Positive Discipline, and Why is it Important?
The Goal of Positive Discipline
Establishing Boundaries
The Dangers of Traditional Discipline
Why Spanking Doesn't Work
What about "Spare the Rod and Spoil the Child?"
A Look at Discipline through the World's Religions
Rewards and Punishments
The Words We Say
Learning to Express Our Needs

Foreword

Many books have been published (ours included) on the subject of attachment parenting. Each one, as it is released and read and practiced, moves the next one forward a notch, or even a few notches. *Attached at the Heart* takes a giant step in moving forward this critical concept: to parent our children well, we need principles, and we need reasons for those principles. Eight such principles are offered in this book.

This will be an ongoing conversation, because even this book will be better once the concept it defines, using these eight principles, is practiced by more and more parents. The principles will become more compelling; anything that could be added, as we get more practice, will most likely fit into one of these well-thought-out and well-stated principles.

When we stumbled onto a reason to get serious about the way we were being called and stretched beyond the neighborhood parenting norm, we knew we would have to write a book- we got creative with the way we responded to our fourth child's temperament. "Immersion mothering" and "involved fathering" morphed into "attachment parenting" and the 7 Baby Bs. All of this happened in the context of our research laboratory—our own (eventually) eight children and a thriving but focused pediatric practice, where we did a lot of note taking. Those notes wound up in one book after another (including *The Baby Book*), and many of you reading this right now contributed, because you came into our office or talked with us on the phone and told us what worked for your

We ask that you pay attention to and heed well this "call to arms" you see so strongly set forth in *Attached at the Heart* as a sort of parenting "manifesto"—by definition, a public declaration of intentions, purposes, or motives by an important person or group. This important person or group is you, the individual reader, and the parents in our culture who truly want what's best for our children, and who want to change the way our culture raises the next generation. In the process of responding to this call, we will each make this a better world, one family at a time.

Dr. William and Martha Sears

Preface

If we are to reach real peace in this world and if we are to carry on a real war against war, we shall have to begin with children; and if they will grow up in their natural innocence, we won't have to struggle; we won't have to pass fruitless idle resolutions, but we shall go from love to love and peace to peace, until at last all the corners of the world are covered with that peace and love for which consciously or unconsciously the whole world is hungering.

Mahatma Gandhi

Over fifteen years ago, we hatched our idea to "save the world." We were and remain hopelessly optimistic (with occasional bouts of despair) that we can effect change in our society. Both of us are parents, with six sons between us, and we both were teachers with experience on the front lines, which gave us the perspective, determination, and passion to begin a grassroots nonprofit organization called **Attachment Parenting International (API).**

Why did we do it? When we were new mothers, we felt so insecure about our abilities. We just didn't feel knowledgeable or prepared, even though we read just about every book we could get our hands on. We both lived far from other family members, so when we became friends, we glommed onto each other for support. We also found support and education from our local La Leche League group (they teach mothers how to breastfeed).

Our experience with La Leche League prepared us in so many ways and provided us with opportunities to learn from other, more experienced mothers. These experiences gave us confidence and skills to be better mothers. At these monthly meetings, we first learned about attachment parenting and read books by Dr. William and Martha Sears. Their books were like a buoy in the ocean—guiding our way, helping us keep our sanity by giving us reassurance that we were doing the right thing. In time, we learned to trust our own innate wisdom and mothering instincts, which allowed us to connect with our children in ways that we would never have thought possible. Of course, we made a lot of mistakes along the way … just ask our sons. But the fact is that we are better for the experience, and our children are better for our experience.

In the early 1990s, we began to read about kids killing kids and kids killing their parents. What in the world was happening to children that would cause them to commit such heinous crimes? Then we read a book called *High Risk: Children without a Conscience* by Ken Magid and Carol McKelvey. This was the first time we learned about Dr. John Bowlby and *attachment theory*, which hypothesized that the lack of emotional connection created all kinds of emotional and social problems, including violence.

The work of Alice Miller awakened our awareness of the influences of culture on the treatment of children. Until we come to terms with how we were treated as children, we will continue to perpetuate the same attitudes and treatment with our own children. The culture in which we live has tremendous power over us, and it takes consistent and conscious effort to go upstream against the current of popular opinions. Dr. Miller has made it her mission to abolish corporal punishment in every country because she believes that will be the only way we can begin to move forward in eliminating violence toward children.

Given all this information and from our own experiences, we knew in our heart of hearts that attachment parenting was the key to creating emotional connection and making families stronger. We believed (and still do) that if parents are given good information about why it is so important to nurture children, the tools to do it, and parent groups that support them in their choices, then we will have a lot of empowered mothers and fathers. Renowned anthropologist Margaret Mead once said, "Never doubt a small group of committed people can change the world; it indeed is the only thing that ever has." Who knows, we parents might just create a paradigm shift in childrearing.

We began going to the library and spending hours, days, months, and years researching and reading articles, books, and magazines from as far back as the 1940s (this was before the Internet was widely used). We called anyone we thought would give us advice or information, and many were more than happy to talk to us. They shared their wisdom and encouraged us all along the way. *Attached at the Heart* is the culmination of over fifteen years of information gathering, investigative research, and practice. We believe that it is critical for parents to have this information in order to make informed decisions for their children in our increasingly complex society. Until recently, we have heavily relied on and trusted others to know what is best for our children. We can no longer rely on others; we have to educate ourselves and rely on our own knowledge of our children.

Since the early nineties, the world seems to have become worse, not better—even more violent and chaotic. People are looking for answers, for something they can do to change this direction, because we can no longer rely on politics and governments. Many realize that it has to begin with each individual and within each family.

The intent of our book is to give you practical answers to everyday problems and to raise your awareness that you might be more conscious and purposeful in interactions with your children. Unless we understand why we do what we do in regard to children, we will undoubtedly continue the same practices, whether they make sense or not. We will be vulnerable to the advice of others who may say things with authority but without any basis for backing up their advice. This book will give you the evidence you need to feel confident in your decisions.

Attachment parenting is an idea whose time has come. What began at the kitchen table as a simple idea has grown into a worldwide network of parent support groups, a comprehensive support group leader training program, and a new curriculum, and it also serves as a national clearinghouse for parents and professionals. API helps parents with every aspect of parenting, from preconception through the teen years, by providing the latest information and research on parenting practices that strengthen parent-child relationships and families. A nonprofit organization founded in 1994, API offers parents information, education, and support to help them in their parenting journeys and to strengthen their relationships with their children. The basic principles of attachment parenting are a blueprint for change and are discussed in *Attached at the Heart*. Rooted in sound science and common sense, these principles provide a framework of an overarching philosophy—*listen to your baby and trust your instincts*!

We have learned that every family is unique with unique circumstances, that there is no such thing as perfect parents. We always carry with us the legacy of those generations who went before. The way we were parented and the wounds that we carry inevitably work their way into our interactions with our children, which is why it's so important to consciously work on those issues. As you read our book, please know that the principles are not intended to be standards of perfection but rather to be used as guidelines to help you feel informed, validated, supported, and confident in your childrearing decisions. It's so important to base your daily decisions on what will strengthen your attachment with your baby (or child), given the current circumstances. Ask yourself, "Will this strengthen my connection with my baby?"

If the situation is not ideal but necessary, then ask yourself what you can do to minimize the impact of the situation for your baby and what you can do to reconnect with your baby or young child.

Enjoy your baby, knowing that the love you give will come back to you in more ways than you can imagine for generations to come.

Barbara Nicholson and Lysa Parker

Acknowledgments

The principles described in this book were created and defined with the collective effort of many parents actively involved with API—support group leaders, many of whom are professionals in social work, psychology, or child development; lactation consultants; childbirth educators; and advisory and other board members. Many wise women and men contributed to our book, and to them we will always be indebted.

We also wish to thank our advisory board members, who recognized early on the importance of our mission and lent us their moral and professional support:

Elliott Barker, MD, founder of the Canadian Society for the Prevention of Cruelty to Children (CSPCC), without whose initial encouragement we likely would never have started API.

Elizabeth Baldwin, JD (deceased), who provided us with legal advice in our formative years and the courage to keep going.

Stephen Bavolek, PhD, researcher, parent educator, and principal author of the Nurturing Parenting Programs, whose experience and wise counsel has been instrumental in moving us forward from a "mom-and-pop" organization to one of professionalism based on research.

Sir Richard Bowlby, Bt, the son of Dr. John Bowlby, attachment advocate, friend, and ally, whose support and encouragement is a powerful validation of the work of API.

Barbara Clinton, MSW, director of the Center for Health Services at Vanderbilt University, who has always been there for us with her professional and motherly wisdom, our staunchest cheerleader and dear friend.

Isabelle Fox, PhD, psychotherapist, our tireless "ambassador" for API, friend, motivator, and role model of determination and fearlessness.

Jan Hunt, MS, author, founder of The Natural Child Project, friend, and strong advocate for children and families.

Alice Miller, PhD, author, therapist, and child advocate, for her pioneering work in awakening our collective conscience to the damage that has been done to children "for their own good." She has given us the missionary zeal we needed to fully engage in our role as parents and as professionals to get this urgent message out to the world.

Peggy O'Mara, editor of *Mothering* magazine, our friend and sister in this cause.

James McKenna, PhD, friend, outstanding researcher, and fearless advocate for the rights of parents and their babies.

Bruce Perry, PhD, MD, strong voice for abused and traumatized children, whose eloquent words have given new awareness to the plight of children.

Raffi, singer, songwriter, recording artist, author, and children's troubadour, whose passion for children and his mission to promote the importance of honoring children has been a shining example to us and to all parents.

William Sears, MD, and Martha Sears, RN, whose work has given us and millions of parents the ability to see children in a new way and to be better parents. They have stuck with us through thick and thin, providing encouragement and advice when we most needed it. Thank you for being there for us.

Michael Trout, MA, director and founder of the Infant-Parent Institute, an early supporter and mentor who has always been there for us. Your work has been an inspiration.

Karen Walant, PhD, author, psychotherapist, and support group leader who practices what she preaches in her family and in her work. We thank you for your years of support, encouragement, and friendship.

We want to thank our tireless operating board members, past and present, staff, and early supporters, for without their constant handholding, encouragement, and dedication, API would have folded its tent long ago: Julie Artz, Miranda Barone, Rita Brhel, Zan Buckner, Kate Byrne, Adrienne Carmack, Beth Nielsen Chapman, Dave and Perry Clennon, Bill Corbett, Melissa Corbett, Mary Elizabeth Curtner-Smith, Carlotta Crawford, Avril Dannenbaum, Kathy and Joe Diaz, Linda Dicus, Lisa Dietlin, Don Duke, Laura Duke, Susan Esserman-Schack, Christy Farr, Lisa Feiertag, Jill and Danny Flowers, Karen Fletcher, Bob and Isabelle Fox, Ann Fundis, Wendy Goldstein, Michael Gomez, Macall Gordon, Kate Green, Samantha Gray, Lu Hanessian, Sarah Harding, Jane Hardy, Meredith Hays, Barbara Heaney, Molly and Don Henry, P. J. and Reedy

Hickey, Amanda Hughes, Joyce Jackson, Jan Jacobson, Tricia Jalbert, Janet Jendron, Kathleen Kendall-Tackett, Kay and Stephen Knight, Rod Kochtitsky, Alison Krauss, Anna Krimshtein, Nancy Lansdell, Brandy Lance, Minda Lazarov, Nancy LeQuire, Liz Lockard, Dorothy Marcic, Susan Markel, MD, Erika Maxwell, Delbert McClinton, Camille McNutt, Wendy Middlemiss, Jennifer Moquin, Ann Murray, Nancy Nance, Christine Orrall, Stephanie Petters, Lauren Porter, Dave and Stephanie Richardson, Anne Ross, Susan Savage, Amy Silver, Amy Scott, Jeanne Stolzer, Pam Stone, Susan Switzer, Sara Tavernise, Jennie Thompson, Anneloes Tijssen, Marian Tompson, Atsuko Uchida, Ray Westerhoff, Chris Wink and Artemisia Yuen.

We are deeply grateful to the hundreds of API support group leaders, past and present, who donated countless hours to facilitate local support groups in order to provide support and education to parents in their communities.

Most importantly, we want to thank our family members, who patiently supported us in this long, amazing journey: Pauline Ellendorff, Tyler and Lori Ellendorff, John and Toni Lowery, John Lowery, Jr., Kathleen Barnes Lowery, Tim Lowery, Les Baxendale, Charles and Jo Pearce, Gary and Morgan Kendrick, and Austin and Cameron Moore.

Introduction
Parents' Call to Arms

The key to successful parenting is not found in complex theories, elaborate family rules, or convoluted formulas for behavior. It is based on your deepest feelings of love and affection for your child, and is demonstrated simply through empathy and understanding. Good parenting begins in your heart, and then continues on a moment-to-moment basis by engaging your children when feelings run high, when they are sad, angry, or scared. The heart of parenting is being there in a particular way when it really counts.[1]

John Gottman, PhD
Raising an Emotionally Intelligent Child

A mother and father hold their newborn baby for the first time. As they gaze at his little face and body, they are in awe of the miracle of life they have created together. The birth of a baby symbolizes a new beginning, a renewed sense of hope, a sense of life's purpose, and a chance to leave a legacy for family and society. They wonder about the future that will unfold as both they and their baby grow. What kind of parents will they be? What kind of relationship will they have with their child? What kind of adult will their child turn out to be? How do they get there from here?

Parenting is the most important job we will ever have. Yet, in our society, it is one for which we are the least prepared and for which we receive the least support. Babies are born without instruction manuals; every baby is unique, and no one book could possibly teach all that you need to know about your particular child. Only your child can teach you about his needs and personality.

Unfortunately, parents today are challenged from all sides by the variety of childrearing advice that is available. Since many new parents rely on the advice they get from others or from reading parenting books,

---

1   Gottman, *Raising an Emotionally Intelligent Child*, 8.

they come to rely less on their own intuitive feelings or understanding of their child. This advice is often conflicting, so it's no wonder that many parents become confused or misdirected. Too often, the most popular parenting advice is based on someone's opinion rather than common sense and sound science. This undermines new parents' confidence in their own innate knowledge of their children. Even worse, in some cases popular advice is harmful to the child as well as to the parent-child relationship.

The Big Picture: How Parenting Affects Society

Parents can't raise children in a vacuum or expect that what they do within the home has no lasting impact. Most of us have experienced the effects of the way we were parented. Ideally, each generation does a little bit better than the generation before. Unfortunately, we still have a long way to go. As a culture, we seem content to spend billions of dollars trying to fix problems rather than to prevent them. It is our hope that as you read chapter 1 you will recognize the endemic disconnect within our society that is at the roots of many of our social ills and the ways in which you, as a parent, play a role in prevention. We begin by examining the state of children in the United States—our most precious and vulnerable population.

Violence against and by children is committed in many parts of the world, yet the United States has the largest percentages of violence, mental illness, and incarceration of any Western culture. According to the National Council on Crime and Delinquency, "The U.S. has less than 5% of the world's population, but over 23% of the world's incarcerated people." These statistics include the highest rate of incarcerated women in the world.[2]

The Children's Defense Fund keeps national statistics on the welfare of children. They've found that *every day* in America:

- Four children are killed by abuse or neglect
- Five children or teens commit suicide

---

2   Hartney, "U.S. rates of incarceration: A global perspective," National Council on Crime and Delinquency Web site.

- One hundred and ninety-two children are arrested for violent crimes

A barometer of the well-being of a society is its rate of suicide. Children who end their lives are the victims of a very sick society.

Childhelp USA receives over 3 million reports of child abuse each year. It is estimated that the actual rate of child abuse is three times this.

America's Cradle to Prison Pipeline, a 2007 report from the Children's Defense Fund, states, "Our 'child and youth problem' is not a child and youth problem; it is a profound adult problem as our children do what they see us adults doing in our personal, professional, and public lives."[3]

Child and adolescent mental health experts are witnessing ever-rising rates of depression, anxiety, attention deficit disorders, conduct disorders, suicide, and other serious mental, emotional, and behavioral problems in the United States. According to the National Mental Health Association, six million children currently suffer serious emotional and mental health problems. The diagnosis of bipolar depression has increased 4,000 percent over the last five-to-seven years, translating into one million children being treated for bipolar disease alone.[4] Something troubling is happening to our children.

The big question is why? Many experts agree that this crisis is due to children feeling a deep lack of connectedness to their parents and their community. In the *Hardwired to Connect* report released by the Commission on Children at Risk in 2003, over thirty researchers, community leaders, and scholars found that this lack of connectedness was of two kinds, "close connections to people and deep connections to moral and spiritual meaning."[5] These problems cross all racial, cultural, and economic status barriers. They are not limited to the uneducated or to those living in poverty. They reflect a more intrinsic kind of poverty—a poverty of the mind and of the *spirit*.

---

3   "America's Cradle to Prison Pipeline, 2007 Report," Children's Defense Fund Web site.

4   "Medicating Kids," PBS.

5   Commission on Children at Risk, *Hardwired to Connect: The New Scientific Case for Authoritative Communities*, 3.

This information gives you a small snapshot of the lives of millions of children. While it may seem overwhelming, there is something that each of us can do, and it begins with growing a strong and indissoluble bond with our children.

> My mother, a psychotherapist, turned me on to Attachment Parenting and sent us a Sears Book [*The Baby Book*] and a note that said "I'd have half the patients I have now if everyone was raised with Attachment Parenting." And she really believed in it. People in her field talk about it a lot, and the importance of the bond between parent and child, expanding outward to parent and family.[6]
>
> Chris Wink
> Cocreator of Blue Man Group

Hope for the Future

Attached at the Heart is not a typical parenting book. Rather than dictate advice, it calls each of us to look deeper into ourselves and how we raise our children. It asks you to rethink your perception of children and to see the world through their eyes. It sounds the alarm that our children are in trouble and that we, as parents and caregivers, are the only ones in a position to change this spiraling trend. Most of all, it is a book about hope. We can make lasting changes in the world by starting at home and strengthening our loving connections with our children, being more empathic with them and with ourselves.

Attached at the Heart offers hope that we can actively participate in reversing this dangerous trend, first by awakening our understanding of the emotional and psychological needs of babies and young children. Secondly, this book offers strategies that define attachment parenting as a way of helping you nurture these needs, to follow your parenting instincts rather than the dictates of our culture.

When you respond to your children's needs in a sensitive, *respectful,* and developmentally appropriate way, the parent-child relationship—

---

6   Parker, "Happy being blue," *Attachment Parenting: The Journal of API.*

and the family as a whole—is strengthened. A baby's first lessons of empathy and trust are embedded early on from his daily experiences of feeling safe, secure, and protected by his parents. Babies need to know that someone will be there for them when they are in need.

Our purpose in writing *Attached at the Heart* is to inform, support, and empower parents. This book will teach you:

- The importance of being aware of how our own childhood experiences influence the way we parent
- How to become more attuned to your child
- To feel confident that you know your child better than any expert
- How research supports attachment parenting practices and the importance of sharing this information with pediatricians and other health care providers
- The importance of making informed decisions about your children without fear of intimidation by others
- How to actively improve your family relationships and communities

Why Attachment Parenting?

As you read this book, you will learn about those who came before us and pioneered the way for children and families. Numerous scientists and leaders have long believed that the parent-child relationship holds the key to the very survival of humanity; some believe it is the key to world peace. We call the type of parenting these scientists have observed in peaceful cultures around the world "attachment parenting."

Why is it called attachment parenting? This style of parenting is designed to stimulate the optimal development of children. It calls for a new consciousness in childrearing and encourages parents to learn to trust their intuitive knowledge of their child to build a strong foundation of trust, allowing the child to develop his capacities for empathy and compassion for others. Attachment parenting will help you create a strong emotional connection or "attachment" with your baby, empowering you as a parent and strengthening your family. Many parents have found that attachment parenting has helped them heal from their own childhood wounds by allowing them to give nurturance to their child that they didn't receive, at the same time educating them about new positive ways of childrearing and communicating. Attachment parenting gives parents "permission" to fall in love with their baby instead of worrying that they might spoil him. When we invest our time in children's early years, we can take comfort in knowing that strong attachment relationships will positively influence your child's future relationships.

The concept of attachment parenting holds tremendous power—in the process of raising our children, we raise ourselves. Gandhi once said, "Be the change you want to see in the world." This sentence can easily be paraphrased to say, "Become the kind of adult you want your child to be." Gandhi understood the power of example that we as parents must provide—the onus is laid squarely on the shoulders of each and every one of us. Children will model our behavior before they will heed our words.

We want to make it clear, however, we are all a work in progress, and we do the best we can with what we know and where we are in our parenting journey. Attachment parenting is not a panacea for all problems, but it provides a good start in giving our children the most loving environment possible to achieve their fullest potential. As our children grow, they will make mistakes as part of their process of discovering who they are—our job is to maintain the heart connection and be there for them when they need us. It may take a few generations to really see the long-term benefit of our efforts, especially if there is a family history of dysfunction, depression, or addictions. Genetic influences such as a child's temperament also play a major role in how he experiences his home environment and the powerful forces of the culture.

Each of us has the potential to change the course of our familial inheritance and the hidden potential within ourselves and our children, but we can't and shouldn't do it alone. We are social beings who need to be connected to others; we need an extended family. There is power in parents helping other parents that builds their confidence and skills. Our goal at Attachment Parenting International (API) is to create a tipping point of change in our society, to transform a world of war and violence into a world of compassion and peace. *It can be done, and we hope you will join us.*

Chapter One

Charting a New Course:
Breaking the Ties that Bind

Charting a New Course: Breaking the Ties that Bind

> *I know the kind of parent I would like to be. I also know*
> *the kind of parent I do* ***not*** *want to be. Many times I*
> *am proud of how we value our children's nature and*
> *avoid doing what was done to us. There are times (more*
> *frequent than I'd like to admit) that I feel hopelessly*
> *adrift and I don't know where I lost my way. I don't*
> *want to do what was done to me, but the power of that*
> *programming is there and it's not easy to ignore.*[1]
>
> Macall Gordon
API News

Don't most of us have the same feelings about being a parent? We want to be good parents; some strive to be a "super parent," while others are just trying to keep their heads above water. The majority of us had no clue what to expect when we became parents because we had little to no experience with babies or children. Maybe you have read a few books here and there, but without prior experience, there's no way of really understanding the day-to-day reality. Most people don't think to discuss the kind of parent they want to be before having children, nor do they discuss the kind of adult they want their child to become. For many parents, the first baby they ever hold is their own. Strangely, we begin this incredible, lifelong journey that radically changes us as adults and most definitely has a lasting effect on our children (not to mention society as a whole) without any experience and very little knowledge.

---

1   Gordon, "Breaking the Ties that Bind," *API News*.

You know you are face-to-face with the unfinished business of your own childhood when you respond with strong negative feelings to your child's behavior…. Disproportionate levels of fear, sadness, anger, or, conversely, elation or relief are signals to the parent that he has just activated an old wound and might do well to investigate further.[2]

Harville Hendrix, PhD, and Helen Hunt, PhD
Giving the Love that Heals: A Guide for Parents

The most natural thing we do is raise our children the way we were raised. You are less likely to be troubled by conflicting advice if you had nurturing childhood experiences. Adults who had difficult childhoods for any reason—trauma, abuse, neglect, or separation due to divorce, for example—may have some challenges to overcome.

You Can't Give What You Don't Have

For some families, implementing attachment parenting practices just seems natural, like it's the right thing to do. However, many parents find it difficult to give emotionally to their children, especially if they didn't receive love and nurturing as a child. All those memories that were thought to be buried may resurface when you become a parent. Children's behavior at certain ages can trigger old wounds or "buttons." When children "push your buttons," it's usually because those buttons were installed a long time ago. You may have *thought* you had them under control—until you find yourself becoming angry, overreacting, or becoming irrational. These buttons, or unresolved issues, are what some call our "ghosts" from childhood. Our early childhood experiences

---

2   Hendrix and Hunt, *Giving the Love that Heals*, 96.

create powerful forces that are extremely difficult to overcome on one's own and will often require professional help. The first step toward healing is becoming aware—a person has to be conscious and aware of the past in order to not repeat it. For those parents who desire to break the cycle of abuse, becoming a parent can be the impetus for change.

Ghosts from the Past

It isn't necessarily just overt abuse or neglect that is damaging. Culturally accepted parenting practices can also be abusive or neglectful. These practices have deep roots that go back hundreds of years and have become traditional and are now being recognized by some as "normative abuse."[3] In most cases, parents cared for their children the way they were told to by the parenting experts of their day. In many cases, they were doing the best they could with what they knew. Similarly, now that we know better, we must try to do better for our children.

When we spoil something, we deny it the conditions
it requires.... The real spoiling of children is not in
the indulging of demands or the giving of gifts, but in
the ignoring of their genuine needs.[4]
Gordon Neufeld, PhD, and Gabor Maté, MD
Hold On to Your Kids

Beginning the process of raising awareness starts with understanding how so many of us got to this point of trying to overcome our past. Until the evolution of our modern Western culture, children had to grow up fast and get to work, usually on the family farm. By the time they were

---

3   Walant, *Creating the Capacity for Attachment: Treating Addictions and the Alienated Self,* 8.
4   Neufeld and Maté, *Hold On to Your Kids,* 185.

eight, nine, or ten years old, their childhoods were over. The period we call adolescence is a stage of development rather newly identified by child development researchers. With the identification of this new stage of development, coupled with new laws earlier in the twentieth century to protect children from abusive work practices, children were allowed to enjoy a longer childhood. All along the way, attitudes about children and parenting practices were largely influenced by strict religious dogma, or experts in the fields of psychology and human development such as Sigmund Freud, L. Emmet Holt and John Watson, the "father" of behaviorism. Their parenting advice had negative and devastating effects on children and their families—sometimes for generations—ranging from sexualizing children to treating them as objects.

So over the years, thousands of parenting books have been written, each claiming to have the answer to raising "good," obedient children, leaving many parents confused, anxious, or guilty and many children feeling disconnected from their parents. For hundreds of years, the treatment of children in many cultures has been harsh and disturbing. We know that the residuals of some of those abusive practices are still present today. Great strides have been made in the treatment of children, but we still have a long way to go.

One classic example comes from the work of psychologist John B. Watson, who admonished parents not to hug, coddle, or kiss their infants and young children in order to train them to develop good habits early on. In 1928, Watson published his hugely popular childcare book, called *Psychological Care of Infant and Child.*

> Treat them as though they were young adults. Dress them; bathe them with care and circumspection. Let your behavior always be objective and kindly firm. Never hug and kiss them, never let them sit on your lap. If you must, kiss them once on the forehead when they say goodnight. Shake hands with them in the morning. Give them a pat on the head if they have made an extraordinary good job of a difficult task.[5]

---

5   Watson, *Psychological Care of Infant and Child*, 81–82.

In her book *Breaking the Silence*, actress and comedian Mariette Hartley writes about the heartbreaking legacy for her family and millions of other families created by the advice of her maternal grandfather, John Watson, or "Big John," as she called him.

> In Big John's ideal world, children were to be taken
> from their mothers during their third or fourth
> week: if not, attachments were bound to develop. He
> claimed that the reason mothers indulged in baby-
> loving was sexual. Otherwise, why would they kiss
> their children on the lips? He railed against mothers
> whose excessive affection made the child forever
> dependent and emotionally unstable. Children should
> never be kissed, hugged, or allowed to sit on their
> laps.
>
> My mother's upbringing was purely intellectual. The
> only time my mother was "kissed on the forehead"
> was when she was about twelve and Big John went to
> war. Although she was reading the newspaper by the
> time she was two, there was never any touching, not
> any at all. Grandfather's theories infected my mother's
> life, my life, and the lives of millions.
>
> How do you break a legacy? How do you keep from
> passing a debilitating inheritance down, generation to
> generation, like a genetic flaw?[6]

Suicide and depression have been the legacies left her by her family, having lost her father, an uncle, a cousin, and almost her mother. Not without her own emotional "demons," Mariette Hartley was able to break the chain through therapy and raising her awareness about life, love, and spirit. She became a loving mother of two children and continues to work as a successful actress while donating her time to suicide prevention.

---

6   Hartley, *Breaking the Silence*, 18.

When "Normal" Childrearing Crosses the Line

Watson's legacy, like others', continues to permeate our cultural psyche in many ways—how we view children, how we speak to them, and how we treat them. In order to discipline children, our culture has accepted numerous ways of keeping kids in line. They are often talked down to or spoken to harshly, hit, humiliated, shamed, ignored, and, in some extreme cases, tortured, such as by placing hot sauce on a child's tongue or forcing a child to stand for long periods of time with his arms straight out. A nurse and lactation consultant at a local hospital recently shared this example:

> I went into a mother's hospital room to help her with
> breastfeeding, and I saw her three-year-old daughter
> with her back to the wall with her arms straight
> out in front of her. I asked the mother if her child
> was playing a game, but she said, "No, she's being
> punished for misbehaving. She has to stand there for
> five minutes." It struck me that the mother thought
> there was absolutely nothing wrong with how she was
> disciplining her child.

These abusive forms of discipline have been so much a part of our culture that we sometimes don't think twice about it. We have learned to desensitize ourselves to the actual physical and emotional pain that it causes children. After all, that's how we were raised, and we turned out okay—right? Maybe we were lucky and turned out well in spite of how we were treated; maybe we still suffer in ways we don't realize are connected to our early childhood years. Some of us were lucky enough to have strong, loving families with parents who did the best they could with what they knew then. We can understand that, embrace it, and even forgive because we know that there are no perfect parents, and their love far outweighs anything else.

Child abuse is a huge epidemic in the United States. Every day, four children die from abuse, and of these, three out of four are under the age of four.[7] We tend to think it only happens in families in poverty, but child abuse crosses all social, educational, and economic barriers and ranges from benign neglect to physical abuse.[8] If we are serious about breaking the cycle of abuse, we have to begin in the family. The Web site Child Welfare Information Gateway lists "nurturing and attachment" as one of the primary factors in preventing child abuse.[9]

Research has demonstrated that five important factors can help families protect children from the risk of child abuse and neglect. [S]trategies to develop and enhance these five factors include: [10]

1. Nurturing and attachment
2. Knowledge of parenting and of child and youth development
3. Parental resilience
4. Social connections
5. Concrete supports for parents

A growing number of therapists are determined to bring attention to the dangers of "normal," or traditional, parenting. In her book *Creating the Capacity for Attachment,* Dr. Karen Walant first described this type of treatment as "normative abuse."

> Our culture allows for a certain threshold of parenting
> practices that I term *normative abuse.* Normative,
> because these are included in some of the basic

---

7   "National child abuse statistics," 2005, Childhelp Web site.

8   "Child abuse and neglect fatalities: Statistics and interventions," Child Welfare Information Gateway Web site.

9   "Protective Factors for Promoting Healthy Families". Child Welfare Information Gateway Web site.

10 Child Welfare Information Gateway, "Promoting healthy families in your community," Prevent Child Abuse Web site.

tenets of child-raising that are endorsed by the
culture in which we live. Normative, because, like
the generations before that believed "a child should
be seen and not heard," these are parts of current
parenting philosophy. Normative, because these are
often tiny moments in a child's life, moments that
may be followed by a loving interaction or a sweet
caress. Normative abuse occurs when the attachment
needs of the child are sacrificed for the cultural
norms of separation and individuation. Normative
abuse occurs when parental instinct and empathy are
replaced by cultural norms.[11]

The word abuse is defined as *treating a living creature, whether animal or human, in a harmful, injurious, or offensive way.*[12] Dr. Walant acknowledges that though normative abuse in and of itself may not be *as* traumatizing as verbal, physical, or sexual abuse, it still has its damaging effects on the overall healthy development of the child.[13] Often we don't realize that damage is being done because we cannot see it.

Yelling, spanking, jerking, slapping, shaming, and humiliating are all ways that we can harm a child's dignity and our emotional connection. (Read more about the effects of physical punishment in chapter 8.) You may know parents who are firm in their belief about the use of corporal punishment and crying-it-out methods as forms of discipline. Our goal is not to be judgmental or make this an indictment against parents who hold these beliefs. We've done some of the same things with our own children out of lack of knowledge and understanding. Our intent in writing this book is to raise awareness. Only when a person's awareness is raised can he begin to make conscious changes in behavior. So how do we get there from here?

---

11 Walant, *Creating the Capacity for Attachment: Treating Addictions and the Alien-ated Self,* 8.

12 "abuse", Dictionary.com Web site.

13 Ibid.

Understanding Bonding and Attachment

Scientists haven't always been aware of attachment in humans but have long recognized the "bonding" that occurs in other mammals right after birth. You may have watched a family dog or cat have babies and noticed how the mother instinctively knew what to do—licking, cuddling, nursing, and protecting. You may have also observed that the babies had their own way of telling the mother what they needed—squeaking, crawling to get closer to the mother, searching for the nearest nipple to suck. Once satisfied, they become perfectly calm and contented. Over time, as the babies grew, you may have noticed a special bond that deepened as they developed; the mother acting very protective and caring while the offspring begin to explore and test their new skills, working toward their independence.

That special bond is called *attachment*, and it is a process that continues for a much longer time in human babies, usually for the first three to five years of life. Why so long? Because only 25 percent of the brains of human infants are developed at birth, which means they will, in a very real sense, continue their gestation outside of the womb, much like a baby kangaroo. Kangaroos are extremely dependent upon the mother for a much longer time than other mammals. Even chimpanzees, our closest genetic relatives, who are born with 75 percent of their brains developed at birth, remain very close to their mothers for several years.

Only in the last sixty years or so have professionals in the fields of psychology, anthropology, child development, and social work begun to recognize and accept how vital this process is in determining who we become. We are learning that attachment is at the core of our humanity.

Nature and Nurture

In the ideal home environment, babies flourish; their cognitive, emotional, and physical needs are being met by loving parents as they experience trust, empathy, and affection. They are stimulated and eager to learn new skills. During the first three years, under these conditions, their brains grow at the fastest rate of their lives—millions of cells waiting for "marching orders" before the brain starts pruning back unused cells. Brain cells designed for language and vision, if not stimulated by the environment by the age of six or seven, disappear forever. Children who are not spoken to or are not modeled language will lose the ability to speak, as scientists have learned from observing feral (wild) children and children neglected in orphanages. The brain is a "use it or lose it" organ, but it's also highly adaptable to even the most adverse of environmental conditions.

The "use it or lose it" principle also applies to learning empathy, affection, and other positive aspects of social interactions and relationships. Brain researchers have found that a baby receives all kinds of sensory information from his mother's face and tone of voice, which is simultaneously associated with the physical sensations the baby is experiencing. If children do not receive love, affection, and responsiveness from their parents (or primary caregivers), or if they experience significant trauma and abuse, they may never learn what it means to love, to be affectionate, or to have empathy for another human being. All the while, their brains are adapting to their experiences (hardwiring), internalizing what their parents have modeled for them, making it more difficult to change as they grow older.

What is most striking is that neuroscientists have found the critical period for the development of certain parts of the brain coincides precisely with the critical period for attachment development—during the first three years of life.[14] One such part is the orbitofrontal cortex, located above the eyes in the forehead area between the left and right hemispheres. Dr. Allan Schore, from the Department of Psychiatry and Biobehavioral Sciences at the UCLA School of Medicine, has described the orbitofrontal cortex as the key component to infant attachment and emotional regulation, playing a central role in the development of empathy and emotional memory.[15] The neurons located in this area are particularly sensitive to the emotional expressions of the human face. Schore believes that the effects of the attachment relationship and the process of mother-infant attunement have a direct impact on the development of the orbitofrontal cortex.[16]

---

14   Karr-Morse and Wiley, *Ghosts from the Nursery*, 37.

15   Siegel, *The Developing Mind: How Relationships and the Brain Interact to Shape Who We Are*, 140–141.

16   Schore, "The experience-dependent maturation of a regulatory system in the orbital prefrontal cortex and the origin of developmental psychopathology," *Development and Psychopathology*.

Not only is the brain affected by the child's environment, but so is his genetic code. In their book *The Relationship Code*, psychologist David Reiss and his colleagues at George Washington University describe the results of their twelve-year genetic study of parenting influences on genetic traits. "Many genetic factors, powerful as they may be in psychological development, exert their influence only through the good offices of the family; we'll be changing a genetic trait by changing the family environment."[17] In other words, "How parents treat a child can shape which of his genes turn on."[18]

New research in the fields of neuroscience, genetics, child development, and psychology continues to provide evidence that there is a lot at stake for children and society. This is where the theory of attachment provides the glue that holds all the elements of child development together.

Just as children are absolutely dependent on their
parents for sustenance, so in all but the most
primitive of communities, are parents, especially their
mothers, dependent on a greater society for economic
provision. If a community values its children, it must
cherish their parents.[19]

John Bowlby
Maternal Care and Mental Health

---

17 Reiss et al., *The Relationship Code*, 49.

18 Begley, "The nature of nurturing," *Newsweek*.

19 Bretherton, "The origins of attachment theory: John Bowlby and Mary Ainsworth," *Developmental Psychology*.

The Legacy of John Bowlby and Mary Ainsworth

Two historical figures are largely responsible for our current understanding of children and what drives human relationships. In the late 1930s and 1940s, it was common for children to be admitted into hospitals without visitations by mother or father for long periods of time. It was the highest priority that hospitals remain germ-free, so parents were only allowed to visit once a week. Nurses were in charge of the physical care of infants and young children, but they didn't have time to hold or coddle the children as they had to keep up with their rigid schedules. As a result, the children began to deteriorate emotionally very quickly. They became sad, depressed, fearful, and unresponsive. James Robertson, a concerned individual in London, England, filmed this process and then shared the film with a British psychiatrist named John Bowlby. These films so disturbed and intrigued Dr. Bowlby that they led to his life's work of advocating for children and parents. Bowlby is considered the founder or father of attachment theory. It was his study of young delinquent boys that led him to understand the links between prolonged early separation from the mother (or primary caregiver) and later "affectionless character." His work was so radical that he was ostracized by fellow psychiatrists, who refused to believe that the environment had anything to do with how children turned out. Rather, they believed it was their genetic makeup.

Throughout it all, Bowlby never wavered in his convictions and maintained his position with confidence and dignity. Still, he had no way of actually proving his theory until Mary Ainsworth came into his life.

Dr. Mary Ainsworth, who was originally from Ohio and educated at the University of Toronto, accompanied her husband to England where she began working for Bowlby as a research assistant. She later went to Uganda to study the weaning practices of mothers and realized that she was witnessing the natural process of attachment (bonding) of babies and mothers. Ainsworth used this knowledge to develop a procedure to assess the quality of the child's attachment to the mother called the "Strange Situation." Thousands of research studies later, this instrument is still being used today and continues to validate Bowlby's early conclusions.

The "Strange Situation"

Researchers have learned that the attachment process is a reciprocal one. In other words, both parent and child take turns initiating cues (signals) and responses—baby smiles, mother smiles back; baby cries, father picks baby up to comfort; baby signals he is hungry, parent responds by feeding; baby gazes at father, father gazes back, responding with loving interactions. All of these seemingly mundane daily activities are the basic elements of creating a secure attachment. It is not only the bond that the child feels toward the parent, but the bond that the parent feels toward the child. Bowlby and Ainsworth learned from studies done in Uganda and in the United States that attachment relationships fit fairly clearly into three categories: secure, insecure ambivalent, and insecure avoidant.[20]

The Strange Situation allowed them to demonstrate that babies behaved in different ways, depending on their relationships with their parents. This procedure is intended to stress the baby for a minute or two by putting the baby with a stranger in a strange location without the mother. The keys to the procedure are 1) record how confidently/ effectively the baby is able to separate from the mother and resume play and exploration of the toys, and 2) record the mother's ability to sooth the baby on reunion. It is the detail of the reunion with mother that is the key to assessing the quality of the baby's attachment to mother—secure or insecure. Securely attached babies will likely cry and protest strongly and quickly (other researchers believe that temperament and gender also play a role in their reactions). The babies become extremely upset, but when the mother returns (within a minute or so), they are quickly quieted and resume playing. Ainsworth noted that these children were the most nurtured at home as well.[21] It is an amazing process to watch, knowing that every action and reaction tells a part of the story.

The findings during the test by no means reflect that the parent-child relationship will always remain secure or insecure since home environments are always subject to change, but it gives a good indication of the parent-child relationship at the time of the assessment and what could be a continuing pattern of interactions.

---

20   Ainsworth et al, *Patterns of Attachment*, 347–362.
21   Karen, *Becoming Attached*, 147–163.

The three categories of attachment that Bowlby and Ainsworth created based on their observations are described here. Within each category, there can be varying degrees of attachment.

1. **Secure Attachment.** The infant actively explores, gets upset when mother leaves, is happy upon reunion, and seeks physical contact with mother. Mothers of secure babies are typically loving and responsive to their infant, quick to pick them up when they cry, and hold them longer and "with more apparent pleasure."[22] [23] [24]

2. **Insecure-Ambivalent (Anxious/Resistant) Attachment.** The infant stays close to mother, explores to a limited extent, becomes very distressed upon separation, and is ambivalent toward mother upon reunion but remains near her. Mothers of anxious babies were observed to be "more mean-spirited to merely cool, from chaotic to pleasantly incompetent. Though well-meaning, these mothers have difficulty responding to their babies in a loving, attuned, consistent way."[25] [26] [27]

3. **Insecure-Avoidant Attachment.** These infants show little distress when separated, ignore the mother's attempts to interact, and are often sociable with strangers or may ignore them as they ignore their mother. These mothers often have an aversion to physical contact themselves and speak sarcastically to their babies.[28] [29]

22 Ainsworth et al, *Patterns of Attachment*, 347–362.
23 Shaffer, *Developmental Psychology: Childhood and Adolescence*, 412–413.
24 Karen, *Becoming Attached*, 159.
25 Ainsworth et al, *Patterns of Attachment*, 347–362.
26 Shaffer, *Developmental Psychology: Childhood and Adolescence*, 413.
27 Karen, *Becoming Attached*, 159.
28 Ainsworth, et al, *Patterns of Attachment,* 347–362.
29 Karen, *Becoming Attached*, 160.

A fourth category was added years later by Dr. Mary Main and her colleagues.

4. **Insecure-Disorganized/Disoriented.** These infants are the most distressed upon separation and are considered the most insecure. They seem confused upon reunion or would "act dazed or freeze"; they might "move closer but then abruptly move away as the mother draws near ..." exhibiting behaviors that appear to be a combination of resistant and avoidant.[30]

Attachment: An Idea Whose Time Had Come

Ironically, during the time Bowlby and Ainsworth were researching attachment theory, similar observations were being made in other parts of the world by professionals ranging from psychiatrists to anthropologists. Studying the dominant parenting practices of cultures around the world has given researchers deeper insights as to why some societies are aggressive and others nonaggressive. In his book *Learning Non-Aggression,* anthropologist Ashley Montagu answers the question of why aggression and violence are totally nonexistent in some nonliterate cultures:

> Years ago Margaret Mead was the first anthropologist to inquire into the origins of aggressiveness in non-literate societies.... [S]he pointed to the existence of a strong association between child-rearing practices and later personality development. The child who received a great deal of attention, whose every need was promptly met, as among the New Guinea Mountain Arapesh, became a gentle, cooperative, unaggressive adult. On the other hand, the child who received perfunctory, intermittent attention, as among the New Guinea Mundugomor, became a selfish, uncooperative, aggressive adult.[31]

---

30   Shaffer, *Developmental Psychology: Childhood and Adolescence,* 413.
31   Montagu, *Learning Non-Aggression: The Experience of Non-Literate Societies,* 7.

Fully recognizing that there are no perfect cultures, through the years we have collected stories from around the world that have indirectly illustrated and validated attachment parenting principles. One of these stories takes place at the end of World War II, when a navy psychiatrist named James Clark Moloney was stationed in Okinawa. He and another doctor were told to be prepared for the devastation they were to see—horrible bombings had forced thousands of people to flee to caves and the wilderness areas, exposing them to starvation, life-threatening injuries, and illness. They were told to expect that the psychological impact would be just as horrific, but to their amazement they found that the people were, for the most part, psychologically healthy. As Dr. Moloney started investigating why the Okinawan people had survived so amazingly well, he found that before the war they had no psychological wards in their hospitals, and there had only been one murder in their largest city in the last seventy-five years.

Dr. Moloney felt a key component to the mental health of the Okinawans was how they parented their children. In contrast to the West, where bottle-feeding was quickly becoming the norm, Okinawan mothers breastfed, not only to nourish their babies but also to give comfort. He noticed how the mothers would carry their babies on their backs in beautiful fabric carriers and let them nurse whenever they needed—not on a strict schedule. Most babies were nursed until at least two years of age or older, and if the babies were not with the mother, they were carried by another family member—always in contact with someone they knew and trusted. Moloney was also impressed by the respect the adults showed for the children—for example, once when he was photographing a young child, he asked the father for permission to film. The father requested that he ask the child's permission—a revelation for this American doctor! Moloney reported that he never saw the use of physical discipline like spanking and referred to the Okinawans as "permissive" compared to standards in the United States. They talked to their children rather than using physical force, threats, or coercion. In spite of the fact that the parents were so "permissive," the children were very well-behaved and rarely cried. He became convinced that their style of parenting was the key to world peace.

Dr. Moloney traveled the countryside for many months, interviewing and documenting his findings in a film called *The Okinawan*. With great enthusiasm and hope, he then took this documentary back to the United States and showed it to standing-room-only audiences in medical schools all over the country. People were fascinated by this "strange" way of raising children, but Moloney's observations were quickly rejected by most in the medical community. However, a small group of doctors at Wayne State University, all members of a group called "The Cornelian Corner," were very supportive and became one of the first groups of mental health professionals to support his conclusions. They taught a few American mothers the Okinawan style of parenting and conducted their own research.[32]

An account of Dr. Moloney's experiences was written in an article published in the November 1949 issue of *Better Homes and Gardens* magazine, titled "Is Your Wife Too Civilized?" To illustrate Dr. Moloney's concept of the Okinawan style of parenting, *Better Homes and Gardens* used a photo of a young American mother with her baby happily secured to her back with a cloth fabric carrier—a very unusual sight in 1949! What Dr. Moloney was promoting then is very similar to what we call attachment parenting today. These pictures show an Okinawan mother wearing her baby on her back, an American mother wearing her baby in the 1940s, and a mother today wearing her baby in a sling.

---

32 "The Cornelians," *Time* magazine Web site.

Traditional Okinawan mother wearing her baby From *Better Homes and Gardens*, November 1949

American mother wearing her baby From *Better Homes and Gardens*, November 1949

Today's AP mother with baby in a sling

In his lifetime, Dr. Moloney didn't witness an overwhelming acceptance of the Okinawan style of parenting, but in the early 1960s he learned about the founding of a mother's breastfeeding group in Chicago called La Leche League International (LLLI) and spoke at one of their first conferences. LLLI was the primary organization promoting attachment parenting until API was founded in 1994. Our culture is at last incorporating some of these ideas, and we are gradually becoming a more nurturing society!

World War II created so much devastation to the world population that scientists and researchers from around the world found unprecedented opportunities to explore and examine human behavior in a variety of contexts. The work of Dr. Alice Miller has greatly shown how culture shapes our attitudes about children. In her book, *For Your Own Good: Hidden Cruelty in Child-Rearing and the Roots of Violence,* she gives us unsettling insight into prewar Germany and the parenting practices that were common at the turn of the twentieth century. She was fascinated that an entire society could fall under the spell of such an extremely authoritarian dictator, and she warns that unless we become more conscious in our parenting, we are destined to repeat the mistakes of past generations.

Dr. Miller researched some of the most popular parenting books in Germany during the years prior to and at the time Hitler and his counterparts were children. She included passages from "parenting experts" of the day in her book, a fascinating yet sad prediction of what laid the foundation for the Holocaust. In the latter part of the 1800s, Dr. Daniel Schreber wrote one of the most popular parenting books of the time, which went through forty printings and was translated into several languages. His advice sounds eerily similar to some parenting books that are on the shelves today.

Here is an example of his advice (emphasis added):

> The little ones' display of temper as indicated by screaming or crying without cause should be regarded as the first test of your spiritual and pedagogical principles.... [N]ow you should no longer simply wait for it to pass, ... but should proceed in a somewhat more positive way by stern words, threatening gestures, rapping on the bed, ... or, if none of this helps, by appropriately mild corporal punishments repeated persistently at brief intervals until the child quiets down or falls asleep.... This procedure will be necessary only once or at most twice, and then you will be master of the child forever. *From now on, a glance, a word, a single threatening gesture will be sufficient to control the child.*[33]

Of course, parents must create safe, developmentally appropriate boundaries for their children. More about this is discussed in chapter 8, Practice Positive Discipline. However, the key goal here is to control the child's will before he remembers that he has a will. Domination, veneration for authority, and blind obedience are a recipe for creating a nation ripe for an authoritarian dictator, and, unfortunately, that's exactly what happened under Hitler's rule. Tragically, just like the children of American psychologist John Watson, Dr. Schreber's own children suffered from severe mental illness as adults—one committed suicide and one became a famous patient of Sigmund Freud.[34]

---

33 Miller, *For Your Own Good*, 5.

34 Freud, *The Schreber Case*.

Changing Course

The good news is that a growing number of parents and professionals have become increasingly interested in a style of parenting that actively promotes compassionate, respectful treatment of children and provides the much needed support for the attachment relationship. The characteristics of this style of parenting are a hallmark of peaceful societies around the world and are more conducive to cooperation, compassion, and peace within the family and society. These practices have been used in some form for thousands of years—some call this kind of parenting "conscious parenting," "natural parenting," "compassionate parenting," or "empathic parenting"—some Native Americans refer to it as "original parenting." In many languages around the world, the word "parenting" doesn't exist. They don't try to define it—it's just something that comes naturally.

The most popularized term today for this style of parenting is attachment parenting (AP), which incorporates what we believe to be the best of most parenting practices from around the world and which have increasingly been validated by research in many fields of study, such as child development, psychology, and neuroscience.

Attachment parenting is a term that was created by pediatrician William Sears and his wife, Martha, a registered nurse, over twenty-five years ago, early in their book-writing career. Martha told us the story of how they came up with the term:

> When Bill wrote *Creative Parenting* (1982), he referred to it as "immersion mothering" and "involved fathering." At a talk one time in Pasadena, a grandmother came up to Bill and said she thought the term immersion mothering was a good one, because some moms find themselves "in over their heads."
>
> When he told me of this, I realized we needed to change the term to something more positive (!), so we came up with AP, since the Attachment Theory literature was so well researched and documented, by [John] Bowlby and others.

William and Martha Sears structured the practice of attachment parenting on what they call "The Baby Bs" and offer them to parents as tools to help them build lasting bonds with their children. The Baby Bs are listed in their book, *The Attachment Parenting Book.* The basis for these tools came from observing and talking to the many parents in their practice who had great relationships with their children. API has, with their blessing and support, used the Baby Bs and expanded them to include additional information that we believe to be important. We have structured them into the eight principles of parenting to provide guidance for parents as they face serious decisions and cultural pressures on a daily basis. These principles were created through the lens of attachment research and are designed to help parents become more attuned and connected to their children.

API's Eight Principles of Parenting

1. Prepare yourself for pregnancy, birth, and parenting
2. Feed with love and respect
3. Respond with sensitivity
4. Use nurturing touch
5. Ensure safe sleep-physically and emotionally
6. Provide consistent, loving care
7. Practice positive discipline
8. Strive for balance in your personal and family life

The eight principles of parenting have been developed for infants and young children up to the age of five years or for as long as you, as a parent, feel they apply. It is our hope and plan to expand these principles for preteens, teens, and adults. The core values will never change—respect, empathy, and affection. We like to think of AP as practicing the *golden rule* of parenting—treat our children as we would want to be treated. Our dream is that one day AP will become the mainstream way to parent, and that as these children grow up, they will be the adults who will permanently change our culture to one of peace and respect for all living beings and the world they live in.

The following chapters are dedicated to defining the principles and providing practical strategies for everyday situations or decisions you will experience in your journey as a parent. We want to arm you with the best information available and provide you with the best resources so that you can investigate the principles more fully. *You* are the expert when it comes to your child. Our hope is that after reading our book you will feel more empowered to make changes and be the kind of parent *and* person you were meant to be.

Appendix to Chapter One: Additional Research and Resource Recommendations

Additional research

The prospect of having a baby brings forth memories of their own childhood and causes them to reflect on the parenting that they received.[35]

New parents' own early childhood experiences have a major impact on their parenting attitudes and beliefs with the possibility of affecting the attachment process with their newborn child.[36]

"The self-organization of the developing brain occurs in the context of a relationship with another self, another brain. This relational context can be growth-facilitating or growth-inhibiting, and so it imprints into the developing right brain either a resilience against or a vulnerability to later forming psychiatric disorders." [37]

Of eighty-six juveniles who were incarcerated for at least one felony, 100% had been exposed to significant childhood trauma.[38]

"Parents of delinquent boys use frequent and violent punishment, issue numerous commands, provide little attention, are vague and inconsistent in giving direction, and practice little supervision of peer-group activities outside the home. That is, the parents of delinquents

---

35   Fonagy, et al., "Maternal representations of attachment during pregnancy predict the organization of infant-mother attachment at one year of age." *Child Development*

36   Ibid.

37   Schore, "The experience-dependent maturation of a regulatory system in the orbital prefrontal cortex and the origin of developmental psychopathology." Development and Psychopathology.

38   Perry et al., Relationships between early experiences and long term functioning: The role of affect development in adjudicated adolescent males. Child Trauma Web site.

tend to be harsh, authoritarian, and lax in monitoring them, and they do not maintain consistent and high standards." [39]

Recommended Reading

A General Theory of Love by Thomas Lewis, MD, Fari Amini, MD, and Richard Lannon, MD.

Becoming Attached by Robert Karen, PhD.

Child Honoring, edited by Raffi Cavoukian and Sharna Olfman.

Creating the Capacity of Attachment by Karen Walant, PhD.

For Your Own Good: Hidden Cruelty in Childrearing and the Roots of Violence by Alice Miller, PhD.

Forgive for Good by Fred Luskin.

Ghosts from the Nursery by Robin Karr-Morse and Meredith Wiley.

High Risk: Children without a Conscience by Ken Magid and Carol McKelvey.

Kids: How Biology and Culture Shape the Way We Raise Our Children by Meredith Small, PhD.

Magical Child by Joseph Chilton Pearce.

Mother Nature: Maternal Instincts and How They Shape the Human Species by Sarah Hrdy, PhD.

Our Babies, Ourselves by Meredith Small, PhD.

Raising America by Ann Hulbert

The Attachment Connection: Parenting a Secure & Confident Child Using the Science of Attachment Theory by Ruth Newton, PhD

The Attachment Parenting Book by William Sears, MD, and Martha Sears, RN.

The Continuum Concept by Jean Liedloff.

The Drama of the Gifted Child: The Search for the True Self by Alice Miller, PhD.

The Science of Parenting by Margot Sunderland.

Why Love Matters: How Affection Shapes a Baby's Brain by Sue Gerhardt.

---

39   Weisfeld, Principles of Human Adolescence, 298.

Useful Web Sites

http://www.americanvalues.org/html/hardwired.html Website for the Hardwired to Connect Report- A report to the nation from the commission on children at risk.

www.attachmentparenting.org: Web site of Attachment Parenting International.

www.continuum-concept.org: Web site to help further understand the concepts from the book by Jean Liedloff.

www.parentingscience.com: Describes cutting-edge research news and practical, science-based tips about child development and child-rearing.

Chapter Two

Principle 1
Prepare Yourself for Pregnancy, Birth, and Parenting: What Every Parent Needs to Know

Prepare Yourself for Pregnancy, Birth, and Parenting: What Every Parent Needs to Know

> *Let's face it: You can do everything "right," eating all the right foods, reading all the right books, and talking to all the right practitioners, yet you still can't control your pregnancy or birth. This can lead you to feel personally responsible when things do not proceed as expected. There is no "right way" to give birth. Birth is not a contest. It is a creative process, and as such, every birth is unique. If we give paints, brushes, easels, and canvases to a group of women and ask them to paint the same scene, each painting will be distinctly different—just as each pregnancy and birth will be a unique experience.... Birth is a normal event and no two are alike.*[1]
>
> Peggy O'Mara
> *Having a Baby Naturally*

The remarkable miracle of new life is a transformative experience for any human being. For most parents, the day their baby joined their family was the most profound experience of their lives. Pregnancy offers expectant parents an opportunity to prepare physically, mentally, emotionally, and spiritually for parenthood. Making informed decisions about childbirth, newborn care, and parenting practices is a critical investment in the attachment relationship between parent and child. Education is the key component of preparation for the sometimes-complex decisions required of parents, and it is an ongoing process as each stage of growth and development brings new joys and challenges.

When preparing for the birth of a child, it is easy to get caught up in the material things associated with pregnancy, childbirth, and newborn care. Cute infant clothing, the latest maternity fashions, and all the baby gear can be an all-consuming part of preparing for a baby, but the lasting investment of preparation involves creating a peaceful, loving environment in which to grow, birth, and care for a new life.

---

1   O'Mara, *Having a Baby Naturally*, xxiv.

Planning For Baby—Preparing Your Body, Mind, and Spirit

Ideally, a couple planning to have a baby will begin to prepare themselves *before* becoming pregnant. Lifestyle choices including eating a nutritious diet, avoiding the use of alcohol and drugs, exercising, and seeking emotional and spiritual health will be a conscious choice for parents anticipating a healthy pregnancy.

Before getting pregnant, a woman will want to prepare her body by eating healthy foods. The amount of processed foods we eat is so much a part of our culture; many young people have never had a home-cooked meal from natural food sources. A practical guideline is to eat a wide variety of foods in as natural a state as possible. For instance, a breakfast of a whole grain cereal, eggs, and toast, or some (preferably organic) fruits and juices is an excellent way to start the day. Think about decreasing caffeinated drinks, or at least limiting them to only breakfast. Sodas and other highly sugared drinks (or carbonated drinks that are artificially sweetened) can be replaced with herbal teas and filtered water. These habits are wonderful to start before pregnancy, so that healthy food choices will already be established when pregnancy occurs.

Because most of us have sedentary lifestyles, exercise is another important addition to a daily regimen. You may only have time for walking thirty minutes a day; this has tremendous advantages, but even better is mixing up your routine to include other forms of exercise like yoga, Pilates, and other stretching and balancing exercises. Good nutrition and exercise will help you be at an optimum weight before conception, so gaining the weight of pregnancy will not be a problem. Mothers who are more physically fit also have a much easier time giving birth.

Emotional preparation is a key factor in beginning a healthy pregnancy. Many women have mixed feelings about having their first baby and are not sure why they feel conflicted. Some women have a great fear of childbirth because of frightful scenes they have seen in movies or on television. A recent study found that far more mothers were exposed to childbirth through television shows than through childbirth education classes.[2] This is a good time to read, ask questions,

---

2   Declercq et al., "Executive summary," In *Listening to Mothers II: Report of the Second National Survey of Women's Childbearing Experiences.*

and do your own research about the normal process of childbirth. Learn about hospital routines in your area, for instance, how common are induced labors, ultrasound, epidurals, and cesarean sections? What are the pros and cons of these procedures, and what are the options in my community? Fear of the unknown is easily dispelled with good information. In her book *Immaculate Deception*, Suzanne Arms discusses the harmful effect of fear on a mother's birth experience:

> [A] positive attitude is important, too. Nature is not prepared to handle inordinate fear and self-doubt. We hear so much about the harmful effects of cocaine and other drugs on a baby in utero, but we hear nothing about the harmful effects of our bodies being constantly flooded with stress hormones that weaken our immune system and inhibit normal birth. If, in addition to making our bodies fit, we do as much as we can to learn about birth as a natural process, we will do much to alleviate unnecessary fears and be able to face birth with calm and courage.[3]

Other issues from your own childhood may arise when thinking about becoming a parent for the first time. Couples can share their stories with each other, and if there are deep concerns, fears, or a history of abuse, this might be a good time to seek professional counseling to help see your birth and parenting experience in a positive light.

Preparing for baby is a perfect time for your spiritual growth; you might read books on spirituality together, talk to a counselor or minister about any questions or concerns you might have, and together share your dreams and hopes for your child. If your partner comes from a particular religious tradition that you do not share, this is good time to discuss each other's spiritual beliefs more deeply, how they will influence your childrearing decisions, what religious traditions will be taught to the children, and what compromises both of you would be comfortable making in order to incorporate the different religious values you both share.

---

3   Arms, *Immaculate Deception*, 25.

Physician and educator Dr. Deepak Chopra offers a profound insight regarding the spiritual nature of the unborn infant when he wrote, "Throughout pregnancy your body is your unborn baby's universe. You are the rivers, sunlight, earth, atmosphere, and sky for this being growing within you. Your baby's body, mind, and soul are intimately intertwined with your own. Together you express the creative flow of life."[4] Embracing this "creative flow" in your life can set the stage for deep personal growth and spiritual development that can give you an overall sense of inner calm, love, and happiness that will have lifelong benefits for you and your unborn child.

What Kind of Birth Experience Do I Want?

It's a good idea, whether you are pregnant or considering pregnancy, to think about the kind of birth experience you want and start looking at the birthing options in your community. In order to get the best prenatal and childbirth options, some couples have made the decision to move to a new area. These options vary widely in different cities and states, so it's important to do the research. If you have an API support group in your community, it is a great way to network with new and pregnant parents to find out about the options that are available.

Attachment parenting advocates know that the most beneficial birth choice is one that has the fewest interventions and allows for the mother and baby to be awake, aware, and able to connect during and after the birth. "Making a decision on where your baby's birth will take place is second in importance only to making the decision to become parents in the first place!" advises Peggy O'Mara in *Having a Baby Naturally*. In making this decision, first look at the birth process through the lens of the attachment relationship. What would be the optimum experience for a baby entering the world? Imagine entering a peaceful, warm, quiet, welcoming environment, a tranquil place that closely resembles the dark, warm, and nurturing environment that the baby has been experiencing for the past nine months. Infants come "hardwired to connect" in that they are programmed to expect the warmth of the human body, the familiar sounds of their mother's

---

4   Chopra et al., *Magical Beginnings, Enchanted Lives*, 38.

heartbeat and voice, and the warmth of mother's milk.[5] Amazing research has shown that when placed on their mother's stomach after birth, an unmedicated baby (no mother's anesthesia) can creep unassisted to his mother's breast, find the nipple, and begin to feed![6]

Most women in the United States use an obstetrician for their prenatal care and the birth of their babies. Some obstetricians are open and encouraging of a nurturing birth environment and have worked within hospital regulations to create a homelike atmosphere for their patients. Another excellent and safe option today in many hospitals, birthing centers, and at home is midwifery care. Whether using a midwife in a hospital setting, birth center, or at home, many women have found that having this option gives them flexibility in their birth experience. For instance, some parents are interested in researching water birth (or laboring in water) as a more gentle approach to childbirth because they have seen videos or heard about the help this provides the mother in having a more relaxed and comfortable birth. It is a good idea for parents to compare different methods and philosophies regarding prenatal care and birth environments, classes offered, and each practitioner's statistical outcomes and costs. Just because a close friend liked a certain provider does not mean it is the best choice for you. Talk to other parents who have had a positive birth experience for recommendations, and then, after coming up with some questions, interview several providers before making a decision. Several books listed at the end of this chapter have excellent sample questions.

5   DeCasper and Fifer, "Of human bonding: Newborns prefer their mother's voices," *Science*.

6   Widström et al., "Gastric suction in healthy newborn infants: Effects on circulation and developing feeding behaviour," *Acta Paediatrica Scandinavica*.

A great resource for developing questions for a health-care provider and making an informed decision about where to have a baby is the "Ten Steps of the Mother-Friendly Childbirth Initiative for Mother-Friendly Hospitals, Birth Centers, and Home Birth Services," published by the Coalition for Improving Maternity Services (CIMS). If there are no "mother-friendly" hospitals, birth centers, or homebirth services close by, investigate whether there are "baby-friendly" hospitals or birth centers by visiting the Baby Friendly Initiative site at www.babyfriendly. org. This initiative, developed by the United Nations Children's Fund (UNICEF), is now being adopted by health care systems all over the world. "Baby-friendly" hospitals and birth centers have implemented the "Ten Steps" set up by UNICEF to ensure that all staff and administrators have made a commitment to educate, support, and encourage mothers to breastfeed their babies, if at all possible. Parents are assured, among other things, that information they receive from all medical staff will be consistent and that the mother will be allowed to room in with her baby.

Ten Steps of the Mother-Friendly Childbirth Initiative for Mother-Friendly Hospitals, Birth Centers, and Home Birth Services

To receive CIMS designation as "mother-friendly," a hospital, birth center, or home birth service must carry out our philosophical principles by fulfilling the Ten Steps of Mother-Friendly Care:

A mother-friendly hospital, birth center, or home birth service:
1. Offers all birthing mothers:
   o Unrestricted access to the birth companions of her choice, including fathers, partners, children, family members, and friends
   o Unrestricted access to continuous emotional and physical support from a skilled woman—for

example, a doula or labor-support professional
- o   Access to professional midwifery care
2. Provides accurate descriptive and statistical information to the public about its practices and procedures for birth care, including measures of interventions and outcomes
3. Provides culturally competent care—that is, care that is sensitive and responsive to the specific beliefs, values, and customs of the mother's ethnicity and religion
4. Provides the birthing woman with the freedom to walk, move about, and assume the positions of her choice during labor and birth (unless restriction is specifically required to correct a complication) and discourages the use of the lithotomy (flat on back with legs elevated) position
5. Has clearly defined policies and procedures for:
- o   Collaborating and consulting throughout the perinatal period with other maternity services, including communicating with the original caregiver when transfer from one birth site to another is necessary
- o   Linking the mother and baby to appropriate community resources, including prenatal and post-discharge follow-up and breastfeeding support
6. Does not routinely employ practices and procedures that are unsupported by scientific evidence, including but not limited to the following:
- o   Shaving
- o   Enemas
- o   IVs (intravenous drip)
- o   Withholding nourishment
- o   Early rupture of membranes
- o   Electronic fetal monitoring

   Other interventions are limited as follows:
- o   Has an induction rate of 10% or less
- o   Has an episiotomy rate of 20% or less, with a

goal of 5% or less
- o Has a total cesarean rate of 10% or less in community hospitals, and 15% or less in tertiary care (high-risk) hospitals
- o Has a VBAC (vaginal birth after caesarean) rate of 60% or more with a goal of 75% or more

7. Educates staff in nondrug methods of pain relief and does not promote the use of analgesic or anesthetic drugs not specifically required to correct a complication
8. Encourages all mothers and families, including those with sick or premature newborns or infants with congenital problems, to touch, hold, breastfeed, and care for their babies to the extent compatible with their conditions
9. Discourages nonreligious circumcision of the newborn
10. Strives to achieve the WHO-UNICEF "Ten Steps of the Baby-Friendly Hospital Initiative" to promote successful breastfeeding[7]

---

7   the Coalition for Improving Maternity Services Web site.

UNICEF's Ten Steps to Successful Breastfeeding (Baby-Friendly Hospital Initiative)

Every facility providing maternity services and care for newborn infants should:

1. Have a written breastfeeding policy that is routinely communicated to all health care staff
2. Train all health care staff in skills necessary to implement this policy
3. Inform all pregnant women about the benefits and management of breastfeeding
4. Help mothers initiate breastfeeding within a half-hour of birth
5. Show mothers how to breastfeed and how to maintain lactation, even if they should be separated from their infants
6. Give newborn infants no food or drink other than breast milk, unless medically indicated
7. Practice rooming-in—allow mothers and infants to remain together—twenty-four hours a day
8. Encourage breastfeeding on demand
9. Give no artificial teats or pacifiers (also called dummies or soothers) to breastfeeding infants
10. Foster the establishment of breastfeeding support groups and refer mothers to them on discharge from the hospital or clinic[8]

---

8   "Ten steps to successful breastfeeding," Baby Friendly Hospital Initiative Web site.

Childbirth Education Classes

One of the first steps toward creating a positive birth experience is deciding what kind of childbirth classes you want to take and finding out what classes are offered in your area, such as the Bradley Method for natural childbirth, Lamaze classes, or others. By interviewing different childbirth educators, find out what their classes have to offer, what various birth options are available, and the health-care providers who are supportive of more natural methods. Ask the childbirth educator if she will help you develop a birth plan. "A birth plan states, in writing, your vision of the upcoming labor and delivery. It crystallizes your beliefs, states your preferences, and outlines any procedures you would like to avoid."[9]

Couples often enjoy the social aspects of these childbirth classes as much as the information offered and can network with each other about this new world of becoming a parent. The list at the end of this chapter suggests books, Web sites, and other resources for finding childbirth instructors and researching their philosophy about childbirth and their methodologies. It's important to remember that a one-time class at a local hospital won't come close to giving you all the important information you need to be prepared. For the best birth outcomes, parents need to be informed and active participants in all decisions that have to be made, as well as the birth.

In 1972 a study was published in the book, *Why Natural Childbirth?* The author, Dr. Deborah Tanzer, was a student of Dr. Abraham Maslow, the theorist who developed the "hierarchy of needs" scale and the theory of the "peak experience." Dr. Maslow defined peak experiences as those that make life worthwhile and give it meaning. Dr. Tanzer was curious to study mothers who were delivering babies by this new method of "natural childbirth," which was being touted as a rapturous experience by some mothers.

In these studies, Dr. Tanzer found that, as soon as the natural childbirth classes were completed, the women who had taken them (called "the takers" in the study) showed greatly improved attitudes toward their pregnancies. Five times as many women reporting positive emotions after the birth had taken the childbirth classes, a statistically

---

9   O'Mara, *Having a Baby Naturally*, 102.

significant difference. Another important finding was that the takers felt they were much closer to being the type of people they wanted to be; in other words, their self-images were enhanced. Ironically, the takers (most of whom had little-to-no analgesia) reported significantly less pain than the nontakers. Almost equal numbers of the two groups reported high pain, but takers outnumbered nontakers eight to one in registering low pain.[10]

The issue that greatly interested Dr. Tanzer was the experience of a peak or rapturous experience. No one in the group that did not take the childbirth classes reported this kind of ecstatic experience, but ten of the takers in this study did. Overwhelmingly, it was the women whose husbands or partners were with them at both labor and delivery who reported a peak experience.

In summary, here are some of the key points from her research. First, certain fears, feelings, fantasies, needs, and responses seem to be common to all women. Second, by the introduction of natural childbirth, the character of the total birth experience is changed radically and in a highly positive direction. Third, these differences in childbirth experiences included how the mother viewed herself, the baby, and the meaning of the experience; the women in the natural childbirth group emerged happier and healthier. And fourth, *the biggest and most positive differences* became apparent in the *later stages of labor and during the actual birth of the baby*, when the woman could begin to push and thus help to expel the baby. The act of pushing, the sense of meaningful activity, the participation in the great drama of the delivery room, the ability to welcome her new child in full consciousness, the joy in accomplishment—these seem to be the truly important facets of natural childbirth and for these mothers were the ultimate in a "peak experience."

Interestingly, we've talked to many women over the years who attended natural childbirth classes, yet for various reasons did not have the "perfect birth" experience that they had wanted. Those women seem to have an easier time dealing with their disappointment than those who wonder what might have happened if they had been more prepared. It seems to be harder on a mother to accept a disappointing or difficult birth when she was not informed enough about the process of labor and delivery, and the doctor was allowed to make all the decisions. We feel strongly

---

10   Tanzer, *Why Natural Childbirth?* 152.

that birth is such a transformative and empowering experience that each pregnant mother deserves to have the best information, enabling her to make the best decisions for her and her baby. The critical time to gather this information is well before the birth.

To encourage positive birth outcomes, the Lamaze Institute for Normal Birth has identified and updated six care practices, adapted from the World Health Organization, that promote, support, and protect normal birth. When adopted, these care practices can have a profound effect—instilling confidence in the mother and facilitating a process that results in an active, healthy baby.

- *Care Practice #1: Labor Begins on Its Own.* Labor is a set of complex, interacting components. Alteration of the natural process can expose a woman and her baby to unneeded risks.
- *Care Practice #2: Freedom of Movement throughout Labor.* Free movement during labor allows a woman to tolerate contractions and assist the baby's rotation and movement through the pelvis.
- *Care Practice #3: Continuous Labor Support.* Current research supports the benefits of continuous emotional and physical support during labor.
- *Care Practice #4: No Routine Interventions.* Supporting the natural, normal, physiologic process of birth requires clear medical indications prior to any medical intervention.
- *Care Practice #5: Spontaneous Pushing in Upright or Gravity-Neutral Positions.* Allowing a woman to find the positions of comfort and encouraging her to push in response to what she is feeling is beneficial to the birth process.
- *Care Practice #6: No Separation of Mother and Baby, with Unlimited Opportunities for Breastfeeding.* When a baby is kept with the mother, there are

physiological benefits to both, including the facilitation of breastfeeding.

Lamaze International recommends that care providers, hospitals, and birth centers adopt these six practices as standards of care and encourages women and their families to choose care providers and birth settings that employ care practices that promote, support, and protect normal birth.

All six revised care practice papers can be found in their entirety in the latest issue of the *Journal of Perinatal Education* or may be downloaded from www.lamaze.org.

What is a Doula?

Parents today have an incredible resource to use for an optimum birth experience: a doula (doo-lah). In the book, *Mothering the Mother,* Klaus, Kennell, and Klaus explain:

> In searching for a term to describe the role, we wanted a word with a nonmedical connotation that would stress the value of a woman companion as attentive and comforting. We turned to the Greek word *doula* meaning "woman caregiver." Our first exposure to the word came from Dana Raphael's use of the term to describe "one or more individuals, often female, who give psychological encouragement and physical assistance to the newly delivered mother." We use the word in the now widely accepted sense of an experienced labor companion who provides the woman and her partner both emotional and physical support throughout the entire labor and delivery, and to some extent, afterward.[11]

---

11   Klaus et al., *Mothering the Mother*, 4.

Doulas of North America is a licensing organization for professional doulas. Their Web site has much helpful information, including the following description:

> Giving birth to a baby is so much more than a physical phenomenon; it engages parents-to-be in a transformational experience, a key life event full of emotion and meaning. A doula who accompanies a woman in labor mothers the mother, taking care of her emotional needs throughout childbirth. A doula also provides support and suggestions for partners that can enhance their experiences of birth. A postpartum doula continues that valuable emotional support and guidance, helping a family make a smooth transition into new family dynamics.[12]

A postpartum doula is one who helps the mother at home after the birth of her child. Postpartum doulas help continue the "mothering the mother" experience in a variety a ways. Some may help with breastfeeding, nutrition, emotional support and encouragement, light housekeeping, or childcare for older children.

Denise Punger, a physician in Florida, shared her birth stories with the readers of *Attachment Parenting: The Journal of API*—one birth without and one birth with doula support. Even though Dr. Punger had delivered over two hundred babies in her residency, she was not aware that having a doula was an option for her first birth. She and her physician-husband attended childbirth classes, and they assumed that they would be prepared to have a wonderful natural birth experience. She invited her mother to be at the birth, not realizing until later that her mother had never witnessed a natural birth and was herself anesthetized for Denise's birth. When the day came to deliver, her labor was very long and difficult. Not having an experienced support person who was able to help her deal with the long hours of labor or, especially, to suggest strategies like walking or changing positions during her last stages left her feeling traumatized by the birth. She was able to deliver her nine-pound baby vaginally, but later, as she recovered

---

12 "What is a Doula?" DONA International Web site.

from the birth, she knew that there must be a better way—to feel more empowered, supported, and nurtured through the birth—even though her family advised her to just try to forget about the experience.

Her next baby's birth was supported by a professional doula. The doula came to her house during her early stages of labor and gave Denise the loving support and wise council that she needed. She described how, with her doula, she walked around the neighborhood, stopping and breathing through contractions, rather than being forced to labor in a bed. As labor progressed, her doula suggested techniques for relaxing and letting her body do what it needed to do. She was amazed and grateful for the soothing words and birthing wisdom from her doula that gave her the confidence to actually enjoy the labor more and helped it progress more quickly. By the time they reached the hospital, she could feel the baby's head crowning and delivered another nine-pounder with a midwife in attendance.

Denise wrote, "In a way, I wish the obstetrician from my first birth had been at Scott's [my second son's] birth. He would have seen the difference a doula could make. If I delivered babies, I would insist that all my patients consider having a doula. It really makes me sad when I hear a mother tell another, 'You'll forget it all anyway.' Giving birth can be a rewarding physical and emotional experience—one that you will never forget."[13]

This model of "mothering the mother" has been found to have tremendous benefits to a mother in labor. Wise women from all cultures and time periods have historically been a key component to any normal birth, and modern society is now recognizing the critical importance of nurturing parents during this transformative event. Health benefits range from shorter length of labor, lower incidence of forceps or vacuum delivery, and lower rate of cesarean birth to less postpartum depression and heightened satisfaction with the overall birth experience.[14] As with choosing any care provider, parents are encouraged to get references from other parents for finding and choosing a doula.

---

13 Punger, "A physician's personal experience with a doula," *Attachment Parenting: The Journal of API.*

14 Klaus et al., *Mothering the Mother*, 33–51.

A Mother's Story: For the "Naturally Birthing Challenged"

I want to offer encouragement to moms who feel they missed the ideal birthing experience and/or who were separated from their babies at birth. I also want to share a few tips that would have helped me the first time and did help me the second time:

- Seek out support for feelings of loss and recognize that you deserve validation.

- Have a doula, even for a scheduled C-section.

- Draw upon your spirituality, faith in your and your child's creator, and the knowledge that your baby will experience your emotional responsiveness for the entirety of his/her life and was birthed how that baby needed to be birthed.

- Have the knowledge that despite all of the positive affirmations and the knowledge that our bodies were created to birth naturally, not all birthing bodies evolve equally through life and you are not a failure because you required medical interventions, and you haven't messed up your kid up for life because you required separation at birth.

- Surround yourself with friends who display empathy and support and are like-minded.

- Realize that our feelings of grief over having a C-section are completely separate from, and do not lessen, the love you feel for your baby. You can feel grief and love and thankfulness, all at the same time.

- My dear husband suggests that in a hospital setting, you should question the staff. Don't expect them to remember your birthing plan (most won't). Kindly stand strong and stand firm because you do have rights, and if there are no complications with your baby, you have all the rights to choose your baby's course of treatment, and in doing so, you can get much closer to the birthing experience you've dreamed about.[15]

Kaylene Karras
Attachment Parenting: The Journal of API

Vaginal Birth after Cesarean (VBAC)

Fortunately, for a mother who has had a cesarean section, the horizontal incision is more stable than the old style of a vertical cut from the navel to the pubic bone. This makes the possibility of a future vaginal birth possible, and thousands of women have experienced a successful VBAC. It will take some research on your part to determine if this is a safe option for you. You will need to talk to physicians or midwives who support mothers in this decision and have delivered VBAC babies. The International Cesarean Awareness Network has excellent information to help you research this option.

A Fit Pregnancy Means a Healthier Baby

Exercise during pregnancy can be a challenge, especially if the mother is working and has limited time; however, the benefits are substantial. Many prenatal classes are offered in the evenings to accommodate working mothers, including prenatal yoga, swimming, and other exercise programs designed for pregnancy. These classes are also a wonderful way for a new mom to meet other pregnant women in the community. Mothers who exercise during pregnancy tend to have healthier pregnancies, and their labors are much easier, and often shorter, than those of women who have not exercised. Preterm births are 50 percent less common in mothers who exercise. Of course, it is always important to discuss your exercise regimen with your medical professional.

---

15 Karras, "The ideal birth for the 'Natural Birthing Challenged,'" *Attachment Parenting: The Journal of API*.

More than any other time, a pregnancy allows a woman the opportunity to fully understand the importance of how nutrition impacts her health and the health of her baby. There is no question that the choices made will also have a direct impact on the birth experience. Research in this area has shown that malnourished mothers tend to have more premature births, lower-birth-weight babies, and more difficult labors. In this day of convenience food, it is surprising to see how many of us are not getting the proper nutrients, especially pregnant women who are now "eating for two." Take this opportunity to change your eating habits for the better.

When a woman has the excuse to eat for two, it's important to remember that overdoing portions will not be in the best interest of mother or baby! Remember that healthy weight gain is very individual and will vary, depending on many factors. Some mothers may actually lose a little weight in the early months, particularly if they have a lot of nausea. Others may put on quite a bit of weight in the early months, or notice a thickening in their midsection due to hormonal changes. If a mother is already too thin or too heavy before conception and uses this opportunity to change her eating habits for the better, she will find that her body will adjust beautifully to the best weight gain for her and her baby. A knowledgeable health care provider will give the guidance needed, including discussing the importance of prenatal vitamins. However, it is still the parents' responsibility to do their homework on what food choices are the best for their family. If there are special dietary needs, such as a vegan diet or other diets not normally within the expertise of many care providers, parents will need to educate themselves and consult with their provider about optimal choices during pregnancy.

Some childbirth classes suggest the mom to keep a food diary every day, which is a very helpful idea. Being conscious about food choices now will set a pattern for the choices made throughout the life of the child. What a lifelong gift for a child to have parents who model good nutrition in the home.

How Will I Feed My Baby?

In chapter 3, another important nutritional and attachment-promoting decision is discussed at length—the decision to breastfeed or bottle-feed your baby. Seventy-eight percent of the young mothers in a recent study stated that they made decisions about breastfeeding before pregnancy or the first trimester.[16] Looking through the lens of attachment, we learn nature's model of what the baby's expectations are from a biological perspective.. A baby's first primary need is to suckle, and he will be rooting and suckling immediately after birth, providing him with his first important immunization from the colostrum. We discuss this more thoroughly in chapter 3, but suffice it to say here that feeding your baby is such an important attachment-promoting behavior, it warrants much thought and careful preparation, especially if the mother has little experience with feeding a newborn—whether from the breast or bottle. A mother who intends to breastfeed is encouraged to attend meetings of La Leche League International, an organization founded in 1957 to educate and support breastfeeding mothers. Most cities in the United States have meetings that are open to all women who are interested in learning more about breastfeeding, whether they have a baby or not. Even adoptive mothers who would like to learn if they can breastfeed (which they can) are welcome. At the very least, talk to a lactation consultant or experienced nursing mother to get accurate information about positioning the baby at the breast and getting off to a good start. Often a mother will prepare for the birth, not thinking about the most important thing that she will do when she meets her baby for the first time—the baby will want to be cuddled and to suck!

The Emotional Highs and Lows of Pregnancy

A pregnancy can evoke strong emotions in parents-to-be regardless of whether the pregnancy was long anticipated or a complete surprise. The knowledge that they are bringing a baby into the world can bring excitement and joy to expectant parents but may also yield less positive emotions. Memories may be dredged up from the expectant parents' own childhoods, from a prior complicated pregnancy or birth, or from a previous loss. Time taken to reflect on individual childhood experiences and current beliefs about parenting is invaluable preparation. Explore different parenting philosophies and discuss parenting approaches that

---

16   Arora et al., "Major factors influencing breastfeeding rates: Mother's perception of father's attitude and milk supply," *Pediatrics*.

best nurture healthy attachments within your growing family. Work through negative emotions surrounding the pregnancy so you can focus on the joy of welcoming the baby. Those experiencing negative emotions regarding the pregnancy or who have a history of depression should seek help from a health care provider. Meditation, centering prayer, yoga, visualization, and other relaxation techniques can help minimize stress surrounding the pregnancy while helping pregnant mothers prepare for the physical rigor of birth.

Studies have shown that the quality of a woman's relationship with her husband or partner has a substantial effect on the emotional and physical well-being of her baby. A Swedish study found that mothers who experienced a positive relationship with their partners expressed more attachment to their infant, and, overall, a mother's positive relationship with her partner had a positive influence on her attitudes towards pregnancy.[17]

The relationship with the spouse or partner will never be tested more than in the parenting journey. This will probably be the first experience of putting one's own needs aside and, together, putting the needs of another human being first—particularly in the early months of parenting when both parents are on call twenty-four hours a day! Some couples make the mistake of thinking that if there are problems in the relationship now, a new baby will bring them closer together. Take this time of preparation to deeply reflect on partnership—not only do you need to share your own childhood stories and reflect on their impact on each other, but also discuss what you might call your "parenting mission statement" or philosophy. For instance, how do you feel about traditional methods of raising children such as letting the baby cry it out? Are you open to reading books and getting information about childbirth, child development, and

---

17   Siddiqui and Hagglöf, "An exploration of prenatal attachment in Swedish expectant women," *Journal of Reproductive and Infant Psychology*.

positive discipline, perhaps by attending parent support group meetings? Becoming parents can be one of the most meaningful, fulfilling times in your relationship, a time of great personal growth and joy.

In their book, *Giving the Love That Heals: A Guide for Parents*, married couple and authors Drs. Helen Hunt and Harville Hendrix share a profound discovery they made when working with couples:

> As we became more and more interested in the relationship between parents and children, we came to a conclusion that amazed us: the people who were most successful in marriage relationships were the same ones who were most successful in parenting relationships. Why? ... The people who did well ... made a commitment to become conscious about the process. They were willing to see what was hidden in themselves and, without prejudice, to understand the connection between past wounding and present functioning. They were able to override their self-protective impulses in favor of responses that were less me-centered and more relationship-centered.
>
> When you allow yourself to recognize the contours of your own emotional history and the shape of your current family interactions, you become empowered. You see yourself for who you really are and see your children for who they really are. Just this increased awareness alone, without any other help, means that you are more likely to avoid mistakes and are better able to act effectively to get what you want for yourself and the children you love.[18]

Preparation for becoming a parent starts with preparing for pregnancy and childbirth; as the journey unfolds, it is essential to learn about the upcoming developmental stages. Reading books about child development allows parents to have realistic expectations for themselves and for their child, allowing parents to be better prepared for the joys

---

18   Hendrix and Hunt, *Giving the Love That Heals*, xviii–xx.

and challenges of each stage. In Part Four of *Giving the Love That Heals*, the emotional developmental stages are thoroughly discussed, giving parents strategies for empathic care.

Advanced preparation and education prompts discussion about parental concerns before they become crises. For example, if parents understand that it is normal for a newborn and young baby to awaken frequently to feed, they soon realize that sleeping through the night is a very unrealistic expectation. So often we see that simply knowing what to expect avoids a lot of anxiety and later discipline issues. This topic is discussed more thoroughly in chapter 8, Practice Positive Discipline.

Postpartum Depression

There has been much in the media recently about mothers who suffer from extreme bouts of postpartum depression or postpartum psychosis. Fortunately, new research is confirming that there is hope for women who suffer from different postpartum challenges. Dr. Kathleen Kendall-Tackett discusses the importance of getting solid information and remembering that prevention should be the number one goal to help new mothers avoid spiraling into depression in her book *Depression in New Mothers*. Sometimes all a mother needs is support during and after her birth, a healthy diet, and plenty of rest to manage her symptoms. Other times, it is unclear whether a mother is depressed or perhaps suffering from a number of other conditions like bipolar disorder, eating disorder, or substance abuse and needs professional help immediately. This book can help parents and professionals sort through these issues. Dr. Kendall-Tackett also has several excellent Web sites to help mothers, including www.breastfeedingmadesimple.com, which has information for breastfeeding mothers who may have questions about depression, medications that are safe for breastfeeding, and alternative therapies.

Important Decisions in the First Days after Giving Birth

So often we focus primarily on the birth of the baby and critical decisions that must be made almost immediately after the birth are not given much thought! Most of these issues will be addressed by a professional childbirth educator, but if not, please be aware of these topics, and do some reading and research to make an informed decision. Remember to consider these decisions through the lens of attachment: how will this affect not only my baby's physical health, but also his emotional and psychological well-being. Examples of key issues to research follow.

For Baby Boys: Circumcision

If you give birth to a boy, you will be asked if you want to consent to his circumcision. This is not a decision you want to make on the spur of the moment, without reading and researching the pros and cons. Unless this is a religious tradition in your family, most parents do not give this much thought and will make the decision based on what the culture dictates. However, you owe it to your baby boy to research the issue. The American Academy of Pediatrics no longer recommends routine circumcision, and, if a baby boy is circumcised, they recommend the use of local analgesia for pain. It is hard to believe that many doctors still perform this procedure without any topical pain medication for the baby. Some major insurance companies do not cover this procedure anymore because of the AAP's position. (You can read the AAP policy statement on their Web site listed in the "Recommended Reading" section at the end of this chapter.) You will need to find out about your coverage, and talk to your medical professional about his or her opinion, too. This procedure has an impact on the emotional and physical health of your child. Resources listed at the end of this chapter may help you research this decision.

The Vaccination Decision

Another almost immediate decision you will have to discuss with your baby's pediatrician is the long list of vaccines that are routine today. *The Vaccine Book* by Dr. Robert Sears is a very helpful resource that lists all the current vaccines and the pros and cons of each shot. This book is a helpful guide to bring with you when discussing this issue with your baby's doctor. One concern is about additives to the vaccines, which has led to controversies about possible links to medical problems in children such as the epidemic rates of autism in the United States. Dr. Sears is emphatic that his book is not an "antivaccine" book but a balanced view meant to be an educational tool for parents and professionals. He made a diligent effort to refrain from bias and do his own investigative research. He examined all the information he could find on each of the approximately fifteen or more vaccines given over the first twelve years of a child's life. He methodically discusses each disease and vaccine:

- What is it?
- How common is it?
- How serious is it?
- When is the vaccine given?
- Why so many doses?
- How is it made?
- What are the ingredients?
- Are any ingredients controversial?
- What are the side effects?
- Should I give my baby this vaccine?

Dr. Sears is concerned about the lack of information that parents and physicians have about this topic, as well as the consequences of not making an educated decision about how and why vaccines are given. He reassures parents that they can still fully vaccinate but should consider a different schedule, where the shots are spaced out. Other resources are listed at the end of this chapter, and you will find many articles on the Internet.

Your responsibilities as a parent can seem like a "baptism by fire" when you are immediately faced with such tough decisions, so it is imperative to take the time to research these issues thoroughly before your baby is born. When you come from a place of education and rational discussion, mixed with good old common sense, you have more confidence in your parenting and will make the best decisions for your baby and your family.

Attachment Parenting International Support Groups

Many times in this chapter we have mentioned the importance of support; it is critical for the birth, for breastfeeding, and for parenting in general. API support groups are now available in many communities in the United States, and online support is available through our Web site. In their book *And Baby Makes Three,* John and Julie Gottman share why support groups make such a difference to the emotional health of a couple when they become parents:

> For inspiration, we looked at the pioneering research done by our friends Carolyn and Philip Cowan at the University of California, Berkley. In their study, they ran support groups for couples that lasted six months, beginning in the last trimester of pregnancy. They compared these couples with a different set of couples in a control group who had no such group experience. Couples were selected at random to be in the support groups or in the control group.
>
> The Cowans found that the couples who experienced the support groups changed in many ways. Perhaps most important, the couples realized that the stresses they encountered were not the result of relationships gone sour. Most of their fellow couples in the groups were colliding with problems just like the ones they were having.[19]

---

19   Gottman and Gottman, *And Baby Makes Three,* 5–6.

In today's world of extended families that live too far away to give the day-to-day support, knowledge, and care that existed in past generations, it is critically important for parents to create this support system for their family. API support groups are one way for new mothers and fathers to create friendships and community. These groups are also safe havens for learning about their roles as parents and partners, and as they become more experienced parents they become mentors to new members of the group. These groups are valuable resources when researching anything from childbirth methods and local medical care providers to family-friendly restaurants and fun activities in the community. Our hope is that all parents will seek out support, and if you don't have a group in your community, go to our Web site (www. attachmentparenting.org) and learn how easy it is to get started.

Appendix to Chapter Two: Additional Research and Resource Recommendations

Additional Research

Our culture has a powerful influence on our perceptions of the optimum birth experience. Declercq et al. (2006) found that "During pregnancy, mothers sought information … through a variety of sources, with first-time mothers naming books (33%) as their primary information source, followed by friends and relatives (19%), their provider (18%), and the Internet (16%).… Fully two-thirds (68%) had watched one or more of eight television shows specially created to depict childbirth, with more than half of the viewers regularly watching at least one of these shows. Far more mothers were exposed to childbirth through TV shows than through childbirth education classes.… [Only] fifty-six percent of new mothers took childbirth education classes.… As women neared the end of pregnancy, most felt confident, but a majority also felt fearful about their upcoming birth." A few other troubling statistics were reported in this survey. "Despite the importance of early contact for attachment and breastfeeding, most babies were not in their mother's arms during the first hour after birth, with a troubling proportion with staff for routine, non-urgent care (39%)." And another surprising finding was that "just a small proportion of mothers visited multiple providers before selecting their own or sought a provider or hospital matching their own philosophy."[20]

The prospect of having a baby brings forth memories of parents' own childhood and causes mothers to reflect on the parenting that they received. New parents' own early childhood experiences have a major impact on their parenting attitudes and beliefs, with the possibility of affecting the attachment process with their newborn child.[21]

Early childbirth education can empower parents to be involved in the

---

20   Declercq et al., "Executive summary," In *Listening to Mothers II: Report of the Second National Survey of Women's Childbearing Experiences.*

21   Fonagy et al., "Maternal representations of attachment during pregnancy predict the organization of infant-mother attachment at one year of age," *Child Development.*

planning of their birth, often resulting in use of less pain medication during labor.[22]

Mothers who experienced a positive relationship with their partners expressed more attachment to their infant. Overall, a mother's positive relationship with her partner had a positive influence in her attitudes towards pregnancy.[23]

The presence of a supportive companion during labor was associated with a striking reduction in the length of labor, with a consequent reduction in the rate of augmentation of labor with oxytocin. Fetal passage of meconium during labor was reduced, and this, together with the effect of the supportive companions on uterine action, resulted in fewer instrumental deliveries and cesarean sections.[24]

Fears about pregnancy and childbirth can increase the risk of emergency cesarean section and increase the risks of emotional instability after childbirth.[25]

Education about childbirth can significantly increase positive attitudes towards birth.[26]

A positive birth experience and strong support system can strongly influence breastfeeding success,[27] as well as reduce postpartum anxiety by helping parents develop strategies and coping skills for this stressful time.[28]

---

22 Enkin et al., *A Guide to Effective Care in Pregnancy and Childbirth*, 25.

23 Siddiqui and Hagglöf, "An exploration of prenatal attachment in Swedish expectant women," *Journal of Reproductive and Infant Psychology*.

24 Enkin et al., *A Guide to Effective Care in Pregnancy and Childbirth*, 177.

25 Melender, "Experiences of fears associated with pregnancy and childbirth: A study of 329 pregnant women," *Birth: Issues in Perinatal Care*.

26 Cleeton, "Attitudes and beliefs about childbirth among college students: Results of an educational intervention," *Birth: Issues in Perinatal Care*.

27 Tarkka et al., "What contributes to breastfeeding success after childbirth in a maternity ward in Finland?" *Birth: Issues in Perinatal Care*.

28 Midmer et al., "A randomized controlled trial of the influence of prenatal parenting education on postpartum anxiety and marital adjustment," *Family Medicine*.

Education of mothers, families, fathers, and health care professionals regarding the benefits of breastfeeding, as well as how to overcome barriers, has a positive impact on the number of mothers choosing to breastfeed.[29]

The decision to breastfeed is significantly related to the father's level of education and to his approval of breastfeeding. The strong approval of breastfeeding by the father was associated with a high incidence of breastfeeding (98.1%) compared to only 26.9 percent breastfeeding rates when the father was indifferent to [the mother's] feeding choice.[30]

Existing scientific evidence demonstrates potential medical benefits of newborn male circumcision; however, these data are not sufficient to recommend routine neonatal circumcision. In the case of circumcision, in which there are potential benefits and risks, yet the procedure is not essential to the child's current well-being, parents should determine what is in the best interest of the child. To make an informed choice, parents of all male infants should be given accurate and unbiased information and be provided the opportunity to discuss this decision. It is legitimate for parents to take into account cultural, religious, and ethnic traditions, in addition to the medical factors, when making this decision. Analgesia is safe and effective in reducing the procedural pain associated with circumcision; therefore, if a decision for circumcision is made, procedural analgesia should be provided. If circumcision is performed in the newborn period, it should only be done on infants who are stable and healthy.[31]

Recommended Reading

A Good Birth, a Safe Birth by Diana Korte and Roberta Scaer.
And Baby Makes Three by John Gottman, PhD, and Julie Schwartz Gottman, PhD.

---

29   Arora et al., "Major factors influencing breastfeeding rates: Mother's perception of father's attitude and milk supply," *Pediatrics*.

30   Littman et al., "The decision to breastfeed," *Clinical Pediatrics*.

31   American Academy of Pediatrics Task Force on Circumcision, "Circumcision Policy Statement," *Pediatrics*.

Bonding: Building The Foundations Of Secure Attachment And Independence by Marshall Klaus, MD, John Kennell,MD and Phyllis Klaus.

Birth and Breastfeeding by Michel Odent, MD.

Birth Reborn by Michel Odent,MD.

Birth Without Violence by Frederick Leboyer, MD.

Born in the USA: How a Broken Maternity System Must Be Fixed to Put Women and Children First by Marsden Wagner, MD.

Building Healthy Minds by Stanley Greenspan, MD.

Depression and New Mothers by Kathleen Kendall-Tackett, PhD.

Eating Well for Optimum Health by Andrew Weil, MD.

Fatherwise by Alice Bolster.

Gentle Birth Choices by Barbara Harper and Suzanne Arms.

Giving the Love That Heals: A Guide for Parents by Harville Hendrix, PhD, and Helen Hunt, PhD.

Great Expectations by Sandy Jones and Marcie Jones

Having a Baby Naturally by Peggy O'Mara.

How to Raise a Healthy Child in Spite of Your Doctor by Robert Mendelsohn, MD.

Husband-Coached Childbirth by Robert Bradley, MD.

Immaculate Deception by Suzanne Arms.

Ina May's Guide to Childbirth by Ina May Gaskin.

Magical Beginnings, Enchanted Lives by Deepak Choprah, MD, David Simon, MD, and Vicki Abrams, IBCLC.

Mind over Labor: A Breakthrough Guide to Giving Birth by Carl Jones, Marian Tompson, and Emmett E. Miller.

Mothering the Mother: How a Doula Can Help You Have a Shorter, Easier, and Healthier Birth by Marshall Klaus, MD, Phylliss Klaus, and John Kennell, MD.

Motherwise by Alice Bolster.

Natural Family Living: The Mothering Magazine Guide to Parenting by Peggy O'Mara.

Our Babies, Ourselves by Meredith Small, PhD.

Our Bodies, Ourselves: Pregnancy and Birth by the Boston Women's Health Book Collective and Judy Norsigian.

Parenting from the Inside Out by Daniel Siegel, MD, and Mary Hartzell.

Pushed, the Painful Truth about Childbirth and Modern Maternity Care by Jennifer Block.

Prenatal Parenting by Frederick Wirth, MD.

Pre-Parenting: Nurturing Your Child from Conception by Thomas R. Verny, MD, and Pamela Weintraub.

Silent Knife: Cesarean Prevention and VBAC by Nancy Wainer Cohen and Lois J. Estner.

Special Delivery: The Complete Guide to Informed Birth by Rahima Baldwin.

Spiritual Midwifery by Ina May Gaskin.

The Birth Book by William Sears, MD, and Martha Sears, RN.

The Birth Partner: A Complete Guide to Childbirth for Dads, Doulas, and All Other Labor Companions by Penny Simpkin.

The Complete Book of Pregnancy and Childbirth by Sheila Kitzinger.

The Secret of the Unborn Child: How You Can Prepare Your Baby for a Happy, Healthy Life by Thomas R. Verny, MD, and John Kelly.

The Thinking Woman's Guide to a Better Birth by Henci Goer.

The Womanly Art of Breastfeeding by La Leche League International.

Your Amazing Newborn by Marshall Klaus, MD and Phyllis Klaus, MD.

Your Best Birth: Know All Your Options, Discover the Natural Choices, and Take Back the Birth Experience by Ricki Lake and Abby Epstein

Recommended CDs

Lullabies for Sleepy Eyes by Susie Tallman.

Traditional Lullabies by Growing Minds With Music.

Welcome Home My Child: Songs for a Mother's Journey by Lu Hanessian, available at www.letthebabydrive.com/cd.php.

Recommended DVDs

The Business of Being Born (2007)
Starring Ricki Lake and Michel Odent, MD
Director: Abby Epstein
Available at www.thebusinessofbeingborn.com
Vaccinations? Assessing the Risks and Benefits
Jay Gordon, MD
Available at www.vaccinationsdvd.com
It's My Body, My Baby, My Birth, a Film about Natural Childbirth
Wisewoman Childbirth Traditions
Available at www.itsmybodymybabymybirth.com

Useful Web Sites

aappolicy.aappublications.org/cgi/content/full/pediatrics;103/3/ 686: American Academy of Pediatrics Circumcision Policy Statement.

www.askdrsears.com: Web site for the Dr. Sears with information about nutrition, pregnancy and childbirth

www.bbholine.com: Web site for the Bringing Baby Home Program.

www.birthcenters.org/find-a-birth-center: Listing of birth centers in the United States.

www.birthpsychology.org/apppah: The Association for Pre- and Perinatal Psychology and Health focuses attention on human development from preparation for pregnancy through the postpartum period.

www.birthworks.org: Web site of the Birth Works childbirth preparation course.

www.bradleybirth.com: Web site of the American Academy of Husband-Coached Childbirth.

www.breastcrawl.org: Amazing footage of a baby crawling on his mother's body to her nipple and beginning to suckle immediately after birth.

www.breastfeedingmadesimple.com: Information for breastfeeding mothers who may have questions about depression, medications that are safe for breastfeeding, and alternative therapies.

www.cirp.org: Circumcision information and resources.

www.dona.org: Web site of Doulas of North America (DONA International).

www.generationrescue.com/studies.html: Web site for parents and professionals for information and research on vaccinations and the possible link to autism.

www.healthconnectone.org: a nationally recognized nonprofit training and technical assistance agency that uses innovative, community-based approaches to support direct-service providers in promoting the health of mothers, infants, and families.

www.HypnoBirthing.com Web site for information about using hypnosis for a relaxed birth.

www.ican-online.org: Web site of the International Cesarean Awareness Network (ICAN).

www.icea.org: Web site of the International Childbirth Education Association.

www.infant-parent.com: The Infant-Parent Institute specializes in clinical services, professional training, and research related to the optimal development of infants and their families.

www.lamaze.org: Web site of Lamaze International.

www.llli.org: La Leche League International provides a network of mother-to-mother support for breastfeeding mothers.

www.mothering.com/articles/new_baby/new_baby_main.html: A wide variety of articles from *Mothering* magazine that are related to many aspects of caring for a new baby.

www.nocirc.org: Web site of the National Organization of Circumcision Information Resource Centers.

http://pediatrics.aappublications.org/cgi/content/abstract/80/2/215: An abstract regarding a survey about making the decision to circumcise.

www.waterbirth.org: Information about water births and how to find a water birth practitioner.

Chapter Three

Principle 2
Feed with Love and Respect:
Beginning the Attachment Process

Feed with Love and Respect: Beginning the Attachment Process

What is established in the breastfeeding relationship...
and the communication the infant receives through the
warmth of the mother's skin constitutes the first of the
socializing experiences of life.[1]

Ashley Montagu
Touching

In his seminal book, *Touching*, anthropologist and human developmentalist Dr. Ashley Montagu beautifully describes the beginning of the attachment process. Most parents today know of the health benefits of breastfeeding, but few understand that the initial feeding is nature's way of laying the foundation for a secure attachment. Whether a parent is breastfeeding or bottle-feeding, the purpose of this chapter is to help you understand how feeding your child enhances your future attachment relationship. We discuss breastfeeding first because it is a natural model of attachment, and then apply many of the attachment principles seen in breastfeeding families to parents and caregivers who are bottle-feeding their babies.

First, feeding a child involves more than providing nutrients; it is an act of love. From satisfying the very intense hunger needs of a newborn to serving meals at the family dinner table, parents can use feeding time as an opportunity to strengthen their bonds with their children. The newborn's rooting, sucking, and crying reflexes ensure the close proximity of a mother or other dependable caregiver to meet his intense needs. The more parents learn to identify and meet their baby's needs, the more secure the parent-child bond becomes. We also discuss how parents can continue to respect hunger cues as their babies start solid foods and are able to feed themselves. It is so important that this process includes offering nutritious foods, modeling healthy eating habits, and making mealtime an opportunity for love and connection.

---

1   Montagu, *Touching*, 92–93.

Why Breastfeeding is the Attachment Model

Again, Dr. Montagu describes what the baby and the mother need at the moment of birth:

> [W]hat the newborn is looking forward to ... is a continuation of the life he enjoyed in the womb—in other words, a womb with a view— ... the child will also, by suckling, confer vital benefits upon the mother ... producing massive contractions of the uterus ... and [the placenta] is ejected ... Psychologically, this intensification serves further to consolidate the symbiotic bond between [the mother] and her child.[2]

In other words, the baby and the mother have a reciprocal relationship from the moment of birth, and the act of suckling the baby soon after birth has tremendous physiological and psychological advantages for both mother and baby.

When a baby is first put in the breastfeeding position, he is experiencing a sensory bath of warmth, touch, smell, taste, and soothing sounds. His head is in the crook of his mother's arm, placing his field of vision approximately eleven inches away from his mother's face. Science tells us that newborns can only focus at about this distance, so we see how this close proximity to the mother is biologically programmed in

---

2   Montagu, *Touching,* 70–74.

the infant's brain.[3] Science also tells us that babies are hardwired to seek the human face as their first "imprint."[4]

Another attachment promoting behavior we learn from the breastfeeding model is the importance of sensitivity to a baby's feeding cues. Since a breastfeeding mother does not have a bottle with ounces to look at, she is trusting that her baby will signal when he's hungry and when he's full. He may want to nurse again in an hour, or perhaps three hours, depending on how much he took in at the last feeding, how well it was digested, whether he just wants to suck a bit more—so many factors! A bottle-feeding parent can also trust that if her baby doesn't finish the bottle, it's important to not force him to eat more, or, alternatively, if he is hungry again in a short time, to be patient with his needs and trust his signals.

Breastfeeding on cue creates a close nursing relationship, ensures that the mother produces enough milk, and provides the baby with the nutrition and loving touch that is naturally designed for optimal brain development and growth. The mother is now the baby's environment. When the mother is holding her baby, she develops a unique ability to read her child's nonverbal cues, which enables her to respond empathically to his needs even before he gets to the crying stage. A baby's cues may include squirming, making fussing sounds, putting his hand in his mouth, rooting, and turning his head toward his mother's breast. This sensitivity fosters a sense of trust; the baby trusts that his signals are being understood, and the mother learns to trust her own ability to read her baby's cues, laying a foundation for all their future interactions.

A healthy, happy baby develops secure attachments with his caregivers because he more easily reciprocates the loving, smiling behaviors that he receives. During times of sickness, breast milk provides the necessary nutrition and antibodies to fight germs, helping to shorten the duration of an illness or to avoid the illness completely. An unhappy or sickly baby may spend so much time and energy in crying or fussing that there is less opportunity for relaxing or playful interactions until he is feeling better. Another amazing factor is that the colostrum (the first milk a mother produces) from the mother of a premature baby is higher in protein and other nutrients than that of a mother of a full-term baby, which suggests

---

3   Brazelton and Cramer, *Earliest Relationship: Parents, Infants, and the Drama of Early Attachment*, 55.

4   Mondloch et al., "Face perception during early infancy," *Psychological Science*.

that even if a baby is too fragile to breastfeed, the mother should be encouraged to pump her colostrum for her baby.[5]

As a mother becomes more adept, she will find that nursing becomes easier, and she will appreciate its convenience—it is available anytime, anywhere, and satisfies many more needs than infant hunger. As discussed in chapter 4, being responsive to a hungry baby is so important in the early weeks, and having the ready breast can be a great help! Bottle-feeding parents have found strategies to meet this need by having a minifridge with prepared bottles nearby, and bottle warmers that can heat a bottle quickly if needed. Be aware that microwaves are not recommended for heating bottles, whether they contain formula or expressed breast milk. Microwaves can cause "hot spots" that can burn the baby's mouth, even if you've checked the temperature on your wrist.

As the child gets older, nursing is a valuable mothering tool as it is naturally comforting to the baby. Nursing when a child is hurt or upset can help calm him and meet his needs quickly. "Comfort nursing" meets the baby's sucking needs and is one of the many wonderful benefits of breastfeeding. This aspect of nursing continues throughout the breastfeeding relationship.

Breastfeeding is also an advantage for the mother's health and well-being. Breastfeeding triggers the release of the attachment-promoting hormone oxytocin into the mother's body. Often called "the mothering hormone," oxytocin has a calming effect on both mother and baby. Research on this amazing hormone gives us insight into the biological foundation for our early emotional attachments. Oxytocin is released through pleasant warmth and rhythmic touch. When a baby suckles at his mother's breast, an amazing chain of events ensues:

> The breast … is stimulated by the suckling of the
> infant. Nerve impulses travel from the breast … causing
> oxytocin to be released into the bloodstream. This blood-
> borne oxytocin reaches the … organized muscle cells
> that lie next to the milk producing cells in the breast.
> These cells then contract and squeeze out the milk. All
> this is a reflex action…. Then when the woman sees her
> baby, hears the infant cry, or even just thinks about him

---

5   Montagu, *Touching*, 75.

> or her, she may experience a tightening in her breast
> from the pressure of the milk, which may even begin to
> flow…. During nursing oxytocin also produces other
> effects … women experience a warming of the torso
> when nursing…. To survive, infants need not only
> nourishment but also warmth, care, and protection.

The good news for a mother or caregiver who is not breastfeeding is that she can still receive oxytocin benefits from holding the baby skin-to-skin, and also by giving and receiving nurturing touch through massage and gentle caress.

Another advantage for mothers is that breastfeeding can reduce the risk of many devastating diseases such as breast cancer and other cancers.[6] We know that postpartum depression can have a harmful effect on mothers and their ability to form secure attachments with their babies. Research in depression is showing a correlation between lower levels of certain hormones in mothers who experience depression, so it appears that anything we can do to increase levels of these natural hormones may be a powerful aid in prevention.

> Prolactin is the hormone associated with the onset and
> maintenance of lactation, and sharply rises postpartum….
> In one study, data were collected from twenty-three
> pregnant women, seventy postpartum women (at seven
> days postpartum), and thirty-eight nongravid [not
> pregnant] controls. Postpartum women had significantly
> greater levels of cortisol, prolactin, thyroxine, and estrogen
> then the nongravid women. The women with postpartum
> depression had significantly lower plasma prolactin levels
> than those who were not depressed. Women who breastfed
> were significantly less depressed than those who did not.
> Also, women with previous episodes of depression had
> significantly lower prolactin and TSH levels than those
> who had not been previously depressed.[7]

---

6   Newcomb et al., "Lactation and a reduced risk of premenopausal breast cancer," *New England Journal of Medicine*.

7   Kendall-Tackett, *Depression in New Mothers*, 51.

Fathers and Oxytocin

Fathers are not left out of the oxytocin equation. It has been shown that a live-in father's oxytocin levels rise toward the end of his mate's pregnancy. When the father spends significant amounts of time in contact with his infant, oxytocin encourages him to become more involved in the ongoing care in a self-perpetuating cycle. Oxytocin in the father also increases his interest in physical (not necessarily sexual) contact with the mother. Nature now provides a way for the father to become more interested in being a devoted and satisfied part of the family picture through his involvement with the baby. With all its powers, oxytocin is but one of a list of many chemicals that nature uses to ensure that baby finds the love and care he needs.[8]

Linda Palmer, DC
Attachment Parenting: The Journal of API

Some adoptive mothers have successfully breastfed their babies! Even if an adoptive mother is unable to produce enough milk to supply all of her baby's needs, by using a device called a nursing supplementer (an SNS or a Lact-Aid are two examples), she is able to put her baby to the breast and feed him.

A supplemental nursing system is a device that allows a baby to nurse at the breast when the mother is not able to produce enough milk to support the baby without supplementation. Silicone tubing attached to a bag or bottle of breast milk [or artificial milk] is then taped to the mother's breast so that when baby latches on to nurse, she receives milk from the tubing in addition to any milk produced by the mother.

---

8   Palmer, "The chemistry of attachment," *Attachment Parenting: The Journal of API*.

This suckling can stimulate a mother's milk supply, especially in situations when an adoptive mother is attempting to relactate for the adopted infant.[9]

It is critical that partners and other extended family members understand how important it is for a breastfeeding mother to feel supported. Studies show that mothers have greater breastfeeding success when partners are knowledgeable and supportive of breastfeeding.[10]

Breastfeeding also helps the environment! There are no bottles to sterilize or products to dispose of, and it preserves another valuable resource—money. A breastfeeding family can save about $150 a month, not to mention savings in health care. Obviously, saving money and the environment can have psychological and emotional advantages!

Can I Continue Nursing if I Become Pregnant Again?

For most mothers, breastfeeding a baby without supplementation will suppress ovulation, protecting her from conceiving another child for a period of time. This can vary from a few months to a few years, and from nature's viewpoint, we see that spacing our children gives the older baby time to grow and mature before a new sibling arrives.

If a mother gets pregnant while she's still breastfeeding, she can usually continue to nurse during a healthy pregnancy. Nursing an older child and a baby is known as "tandem nursing." Deciding to nurse through a pregnancy can provide definite advantages to the attachment relationship between the mother and child. If the baby is still very young and breast milk is still a major part of his diet and emotional well-being, a mother might have an easier decision to continue. If the child is eating a lot of solid food and drinking from a cup, a mother may want to consider if her toddler is still needing to nurse, and if so, how often. Many mothers have found that their milk may diminish to the point that their toddler loses interest in nursing and gradually weans on his own. Every nursing mother and child pair is different, and it is important for a mother to get the support and information she needs to help her make the best

---

9   Artz, "Adopting a high-risk child," *Attachment Parenting: The Journal of API.*

10   Arora et al., "Major factors influencing breastfeeding rates: Mother's perception of father's attitude and milk supply," *Pediatrics.*

decision for her and her child. The key is that the weaning process ideally be handled gradually and with empathy and love.

If the older baby or child has weaned by the time a new baby is born, it is not unusual for him to want to nurse again when he sees a new sibling at the breast. Parents may refer to La Leche League International publications *The Womanly Art of Breastfeeding* and *Adventures in Tandem Nursing: Breastfeeding during Pregnancy and Beyond* for thorough discussions of the issues surrounding the decision to nurse through a pregnancy and beyond.

Bottle Nursing—Using Breastfeeding Behaviors to Bottle-Feed

We have been contacted by many parents and caregivers who want to incorporate the most loving behaviors into their feeding practices with their babies. Our culture often supports practices that create disconnection from our children. For instance, some parents have shared with us that they were given baby gear to encourage a "hands off" style of parenting, including devices to prop a baby bottle so the baby does not have to be held during feedings. An API support group meeting may be the first place where a parent hears how important it is that babies be fed in the arms of a loved one.

API developed guidelines for bottle-feeding with a unique viewpoint. Because we encourage all parents to look at their parenting choices through the lens of attachment, we have coined the term "bottle nursing" because it reflects breastfeeding behaviors and has tremendous advantages to the parent or other caregiver and baby. These recommendations are applicable to infants who are bottle-fed breast milk, formula, or a combination.

To simulate breastfeeding, parents hold the baby in the crook of the arm, positioning the bottle alongside the breast. This position places the baby's face and cheek in contact with the parent's arm, and this skin-to-skin contact helps parent and baby feel more connected. Holding the baby during feeds also helps to prevent the baby from developing "flat-head syndrome," or *plagiocephaly*, which can happen when a child is left on a flat surface too frequently. When a baby drinks from a propped bottle,

75

mother and baby also miss an important opportunity to strengthen their emotional connection. Propping the bottle can also be a choking hazard.

Try to make feeding time a special time of calm for both parent and child. Maintain eye contact while feeding when the baby is alert and interested, and switch positions from one side to another; these help strengthen the baby's eye muscles. Talk softly and lovingly to baby at feeding times. Parents should respect their child's hunger cues by avoiding feeding schedules. Following the child's cues helps to strengthen the attachment relationship and shows the baby that his needs are understood.

A Foster Mother's Story

We take care of our foster babies as if they were our birth children in every way, except that they are bottle-fed. We hold them as much as we can; I wear them in a sling all of the time when I am out in public, and we never take the car seat out of the car. We sleep in close proximity to them; we have a porta-crib next to our bed. We feed them bottles but use a breastfeeding model, holding them close, never propping the bottle, changing sides for eye-hand coordination, … demand-feeding, yet being careful not to overfeed them formula (which is not a concern with breast milk). We answer their needs as quickly as is humanly possible, helping them to feel as if they are the most precious beings on this earth.[11]

Reedy Hickey, foster mother of thirty-two infants
Attachment Parenting: The Journal of API

Some mothers (or primary caregivers) who bottle nurse choose to follow the breastfeeding model closely so the baby associates feeding with being held; therefore, the mother is the primary person who feeds him while using the bottle. This approach to bottle-feeding produces many benefits for mother and child. The mother will have an opportunity to sit down, to

---

11   Silver, "Interview with Reedy and P. J. Hickey," *Attachment Parenting: The Journal of API*.

have a special time to bond and rest, just as a breastfeeding mother would be "allowed" to do. A new mother sometimes needs this excuse to rest, instead of feeling that she must do all the housework or other tasks while letting someone else feed the baby. With this behavior, the baby benefits from the consistency of his mother's presence while feeding and is able to gaze at her face, smell her scent, and feel secure in her arms. This enables their precious attachment relationship to deepen. A mother might say to a well-intentioned relative or friend who wants to feed the baby that this is their special bonding time and a rest time for Mom.

Sucking can remain a strong need well past the first year or two. Pacifiers, when used appropriately, can satisfy that need until the child outgrows it. Breastfeeding babies suck at the breast for comfort, so parents of bottle-fed babies can enrich their child's experience by either holding the baby in the feeding position when giving a pacifier or simply holding and comforting an older child. These modifications increase close physical contact and bonding time and can make weaning from the pacifier a more natural and gradual process.

As the baby gets older and is able to hold his own bottle, the parent may be tempted to allow the baby to feed himself or to let him walk around with a bottle rather than providing the comfort the child is seeking. If a child doesn't associate the bottle with being held or having undivided attention by the parent, he might use the bottle or a pacifier as a comfort tool, or "transitional object." Toddlers who use the bottle, pacifier, or thumb for comfort—rather than being comforted by the parent—may have a much harder time giving up the bottle, pacifier, or thumb down the road. If they learn to come to their parent for comfort or cuddle time and perhaps a short time of sucking on their bottle or pacifier, eventually they will prefer the cuddle and gradually wean from the transitional object, much like a breastfeeding toddler weans from the breast. In the case of a baby or child who must be separated from their parents during part of the day, it is important that the parent evaluate how important a pacifier or other transitional object is for the security of the child. In some cases, it would be cruel to forbid the use of these comforts, so parents must use their best judgment.

Nurturing Yourself while Feeding Your Baby

Feeding time is the ideal time to take a break, rest, and refuel. For example, mothers can nurture themselves when feeding the new baby by sitting in a comfortable chair, having something to drink (like water or herbal tea), and taking this special time to connect with their baby. As mentioned earlier, the distance from a baby's eyes to his mother's eyes while feeding is about eleven inches, the perfect focal length for newborn vision. Nature provides this perfect visual field for baby to study his parents' faces, allowing baby to fall in love with his parents through sight, taste, touch, smell, and sound.

Just as a baby flourishes when fed by his mother, the new mother flourishes when nurtured by her partner. Sometimes mothers become so involved in the care of their infants that they don't recognize their own needs until they are in emotional or physical trouble. Mothers need frequent rest, plentiful fluids, and adequate nutrition.

A father's relationship with the baby is unique and extremely important in the child's overall development. It is important that fathers (especially those whose babies are breastfed) know they can still develop a close relationship with their baby in many ways other than feeding—such as holding or burping the baby after he has eaten, bathing the baby, changing a diaper, practicing infant massage, taking walks and naps together, and playfully interacting with the baby. Also, when the father nurtures the mother, he nurtures his baby as well.

Introducing Solid Food

What does starting babies on solid food have to do with attachment parenting? A parent's sensitivity and attunement to the baby will be important in determining whether he is ready for solid food. As with all decisions, a parent must examine available options and make the best choice for the child—in this case, parents must opt for foods conducive to optimal brain and physical development. Babies fed the healthiest diet are sick less often, have fewer discipline problems, and achieve more in school. Babies start to show interest in solid foods toward the second half of the first year. Signs of readiness include getting a few teeth, drooling, interest in what the parents are eating, nursing more frequently, sitting up unassisted, and the ability to pick up small pieces of food. Until these external signs are in place, it is unlikely that the baby is fully ready. It is important to remember that the child will let his parents know when he is ready. For instance, some babies who are prone to allergies may naturally reject solid foods until they are older.

Many experts agree that a baby is ready for solid food when he no longer thrusts out his tongue, and he is able to pick up small items like dry cereal with his thumb and forefinger. When a baby is just learning to eat solids, offer breast or bottle first, followed by one solid food. Start slowly with foods that are not likely to cause allergies (delay dairy, eggs, fish, soy, peanuts, and any foods that other family members are allergic to). Introduce gluten-containing foods (wheat, barley, and rye) with caution. Gradually introducing gluten reduces the risk of celiac disease (an allergy to wheat gluten). Watch for signs that new foods agree with the baby and that he shows a genuine interest in them. Introduce new foods one at a time for at least five days before introducing another food. This allows time for any allergic reaction to manifest. Be aware that some babies do not like to be spoon fed solid food. They would prefer to feed themselves, so give them the opportunity to have small bits of food on their plate or high chair tray to try themselves. This is one way they learn to manage the amount of food they want to eat.

While the American Academy of Pediatrics recommends introducing solids at six months of age, breast milk or artificial milk will likely be a baby's primary nutrition source until about one year of age. It is normal for your child to eat only small quantities of solid foods during this time. Regardless of the amount consumed, mealtimes are an important opportunity for the child to explore new tastes and textures, to develop feeding skills, and to learn the social behaviors of the family's mealtime routines. More information about introducing solids is available through the resources listed at the end of this chapter.

Watch Out for Allergies

An important part of being attuned to your child and his sensitivities is to be conscious of how food can affect his moods, energy levels, and physical problems. Wheat, eggs, and dairy have been identified as the three most common allergens; however, acidic fruits or vegetables may also cause your child discomfort. Don't be alarmed if your child shows no interest in food before one year of age.

Some children need more time for their immune systems to develop before they are able to digest solid foods. Some of the signs of a food allergy are runny nose, itchy nose or eyes, rash, irritability, sleeplessness, diarrhea, or refusal to eat a certain food. Let your child be your guide, and allow your child to develop his taste for food naturally.

Food Additives and Hyperactivity?

For years parents have reported to their doctors their concerns about hyperactivity in their children … and could it possibly be related to the foods they were eating? Most doctors did not see a relationship, but recently the prestigious British medical journal, *The Lancet*, published a study on children's behavior and artificial food additives. The researchers concluded the following:

> For many of the assessments, there were small but statistically significant differences of measured behaviors in children who consumed the food additives compared with those who did not. In each case, increased hyperactive behaviors were associated with consuming the additives. For those comparisons in which no statistically significant differences were found, there was a trend for more hyperactive behaviors associated with the food additive drink in virtually every assessment. Thus, the overall findings of the study are clear and require that even we skeptics, who have long doubted parental claims of the effects of various foods on the behavior of their children, admit we might have been wrong.[12]

---

12 McCann et al., "Food additives and hyperactive behaviour in 3-year-old and 8/9-year-old children in the community: A randomised, double-blinded, placebo-controlled trial," *The Lancet.*

Nurturing a Taste for Nutritious Food

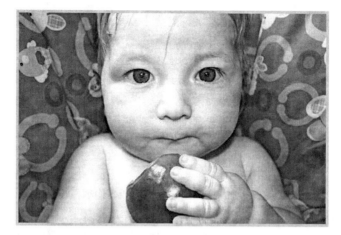

Breast milk prepares infants for the varying tastes of solid foods because it is flavored by the foods eaten by the nursing mother. Generally, children develop their eating patterns from their parents; therefore, it's never too early for parents to begin improving their own habits. When parents offer only nutritious foods in the early years, children will develop a natural taste for these foods and learn important lessons about good nutrition.

What is considered "nutritious" food? Generally a good rule of thumb for identifying nutritious foods is those foods that are in the most natural state (least processed) possible. Ideally, these foods are grown or raised organically (avoiding pesticides and growth hormones). Children who tolerate dairy products usually love cheeses and yogurt. Consider cheeses that are natural, such as Swiss, rather than processed cheeses like American cheese. Plain yogurt sweetened with a little maple syrup and fresh fruit makes a healthy snack. Foods containing dyes, preservatives, excess salt, and sugar should be avoided. Parents don't have to rely on baby food that comes prepackaged. By six months of age or older, babies are often interested in eating what their parents eat. Cooking foods with minimal seasoning can provide meals for the family and for the baby without any extra work or expense. Adults can always add additional spices or embellishments after cooking. Mashing or blending some foods prepared for an adult meal may make them palatable for a baby. They then can be frozen in small portions in an ice tray for future meals.

Remember that it is the parent's job to provide healthy choices and model eating nutritious meals. The child should be allowed to choose what to eat from these healthy choices and how much to eat. A growing child requires nutritious snacks (such as prepared finger foods) and meals throughout the day. Snacks or drinks that contain sugar will curb the child's appetite and negatively impact their willingness to eat more nutritious foods. Encourage your child to follow his bodily cues of hunger and thirst; this teaches him to eat when he is hungry and stop when he is full. Forcing your child to eat when he is not hungry, or to eat foods he does not want to eat, can lead to unhealthy eating habits and potentially to eating disorders. Never use food as a reward or punishment or make food or dessert contingent on behavior. Rather than restricting access to foods, consider having only healthy foods available in the home. Toddlers are busy and burn a lot of calories; they need to eat multiple small meals during the day and should not be expected to sit at a dinner table for long periods of time. Studies have shown that when offered a variety of healthy food choices, children will, over time, select a balanced diet (even if they only eat peas for one week and chicken for the next). Parents who have concerns about their child's eating habits, diet, allergies, or general health should refer to the resources listed at the end of this chapter.

Gentle Weaning

The American Academy of Pediatrics 2005 Breastfeeding Policy Statement advises, "It is recommended that breastfeeding continue for at least twelve months, and thereafter for as long as mutually desired." They also state, "There is no upper limit to the duration of breastfeeding and no evidence of psychological or developmental harm from breastfeeding into the third year of life or longer." The World Health Organization goes on to add that even though in Western cultures it may be unusual to see a child nurse past one year, worldwide it is normal for children, and it continues to be important nutritionally, immunologically, and emotionally to nurse beyond one year.[13]

As surprising as it may seem to some, nursing beyond one or two years of age is normal human behavior and continues to offer many advantages, not the least of which is to satisfy a strong sucking need. Although weaning begins the moment solid foods are introduced into a baby's diet, breast milk remains a beneficial component of the child's nutrition and overall good health. It is also an effective comforting tool, providing both mother and child with a special, relaxing time together to reconnect.

Food increasingly takes the place of breast milk in terms of caloric need, but nursing continues to meet many other needs such as security and connection. La Leche League International and API recommend that weaning occur only when a child outgrows the need. In other words, the child is showing signs of readiness and may be nursing more out of habit than need. For instance if you find that your toddler has been nursing every time you get on the phone, you might choose to find a quiet activity that replaces nursing at this time. If a child finds that this is the only way he can get your attention, you begin to see the difference between a habit and a need.

If weaning is initiated by the mother, it should be done gradually and sensitively. If there comes a point where the mother needs to wean before the child has displayed a readiness to wean, gentle techniques such as distraction, substitution, extension of time between sessions, night weaning, response by the father to baby's nighttime needs, or shortened nursing sessions may help. Local API or La Leche League support groups may offer more ideas or suggestions for weaning. Fathers and other caregivers can also help the mother at this time by becoming more involved in the care of, and activities with, their older child. If the child

---

13   World Health Organization, "Breastfeeding," World Health Organization Web site.

reacts strongly to this change, parents should assess the situation and the child's unmet needs and re-evaluate the child's true readiness.

An empathic mother understands that abrupt weaning from breast or bottle can affect the attachment relationship with her child, so it is important for parents to develop strategies for replacing the nursing frequency with extra attention. This may include more time for cuddling and reading stories, drinking from a cup when thirsty, and playing together.

Children under one year of age will need to be weaned from breast to bottle, and bottle-fed children should be weaned as gently from their bottles as breastfed babies are from the breast. Parents should remember that the weaning process takes time and patience; every child is different, so there is no set timetable. Parents can learn more about these techniques in La Leche League International's book, *How Weaning Happens* by Diane Bengson.

Mealtime—A Time for Promoting Connection in the Family

Many cultures around the world have preserved the tradition of family mealtimes as one of the most important times of the day. So often in American families, the TV is on and the family may sit in the living room or even go off to their bedrooms to eat their meals. Gordon Neufeld and Gabor Maté, in their book *Hold On to Your Kids*, remind us of why this time is so important in family life:

> Since our sojourn in Provence, France, I have come to consider the family sit-down meal as one of the most significant attachment rituals of all. Attachment and eating go together. One facilitates the other. It seems to me that the meal should be a time of unabashed dependency: where the attachment hierarchy is still preserved, where the dependable take care of the dependent, where experience still counts, where there is pleasure in nurturing and being nurtured and where food is the way to the heart....

What other activity can provide something for our
children to hold on to, and invite our children to
depend on us? What other activity provides us the
opportunity to collect the eyes, coax the smiles, and
get them nodding?[14]

Make mealtimes with your baby and child an important family
gathering time. Try to make at least one meal a day (dinner time for most
families) a time for connection and community. A couple can begin this
ritual of creating a special time even before their baby arrives by turning
off the TV, making a conscious choice to not answer the phone, and
being present for each other at mealtime. Once this habit is started, it
will be a natural part of the child's experience as he grows up. If parents
keep their conversation positive, loving, and interesting, everyone will
have a pleasant association with mealtime, which will help not only in
good digestion but will also enhance the attachment relationships that
were started when giving baby his first feeding soon after birth.

---

14   Neufeld and Maté, *Hold On to Your Kids*, 207.

Appendix to Chapter Three: Additional Research and Resource Recommendations

Additional Research

Attachment researchers Mary Ainsworth and Silvia Bell conducted a study of twenty-six mother-infant pairs during the first three months of life, their feeding behaviors (whether they scheduled the feedings or were flexible according to the baby's signals, called demand feeding), the correlation of periods of crying (duration, frequency), and the relationship to security of attachment when the infants reached one year of age. Some of their findings are summarized below:

> [T]he first two patterns of feeding interactions (the consistent-demand feeding and the flexible-schedule feeding) are the two associated with the least crying. The babies in these two groups are conspicuous for the little amount of crying during feeding, and this seems to be related to the sensitive pacing and the prompt response to signals which characterized the mothers' feeding practices.

> [The arbitrary] feeding pattern ... is especially associated with long duration of prolonged crying before feeding.... This reflects the fact that the mothers of these babies tended to be very slow in responding to hunger cues. They were also slow to respond to crying generally; the overall cries tend to become very prolonged.

> It is evident that the ... feeding patterns in which the mothers were relatively sensitive and responsive to the babies' signals and communications, are associated with relatively little crying, while the other ... feeding patterns in which the mothers were relatively

insensitive or unresponsive, are associated with a relatively large amount of crying.

[Report on results of Strange Situation administered at one year of age.] Babies whose mothers were especially sensitive and responsive to them in the early feeding situation, and indeed generally, manifested attachment to their mothers (without conspicuous behavioral disturbance) through active efforts both to regain contact after a brief separation and to maintain contact once gained by clinging and resisting release.

Babies whose mothers were relatively insensitive and unresponsive to them in the early feeding situation, tended, at the end of the first year, either to lack interest in regaining and in maintaining contact with their mothers when reunited after an absence, or to intermingle contact-seeking behavior with rejection of her—either tending to go away and to look away from her or to angrily push away or to push away the toys offered by her.

[In conclusion], although for most babies the feeding situation has become a relatively unimportant occasion for mother-infant interaction by the end of the first year, the baby's experience in influencing his mother's behavior through his own actions—an experience which begins in the earliest weeks of life—seems likely to influence the nature of his attachment.

The findings presented here suggest an early experience can have a significant effect on later development.[15]

---

15 Ainsworth and Bell, "Some contemporary patterns of mother-infant attachment interaction in the feeding situation," In *Stimulation in Early Infancy*, 133–170.

The World Health Organization ranks methods of infant feeding in order of preference based on best health benefits to the baby:[16]

- The first choice is nursing
- Second choice is pumped breast milk in a bottle or supplemental feeding system
- Third choice is breast milk from another lactating mother
- And, if none of these methods is available, artificial milk

Animal studies have found that oxytocin promotes the initiation of maternal behavior and bonding between mother and baby. Oxytocin not only stimulates maternal behavior, but it has also been found to have sedative, antistress effects on the mother, with oxytocin levels correlating with levels of anxiety and aggression. Breastfeeding mothers have reported that they feel calmer due to breastfeeding and are less likely to overreact to everyday stressors, probably due to decreased blood pressure and cortisol levels that occur in response to breastfeeding.[17]

Education of mothers, families (especially fathers), and health care professionals regarding the benefits of breastfeeding, as well as how to overcome barriers, has a positive impact on the number of mothers choosing to breastfeed. Seventy-eight percent of women stated that they made decisions about breastfeeding before pregnancy or during the first trimester.[18]

Breastfeeding significantly decreased rates of many illnesses, including diarrhea[19] and sudden infant death syndrome (SIDS).[20]

---

16   World Health Organization, *Global Strategy for Infant and Young Child Feeding*, 7.

17   Uvnäs-Moberg and Eriksson, "Breastfeeding: physiological, endocrine and behavioural adaptations caused by oxytocin and local neurogenic activity in the nipple and mammary gland," *Acta Paediatrica.*

18   Arora et al., "Major factors influencing breastfeeding rates: Mother's perception of father's attitude and milk supply," *Pediatrics.*

19   Lerman, "Epidemiology of acute diarrheal diseases in children in a high standard of living settlement in Israel," *Pediatric Infectious Diseases Journal.*

20   Ford et al., "Breastfeeding and the risk of sudden infant death syndrome," *International Journal of Epidemiology.*

Lack of breastfeeding has been associated with increased risks of developing multiple sclerosis,[21] respiratory infections, otitis media,[22] childhood cancer,[23] and insulin-dependent (type I) diabetes (formerly referred to as "juvenile diabetes").[24]

Breast milk provides a protective effect against Hodgkin disease among children who are breastfed at least eight months.[25]

In general, breastfed children do better cognitively as well, with significantly higher IQ scores.[26]

Researchers found an 11 percent decrease of breast cancer in premenopausal women who breastfed for up to twelve months. It was suggested that if women breastfed up to twenty-four months, the breast cancer rate could be reduced by close to 25 percent.[27]

Women who were breastfed as infants, even if only for a short time, showed approximately a 25 percent lower risk of premenopausal and postmenopausal breast cancer than did women who were bottle-fed.[28]

The decision to breastfeed is significantly related to the father's level of education and to his approval of breastfeeding. The strong approval of breastfeeding by the father was associated with a high incidence of

---

21 Dick, "The etiology of multiple sclerosis," *Proceedings of the Royal Society of Medicine.*

22 Alho, "Risk factors for recurrent acute otitis media and respiratory infection in infancy," *International Journal of Pediatric Otorhinolaryngology.*

23 Davis, "Infant feeding and childhood cancer," *The Lancet.*

24 Young et al., "Type 2 diabetes mellitus in children: prenatal and early infancy risk factors among native Canadians," *Archives of Pediatric and Adolescent Medicine.*

25 Schwartzbaum, "An exploratory study of environmental and medical factors potentially related to childhood cancer," *Medical and Pediatric Oncology.*

26 Lucas, "Breast milk and subsequent intelligence quotient in children born preterm," *The Lancet.*

27 Newcomb et al., "Lactation and a reduced risk of premenopausal breast cancer," *New England Journal of Medicine.*

28 Freudenheim, "Exposure to breast milk in infancy and the risk of breast cancer," *Epidemiology.*

breastfeeding (98.1%) compared to only 26.9% breastfeeding rates when the father was indifferent to [the mother's] feeding choice.[29]

Mothers who don't breastfeed at all during a baby's first year are more than twice as likely to be depressed. Those mothers who exclusively breastfed their infants had lower scores on perceived stress tests.[30]

Newborns' preferences were influenced both by the visibility of the stimuli and by their resemblance to a human face. There appears to be a mechanism, likely subcortical, predisposing newborns to look toward faces. Changes in preferences at six and twelve weeks of age suggest increasing cortical influence over infants' preferences for faces.[31]

Animal studies have found that oxytocin promotes the initiation of maternal behavior and bonding between mother and baby.[32]

Oxytocin not only stimulates maternal behavior but has also been found to have sedative, antistress effects on the mother, with oxytocin levels correlating with levels of anxiety and aggression.[33]

Breastfeeding mothers have reported that they feel calmer due to breastfeeding and are less likely to overreact to everyday stressors, probably due to decreased blood pressure and cortisol levels that occur in response to breastfeeding.[34]

Early breastfeeding was associated with higher quality mother-infant interactions at twelve months.[35]

---

29   Littman et al., "The decision to breastfeed," *Clinical Pediatrics.*

30   Mezzacappa and Katkin, "Breastfeeding is associated with reduced perceived stress and negative mood in mothers," *Health Psychology.*

31   Mondloch et al., "Face perception during early infancy," *Psychological Science.*

32   Uvnäs-Moberg and Eriksson, "Breastfeeding: physiological, endocrine and behavioural adaptations caused by oxytocin and local neurogenic activity in the nipple and mammary gland," *Acta Paediatrica.*

33   Ibid.

34   Ibid.

35   Else-Quest, "Breastfeeding, bonding, and the mother-infant relationship," *Merrill-Palmer Quarterly.*

When some aspects of care giving are not good enough, breastfeeding may provide detectable benefits for the mother-infant relationship.[36]

Recommended Reading

Adventures in Tandem Nursing: Breastfeeding during Pregnancy and Beyond by Hilary Flowers.

Baby Matters: What Your Doctor May Not Tell You About Caring for Your Baby (2nd ed.) by Linda F. Palmer, DC.

Birth and Breastfeeding by Michel Odent, MD.

Eating Well for Optimum Health by Andrew Weil, MD.

Eat Healthy, Feel Great by William Sears, MD, and Martha Sears, RN.

Eat Well and Lose Weight while Breastfeeding by Eileen Behan.

Feeding the Whole Family: Whole Recipes for Babies, Young Children, and Their Parents by Cynthia Lair.

How Weaning Happens by Diane Bengson.

Mothering Multiples: Breastfeeding and Caring for Twins or More! by Karen Kerkhoff Gromada.

Mothering Your Nursing Toddler by Norma Jane Bumgarner.

My Child Won't Eat by Carlos Gonzalez, MD.

The Baby Book by William Sears, MD, James Sears, MD, Robert Sears, MD, and Martha Sears, RN.

The Breastfeeding Book by William Sears, MD, and Martha Sears, RN.

The Family Nutrition Book by William Sears, MD, and Martha Sears, RN.

The Healthiest Kid in the Neighborhood by William Sears, MD, Martha Sears, RN, James Sears, MD, and Robert Sears, MD.

The Womanly Art of Breastfeeding by La Leche League International.

The Ultimate Breastfeeding Book of Answers: The Most Comprehensive Problem-Solving Guide from the Foremost Expert in North America by Jack Newman, MD, and Teresa Pitman.

Touching: The Human Significance of the Skin by Ashley Montagu, PhD.

Whole Foods for Babies and Toddlers by Margaret Kenda.

Whole Foods for the Whole Family by La Leche League International.

Why Your Child is Hyperactive by Ben Feingold, MD.

---

36   Ibid.

Useful Web Sites

www.attachmentparenting.org: Information on feeding babies, toddlers, and small children available on the Web site of Attachment Parenting International.

http://www.granitescientific.com/BreastfeedingCSASurvivor. pdf: Important information for mothers of child sexual abuse and breastfeeding.

www.llli.org: La Leche League International provides a network of mother-to-mother support for breastfeeding mothers. (*A note from the authors: API does not dispense breastfeeding advice to parents beyond general discussions about breastfeeding and attachment issues. We refer mothers to La Leche League International and their support groups to get expert advice and education about breastfeeding.)

www.AskDrSears.com: Web site of Dr. William Sears and family, providing information on feeding the baby and young child, including information on supplemental nursing systems.

www.bfhi.org: Baby Friendly Hospital Initiative of UNICEF, which includes information on helping establish good feeding practices as soon as the baby is born.

www.breastfeedingmadesimple.com: Kathleen Kendall-Tackett's excellent resource for breastfeeding, including tips for moms who may have depression and want guidance on breastfeeding, safe medications, and alternative therapies.

www.who.int/nutrition/topcis/infantfeeding_recommendation/ en/index.html: World Health Organization site providing information on infant feeding.

Chapter Four

Principle 3
Responding with Sensitivity:
Learning the Language of Love

Responding with Sensitivity: Learning the Language of Love

> *Here's how the early mother-infant communication system works. The opening sounds of the baby's cry activate a mother's emotions. This is physical as well as psychological. Upon hearing her baby cry, a mother experiences an increased blood flow to her breasts, accompanied by the biological urge to pick up and nurse her baby. This is one of the strongest examples of how the biological signals of the baby trigger a biological response in the mother. There is no other signal in the world that sets off such intense responses in a mother as her baby's cry. At no other time in the child's life will language so forcefully stimulate the mother to act.[1]*
>
> William Sears, MD
> *Attachment Parenting: The Journal of API*

Of all the eight principles of parenting, we believe responding with sensitivity is one of the most important. It is the foundation that strengthens all the other principles, and it is the foundation of developing a secure attachment relationship with your children. Sensitive responsiveness implies the ability to set aside one's own needs for the needs of the baby; it presupposes a change in consciousness of the parents and the capacity to feel empathy—to see the world through the eyes of their child. Babies communicate their needs in many ways, including body movements, facial expressions, and crying. They often try to tell us that they need our attention long before they begin to cry, if we only understood their attempts. As you learn to understand and respond to your infant's cues (signals), through consistency you will build a strong foundation of trust and empathy.

---

1   Sears, "Bonding with your newborn," *Attachment Parenting: The Journal of API.*

There is the language of the embrace, the language
of the eyes, the language of the smile, vocal
communications of pleasure and distress. It is the
essential vocabulary of love before we can speak love.[2]

Selma Fraiberg
In Defense of Mothering: Every Child's Birthright

Researchers have found that human infants are born with the expectation to be responded to rather quickly. When responses are consistent, babies begin to learn the first lessons of empathy and trust. Often parents wait until their baby is crying before responding, and then they have a very distraught baby on their hands who is much harder to calm down. For instance, a hungry baby (or one who needs comforting) will typically turn his head toward the breast and open his mouth wide, he may put his fists in his mouth and suck on them, or he may simply start making sucking movements with his mouth. By paying attention to his subtle signals, you will begin to understand what he is trying to communicate long before the tears begin to flow. If a baby fusses and seems restless but quiets down when you pick him up, you are fulfilling his need for closeness, warmth, and comfort.

---

2   Fraiberg, *In Defense of Mothering: Every Child's Birthright*, 29.

What is Empathy?

The word *empathy* means *the experiencing as one's own the feelings of others, or the capacity for this.*

When you respond to your baby (or any other human being for that matter) with empathy, you convey these implicit messages:

I want to understand how you feel
I hurt when you hurt
We're in this together
Your feelings matter to me
I trust you
I respect you
I will help you feel better
I honor you
I care about you
Let's work this out together
I'm here if you need me
You can trust me
You matter to me
You can count on me
I see the world through your eyes
I'll always be here for you
I love you no matter what you do

The implicit messages of empathy to yourself as a parent:

I see myself in you
I was once in your booties
I understand myself
I accept myself
I am strong even in my weakness

I am not afraid to feel
I am not afraid of your feelings; I am secure in myself
I honor myself
I trust myself
I know myself
I accept you in all of your expressions
I do not reject you when you are not reflecting back what
I wish or need

By Lysa Parker and Lu Hanessian

Building a Strong Connection with Your Baby

Harville Hendrix, a renowned psychotherapist, and his wife, Helen Hunt, wrote *Giving the Love that Heals* to help parents understand how imperative it is that they strengthen the attachment with their baby. This advice comes from many years of experience working with individuals and couples using Imago therapy, which they developed. They are also the parents of six grown children.

> For the first eighteen months after birth, your baby is totally dependent. He is bonding with you and learning that his needs will be met. *During this period, the most important thing you can do is be reliably available and reliably warm* [their emphasis]. This means responding to what he needs when he needs it, regardless of whether it is convenient. When you do this, you are ensuring that your baby will survive and that he will maintain that sense of connection with the universe that is the foundation of his future security in the world.[3]

---

3   Hendrix and Hunt, *Giving the Love that Heals*, 201.

Building a strong connection with your baby involves not only responding consistently to his physical needs but also spending enjoyable time interacting, talking, and playing with him, a natural and fun way to meet his emotional needs. When a baby gazes into your eyes, it is his invitation to you to connect with him; he may smile at you with the expectation that you will smile and talk back to him. Later, as he begins

to understand the rhythm of the sounds of language, he will attempt to make his own sounds to communicate back to you in the form of babbling, expecting you to talk back. Hendrix and Hunt advise that parents meet the emotional needs of their baby by speaking in a soothing, soft tone of voice:

> As the baby begins to experiment with facial
> expressions and sounds that will eventually enable her
> to verbalize her communications, it is important for
> the parents to validate her nonverbal communication
> by mirroring them. This means reproducing the
> sounds and expressions in order to allow the baby
> to gain confidence in her experimentation. When in
> doubt how to mirror, smiling works wonders.[4]

Interestingly, researchers have found that mothers who are depressed have difficulty picking up on a baby's facial or body signals and are out of synchrony with their babies.[5] When a baby's frustrated attempts to engage his mother are not responded to, he will eventually stop trying to communicate his needs to her. This can affect his brain

---

4   Ibid., 202.

5   Isabella and Belsky, "Interactional synchrony and the origins of infant-mother attachment: A replication study," *Child Development*.

development, lower his IQ, and put him at risk of becoming depressed as well.[6] Researchers have also found that when mothers respond quickly and appropriately to their baby's cues over time, these children develop better language, cognitive abilities, and self-esteem.[7]

Many societal challenges can interfere with a parent's ability to develop a responsive relationship with his or her baby. For example, parents may believe myths about spoiling a baby, or they may follow advice (often unsolicited) from well-meaning family, friends, and medical professionals, the media, and self-proclaimed "parenting experts." More often than not, this advice conflicts with the science of normal child development. The parents' own intuitive feelings become suppressed, which can undermine their confidence and create unnecessary stress.

In the course of a child's development, he begins to form attachments with the person who spends the majority of time nurturing and caring for him. Frequent holding throughout the day and playful interactions with your baby will increase bonding and promote a secure attachment. Many new parents are relieved to learn that most babies need a lot of close physical contact.

It is impossible to spoil a baby when satisfying his need to be held. When you listen to your baby, you will find he is most content and happy when being held close to you—this is because he is experiencing life as a part of you, not as a separate being. Who doesn't want a happy, contented baby? Soon enough, your baby will be squirming in your arms to be put down.

In the first six months or so, your baby may seem perfectly happy being held by and interacting with other people. Then, around eight to nine months of age, he may suddenly begin to respond with fear and anxiety to strangers and less familiar family members. Attempts to separate him from Mom will be met with desperate clinging and crying. Rest assured, this is normal developmental behavior, which most babies experience as they develop more awareness of the world around them. It is actually a good sign that he wants to remain close to the person with whom he has become attached. Knowing this should make it easier to cope with, rather than allowing yourself to become overly concerned or frustrated. This is

---

6   Kendall-Tackett, *The Hidden Feelings of Motherhood*, 25.

7   Lester et al., "Developmental outcome as a function of the goodness of fit between the infant's cry characteristics and the mother's perception of her infant's cry," *Pediatrics.*

an important phase of development, and baby's feelings require that you continue to be sensitive in your responses, to help him feel safe and secure. This is *not* the time to teach your baby to be independent or to self-soothe. The intense fears of separation will gradually subside as your child matures over the next few years, depending on the temperament of the child. It may take considerably longer to pass for more sensitive children, especially if they have to learn to be comfortable in the care of nonparental adults. Follow your child's cues rather than force him to accept the well-meaning actions of strangers or expecting him to overcome stranger/separation anxiety before he is developmentally ready. This can also be an intense time for Mom; she will need a lot more support and understanding from her family and friends.

Responsiveness and Development

Responding sensitively to your baby teaches him that he is loved and that he can trust you to be there for him. In the beginning, infants don't understand what love is. What they know is that when they feel hungry, uncomfortable, insecure, and frightened, they need someone to respond to them. From a biological perspective, they are born with three basic survival needs: proximity (close physical contact to Mom or the primary caregiver), protection (the need to feel safe and secure), and predictability (knowing that Mom or Dad is consistently available and that their needs will be met.)[8]

From a neurological perspective, it's important to understand how responsiveness plays a significant role in brain development. As we discussed in chapter 1, a baby's brain is greatly underdeveloped at birth (only 25 percent is developed), making him highly dependent upon his parents for everything, especially food, warmth, and comfort. Brain researchers have found that the mother's face, emotional expressions, and tone of voice have a direct impact on the development of the brain. The development of critical parts of the brain coincides with the period of time that attachment develops—during the first three years.[9]

---

8   Concept originated by Isabelle Fox, PhD.

9   Schore, "The experience-dependent maturation of a regulatory system in the orbital prefrontal cortex and the origin of developmental psychopathology," *Development and Psychopathology.*

Emotional Regulation

Due to their neurologic immaturity, infants cannot be expected to figure things out on their own—to soothe themselves—especially during the early weeks, months, and sometimes years. *You* are the emotional regulator for your child until his brain growth has caught up and he is developmentally capable of regulating his own feelings. This is a gradual process that happens over the first few years.

When faced with stressful or fearful situations, your baby or young child needs calm, loving, and empathic parents to speak affectionately and reassuringly to him. Using comforting touch such as holding, massage, or stroking also helps children learn to regulate their emotions and intense feelings. The sucking reflex remains strong for babies and toddlers and goes a long way in helping to comfort them.

Sue Gerhardt, author of *Why Love Matters: How Affection Shapes a Baby's Brain*, describes a parents' role: "Parents are really needed to be a sort of emotion coach. They need to be there and to be tuned in to the baby's constantly changing states, but they also need to help the baby to the next level." For instance, she writes that with the help of parents, children will begin to identify specific feelings with words like frustration, irritation, anger, silly, funny, joyful—a wide range of emotions. Parents can do this by "helping the baby to become aware of his own feelings, talking in baby talk, and emphasizing and exaggerating words and gestures so that the baby can realize that this is not mum and dad just expressing themselves, this is them 'showing me' my feelings."[10]

---

10   Gerhardt, *Why Love Matters: How Affection Shapes a Baby's Brain*, 24–25.

911 for a Crying Baby

Dr. Harvey Karp, in his book, *The Happiest Baby on the Block*, writes that by recreating the womb environment for the newborn, you can trigger what he calls the "calming reflex." To accomplish this, he has created the five *S*'s that have proven to work amazingly well for calming an inconsolable, crying baby:

1. Swaddling
2. Side (side/stomach positioning while being held in the parent's arms)
3. Shushing (to mimic the loud noise in the womb)
4. Swinging
5. Sucking[11]

When done correctly, babies often quickly calm down and go to right to sleep. Please refer to his book or DVD for instructions on how to implement the five *S*'s correctly.

Note: Attachment parenting strategies incorporate many of these behaviors, for example, using a sling type carrier creates a swaddling effect with movement and nursing provides the sucking needs. Attachment parenting practices are more likely to prevent extended bouts of crying unless a physical problem is causing the discomfort. The "shushing" and "white noise" can be helpful additional strategies to mimic the sounds in the womb. We encourage limiting the use of other swing devices.

The "Fussy" Baby

Most parents find that caring for their baby is more intense than they expected. If you have a so-called "fussy" baby, then that intensity is magnified, and you can find yourself quickly overwhelmed. "High-need" is a term used to describe a certain temperament of baby who

11 Karp, *The Happiest Baby on the Block*, 190–192.

is very sensitive and who may experience more periods of fussiness than other babies. Your baby can become overstimulated in a variety of ways, such as cold air, bright lights, sudden noises or movements, or too many different adults giving her attention.

Sensitive babies tend to be more vocal about what they need, and adults may incorrectly perceive them as too demanding. Instead of perceiving his "fussiness" as disapproval, try to see it as a signal that he is overwhelmed with his own feelings and needs and is seeking help to find his equilibrium. High-need babies may well require more soothing, but in the aftermath of such consistent responsiveness, these children often develop a peace about them that shows they have been deeply nurtured. Margot Sunderland, a child psychotherapist and author of *The Science of Parenting*, describes the mechanisms that work in a baby's brain to help him cope with stress later in life: "If you consistently soothe your child's distress over the years and take any anguished crying seriously, highly effective stress response systems can be established in his brain."[12] So don't worry that you might be "giving in" by responding to their cries; they often grow up to be delightful, spirited children with strong leadership qualities. In time, as your baby matures and you become more attuned (tuned in), you will know intuitively when he gradually becomes capable of waiting a few minutes for your response.

Responding at Night

Cultural expectations have led us to believe that babies should sleep through the night for at least a good six-to-seven hours. This on-going myth keeps many parents frustrated and can cause them to become desensitized and less responsive if they feel they are reinforcing a negative behavior such as waking, fussing, and crying. Researchers have found that infants have different sleep rhythms, with more periods of light sleep, and aren't naturally designed to sleep for long stretches of time in their early months—especially breastfed babies.

The reality is that your baby still needs to be cared for during the night. Allowing a baby to cry for prolonged periods of time with the intention of teaching him to sleep on his own causes the baby to experience abnormally high levels of stress hormones (cortisol), creating

---

12 Sunderland, *The Science of Parenting*, 37.

an unbalanced chemical state in his brain. Researchers have found that responsive mothers help a baby's stress hormones normalize more quickly.[13] Minimizing stress for your baby is important; children who experience high levels of cortisol are at risk for emotional problems later in life.[14] More information on responding to a child's nighttime needs is available in chapter 6, *Ensure safe sleep-physically and emotionally.*

When Baby's Cries Overwhelm You

Remaining sensitive and empathic when faced with a crying, inconsolable infant can be very hard for many parents. It calls for awareness and a lot of patience. This doesn't typically come easily or naturally—especially if you weren't raised that way. At times, you may find it difficult to be emotionally responsive, especially when you are feeling exhausted or are experiencing a lot of stress in other areas of your life. Hendrix and Hunt write in *Giving the Love that Heals*, "If you find yourself reacting strongly to your child's dependence on you, then you may have been wounded at this stage [of development]. You can use this insight to focus your attention on issues that you need to work on in your efforts to become a conscious parent."[15]

Whether you are balancing the needs of a new baby and an older sibling or the demands of being emotionally responsive to a high-needs baby, fatigue, frustration, and exhaustion can cause you to overreact so don't take this lightly! Even the best of parents can become dangerously overwhelmed without support and rest. Call in the reserves (Dad, Mom, friend), and allow yourself some time alone to rest, collect your sense of calm, and practice personal reflection so that you don't take your baby's crying personally or fall into the mindset that the baby is being manipulative.

Symptoms of burnout or inability to cope with baby's needs are signals that you need extra support or professional help. We discuss this in more depth in chapter 9, Strive for Balance in Your Personal and Family Life.

---

13 Albers et al., "Maternal behavior predicts infant cortisol recovery from a mild everyday stressor," *Journal of Child Psychology and Psychiatry*.

14 Gerhardt, *Why Love Matters: How Affection Shapes a Baby's Brain*, 78.

15 Hendrix and Hunt, *Giving the Love that Heals*, 201.

Why Do Babies Cry?

Remember that infants cry to communicate their needs and feelings. Here is a list of some of the most common reasons babies cry or appear "colicky." In time, you will develop a mental checklist and go through it quickly as you try to determine how best to help your fussy baby. It is helpful to try different approaches—baby will let you know when his need is being met. Sometimes the only thing you can do is hold your baby.

- ☐ hunger
- ☐ fatigue
- ☐ loneliness
- ☐ a need to be held
- ☐ a need for skin-to-skin contact
- ☐ discomfort, irritability, or gas (also known as "colic")
- ☐ feeling too hot or too cold
- ☐ perception of the mother's stress
- ☐ stress from too much stimulation
- ☐ understimulation (needs more loving interactions with parents)
- ☐ surprise from loud, sudden noises
- ☐ food sensitivity to something directly ingested or passed through the mother's milk
- ☐ unidentified pain or medical problem such as ear infection, gastroesophageal reflux, urinary tract infection, or anemia

Toddlers and Beyond

Toddlers still need a sensitive and responsive parent as their bond to you continues to grow. You can maintain your responsiveness by using the following tips:

- As your child grows, responding with empathy, respecting your child's feelings, and trying to understand the need underlying his outward behaviors will help you continue the close connection you nurtured when your child was a baby. Young children continue to need a lot of loving attention.

As toddlers begin to demonstrate more independence, parents can support their explorations by providing a safe environment for discovery and staying nearby to respond when the child needs it. By showing interest in their toddlers' activities, participating in child-directed play, and sharing in their excitement, parents build their children's confidence and help them develop skills. Throughout the early years, children require frequent feedback from their parents as they try new things.

- Parents are instrumental in helping their children develop social skills. Parents can set up appropriate play "dates" for their child, monitor the children's play, and intervene using positive discipline techniques to keep the children safe and teach effective communication techniques and concepts of fair play. While some toddlers are ready for, and do enjoy, more formal "preschool" environments, it is not necessary for "socialization" of young children. When evaluating any program in which parents are not included, consider your child's readiness to separate from you and the amount and type of support provided by the adults supervising the program.

- Parents are the child's first teachers and begin teaching from birth. Enrich your child's experiences on a daily basis as much as possible. Seek out activities that you can do simply that don't require spending money. Children really love learning, and soak up everything like a sponge. Parents who are attuned intuitively help stimulate that learning environment by following their child's current interests, answering questions, and responding to daily "teachable moments." You can read, sing, play learning games, create projects, and follow your child's lead in play.

- Toddlers are also capable of playing alone or alongside Mom or Dad as they do other chores around the house. Toddlers love to mimic what they see you do, so give them opportunities to perform tasks like folding towels or washing the car. They learn that working can be fun, and it makes them feel like they are a helping member of the family.

Responding to Toddler Tantrums and Strong Emotions

You've seen it happen: you're in the grocery store or restaurant, and a young child has a meltdown—whining, crying, or maybe screaming on the floor. You may have thought, "That child just needs a good spanking," but in reality, that child needs a parent who remains calm. It is critical to respond to children's strong emotions, even when they act out with negative behavior or tantrums. How do you do it? You can start by not taking his behavior personally and trying to see the world through his eyes, with the understanding that it's up to you to help your child regulate his emotions. The best prevention is to avoid putting yourself and your child in a situation you know will likely lead to a meltdown, such as shopping when your child is tired or hungry. Plan ahead as much as possible and keep in mind the low tolerance level of children; they can get bored rather quickly.

If you do have to go shopping, talk to your child ahead of time and explain what you're going to do and what your expectations are for him. Make sure he is fed or you have snacks with you. Try creating a game of shopping by giving your child some item to look for in the store. Keeping their little minds busy (distraction is easy at young ages) will keep them from getting quickly bored and becoming cranky.

Parents bring the baby into this more sophisticated emotional world by identifying feelings and labeling them clearly. Usually this teaching happens quite unselfconsciously.[16]

Sue Gerhardt
Why Love Matters: How Affection Shapes a Baby's Brain

Temper tantrums are an outlet for emotions that are too powerful for a young child's undeveloped brain to manage in a more acceptable way. Tantrums represent real emotions and should be handled empathically. A parent's role in tantrums is to acknowledge and validate his feelings and comfort the child, not to get angry or punish him (even if you feel the urge). Remember that as children grow they develop empathy and improved social skills when you respond with love and affirmation.[17] In the heat of the moment, it is likely that your child will not be able to talk about his feelings or will need your help to give his feelings the right words. He might respond best to soothing words and physical comfort. In order to calm an upset child, remain calm and try techniques such as distraction, cuddling, or, if it is more comfortable for the child, holding or sitting next to the child while talking gently to him (assuming you're not in the middle of the grocery store). You will likely have to experiment to find out how your child responds best—every child is different as is the situation. You *can* learn to model appropriate ways to deal with young, fragile emotions by using empathy and compassion for the child who is tired, frustrated, hurt, or angry. You can read more information about handling tantrums and strong emotions in chapter 8, Practice Positive Discipline.

---

16   Gerhardt, *Why Love Matters: How Affection Shapes a Baby's Brain*, 25.

17   Zhou et al., "The relations of parental warmth and positive expressiveness to children's empathy-related responding and social functioning: A longitudinal study," *Child Development*.

Helping Children Learn to Express Feelings

Children learn empathy from parents who have been responsive to them. Once the child is out of the toddler stage at three, four, and five years old, parents are better able to use language and reason to express empathy; this helps children understand their feelings and the feelings of others. The seeds of empathy are growing during the early years, and you will begin to see the results of your efforts when your child begins to show kindness toward another child or concern for a child who is hurt.

Many parents tend to forget that children, like adults, need to learn how to express their feelings. It's hard to do without the appropriate words, and many adults are not even literate when it comes to adequately expressing their needs and feelings. A program called Nonviolent Communication (NVC), also called Compassionate Communication, offers resources to teach adults successful ways of expressing feelings that meet deep emotional needs. (Read more about NVC in chapter 8 and visit the Center for Nonviolent Communication's Web site, listed in the appendix at the end of this chapter.) Being sensitively responsive to your baby is the beginning of teaching compassionate communication skills for life.

Just for Dads

In the early weeks and months, a father can feel like second fiddle to Mom and baby. They seem to have a nice thing going, but when and where do fathers come in? According to Dr. William Sears, fathers are often portrayed as well-meaning but bumbling when it comes to caring for newborns. He has found that "fathers have their own unique way of relating to babies, and babies thrive on this difference."

> Studies on father bonding show that fathers who are given the opportunity and are encouraged to take an active part in caring for their newborns can become just as nurturing as mothers. A father's nurturing responses may be less automatic and slower to unfold than a mother's, but fathers are capable of a strong

> bonding attachment to their infants during the newborn period.[18]
>
> William Sears, MD
> *Attachment Parenting: The Journal of API*

Attachment researchers have found that babies are born with a drive to initially form a close emotional bond (attachment) to one person, usually the mother or the primary caregiver. As the baby matures, he is more able to expand his universe to be more inclusive of the father and others in his life.

Mothers can and should actively promote bonding with fathers. Dads can be great at comforting, burping, bathing, dressing, and diaper changing. In fact, fathers' unique styles of interacting and playing with baby should be honored and encouraged. You may find the child begins to prefer Dad for diaper changes or giving a bath. Nestling on Daddy's chest for comfort or sleep creates a very special bond that is sacred. But when hunger pangs begin or discomfort occurs, your baby will likely cry for the parent to whom he is most attached—usually Mom. Fathers are more likely, but not always, to remain the secondary attachment figure in the child's life until two-to-three years of age, or sometimes

longer, depending on the temperament of the child. But take heart, this is normal child development. Before long, your child will be begging to go with Dad or do things with him that will create precious lifelong memories for everyone.

---

18   Ibid.

Research on Fathers

The Fatherhood Initiative reports that the degree of father closeness determines the likelihood of adolescents engaging in risky behaviors such as drinking, smoking, and using hard drugs and inhalants.

> Given that father closeness reduces adolescent drug use, and that father closeness is highest in intact families, adolescents in intact families are at the lowest level of risk for engaging in drug use. The level of risk of adolescent drug use increases in blended families, is still higher in single-parent families, and is highest in no-parent families [families where neither parent is involved, such as a state-run institution].

> On measures of smoking, drinking, and the use of inhalants, father closeness has independent, positive, and powerful effects on adolescents. On the other hand, there is no direct correlation between mother closeness and any of the measures of adolescent drug use. In other words, efforts to reduce adolescent drug use must emphasize the strengthening of father-adolescent relationships, regardless of the type of family structure in which the adolescent lives. The strengthening of father-adolescent relationships is especially important for the millions of adolescents living in father-absent homes, where limited contact with nonresident fathers is inadequate.[19]

---

19 "Family structure, father closeness, and drug abuse: A report from National Fatherhood Initiative," National Fatherhood Initiative Web site.

What about Boys?

As a culture, we have always had different perceptions and expectations of boys. People often fear that if boys are nurtured too much, it somehow warps their personalities and makes them too dependent and too sensitive. Conventional attitudes about boys permeate all aspects of society (parents, grandparents, teachers, and coaches, for example) and has created what William Pollack calls a "boy code"—myths such as that boys' behavior is driven solely by their hormones and not the environment; that boys need to learn to be tough at an early age; and so on. This code has only served to force boys to become disconnected from their feelings—less sensitive and more aggressive. New research has begun to reverse that trend by emphasizing the importance of mothers and fathers in nurturing strong emotional connections with their sons. For instance, Dr. Pollack found from his research that "the absence of a close relationship with a loving mother puts a boy at a disadvantage in becoming a free, confident, and independent man who likes himself and can take risks, and who can form close and loving attachments with people in his adult life."[20] Research conducted by the Fatherhood Initiative showed that "adolescents who are close to their moms and dads have less of a need to seek out affirming relationships outside of the home, which can lead to risky behavior (gangs, smoking, drinking, and drugs)."[21]

---

20 Pollack, *Real Boys: Rescuing our Sons from the Myths of Boyhood*, 83.

21 "Family structure, father closeness, and drug abuse: A report from National Fatherhood Initiative," National Fatherhood Initiative Web site.

It is easy to slip into the habit of touching an infant boy mainly when he needs to be fed, cleaned up and changed, or comforted in irritability…. Every boy needs a lot of touching given just for the pleasure it will provide; and a parent needs the heartwarming feedback of a happy boy.[22]

Eli Newberger, MD
The Men They Will Become

This research points to the protective benefits of nurturing a strong connection with young boys by both mother and father. If you have a family where the father is not involved, it's important for your child to develop a loving relationship with a father figure, such as a brother, uncle, or grandfather. Your sons may be fathers themselves someday, modeling what they learned from both genders—the skills to nurture their own children.

How to Be Responsive in Spite of Life's Challenges

When life throws you some curves, you do the best you can with what you're given. Some situations may not be ideal for raising your child. If your life situation puts an emotional strain on your relationship with your child, your efforts to maintain sensitivity and responsiveness with your baby will help minimize the negative effects.

Single parenting: There are no two ways about it, single parenting is really tough! If at all possible, consider moving in with grandparents or other family members to have a built-in support system for parent and child. Another option is for single parents to seek out other single parents to share an apartment or home with, as well as support each other in parenting. It's critical to be on the same page as far as parenting values and childcare for these types of arrangement to work successfully. Single parents may find that cosleeping with their baby after work or school provides a wonderful opportunity to reconnect and be responsive at night. If grandparents or others care for the baby during the day, be

---

22 Newberger, *The Men They Will Become*, 42.

sure they know that you want them to be consistently and sensitively responsive to your child, because crying it out is not acceptable.

If you feel alone and isolated, create your own extended family with your network of friends or seek out other single parents in person or online. Find a local API support group or consider starting one with other like-minded families.

Adoption: Adopted infants will bond sooner if the care and responsiveness of the parents is consistent and loving. If an adopted child has a history of trauma, developing trust may take longer, and his needs may be more intense. Regardless, it is critical that the adopted baby learn that his new parents are consistently available and responsive. If adoptive parents find this challenging in any way, then professional help from therapists knowledgeable about adoption and trauma can be a valuable and critical resource. Children who are adopted from foreign countries adjust much more easily if the adoptive parents bring an item from the orphanage that will help make the child feel more secure, like a special blanket or toy. If the child is eating solid foods, continue to provide similar foods until the child becomes adjusted to his new life and new experiences. The following website offers a lot of good information about attachment parenting for the adopted child, www.adoptivefamilies.com.

Divorce: Here again, consistency is key. Divorce situations can be very difficult and will vary depending on the parents involved. In order to prevent breaks in the attachment process, it's important that both parents commit to open communication, keeping prolonged separations to a minimum, with day and nighttime routines as consistent and as developmentally appropriate as possible. For the children to make a reasonably healthy adjustment to losing the intact family, both parents will have to make their child's emotional welfare the top priority. In many cases, this means setting aside differences and working together to be active in your child's life and activities. Most important of all, both parents need to remain sensitive to their child's feelings and be responsive to his emotional needs. API's Web site contains information regarding visitation and overnights. A strongly recommended book that focuses on maintaining the attachment relationship is *Creating*

Effective Parenting Plans: A Developmental Approach for Lawyers and Divorce Professionals by John Hartson, PhD, and Brenda Payne, PhD. It can be purchased through the American Bar Association Web site (www.abanet.org). Also recommended is *The Unexpected Legacy of Divorce: A 25 Year Landmark Study* by Judith Wallerstein, Julia M. Lewis, and Sandra Blakeslee and *What About the Kids?: Raising Your Children Before, During and After Divorce* by Judith Wallerstein.

Children with special needs: Children born prematurely, with physical handicaps or challenges, or with other forms of disability are no different than nonchallenged children in their psychological and emotional needs. It's important to understand that *you* are the expert in your child and that when you feel connected and tuned-in to what your child needs, you will respond intuitively. Challenged children often spend much of their childhood experiencing a maze of different doctors, hospitals (sometimes multiple surgeries), therapists, and teachers. As a result, it's critical that parents establish a strong bond with their child because it will strengthen their ability to be fierce advocates for him, and that bond will give their child the love, support, and courage he will need. You can find additional resources about this topic and others at the end of this chapter. Also, visit our parent forums on this and other topics at www.attachmentparenting.org/forums/

Having more than one child, twins, and other multiple births: If you've had your first baby, you may now wonder, "How will I be able to parent the next one with the same devotion, care, and empathy? Won't the older child suffer when a new baby takes his place? How should I space my children for optimum attachment? What about birthing twins, triplets, or other multiples? Is it possible to practice the attachment parenting principles when there are so many needs to fulfill?" These are common questions for all parents, no matter what philosophical view they may have about parenting.

Most of us will have one baby at a time, and spacing our children is a definite consideration when thinking about the attachment needs of each child. Many child development experts feel that at least two-and-a-half-to-three years between children is beneficial, because the older child has the language and cognitive skills to understand the needs of an infant and can more easily delay his needs than a younger child. The older child may have less jealousy and be able to help in some ways, like bringing diapers or sitting with books and toys while the baby is being fed. Having babies really close together is almost like parenting twins, because they will have similar needs and will probably be in fairly close developmental stages. We advise parents of closely spaced babies to get a lot of help and support, just as if they had given birth to multiples, because the older child will probably not want to be separated from Mom for very long. This is especially true if he is still nursing or is too young to understand where Mom has gone. He only knows that he needs his mother, and Mother needs to be supported in parenting both babies.

We are always amazed to hear the stories of parents who have successfully parented multiples—their stories inspire the rest of us with "singletons," and we can learn a lot from their experiences. Organization, prioritizing, and support seem to be the key components to keeping balance in the family. One mother of triplets (and an older child) we worked with said that if it weren't for the volunteers from her church, she never would have been able to successfully breastfeed her babies. She was able to pump enough milk so that while she was nursing two, the third baby could get a bottle if needed, and by the time they were a few months old, she was able to nurse them all without bottles. Volunteers did her laundry, took her older son for outings and preschool, and brought her family meals. When Mom and Dad can focus on the children and their needs, and the community helps support the parents, everyone can keep their sanity, their sense of humor, and their stamina! Best of all, the attachment needs of each child can be met, and parents find that somehow they do have the ability to give tremendous stores of love to each child they are blessed to parent.

A Mother's Story: Sacred Love

Within hours of my firstborn child's birth, I got the distinct sense that he wanted a fourth trimester. Here I was, full of breathless anticipation, unspeakable bliss, and mortal terror, and there he was looking at me square in the eye, as if to say, "*Work with me, Ma.*"

I had prepared as so many mothers do for their first baby. But I could have never known the profound effect of meeting someone else's needs because I took the time to know what they were in the first place.

My son was poised to show me the difference between unmet needs and fulfilled ones, from the time he was a newborn to today, nearly ten years later, as a boy embracing his emerging self-reliance.

They called him a "high-need" baby. What did that mean? *Aren't we all high-need humans?* I thought. They called him "fussy." *Isn't that a judgment of him?* I reasoned. And in calling our babies names—fussy, demanding, good, easy—wouldn't this usher in our fears, fueling our defenses? How could I love my baby unconditionally, I wondered, if part of me was *afraid* of him? And wouldn't he sense that subtle rejection somehow?

As with any burgeoning conviction, I was tested.

In those early months, he was averse to the car, the bath, clothes, diaper changes, the telephone ringing, lights, appliances, distant lawnmowers outside his window, being rocked back and forth as opposed to side to side, and the sound of his Velcro diaper tab being pulled ten times a day. Friends, relatives, our pediatrician, and perfect strangers told me to "put him down or he'll think the world revolves around him."

117

What they (and we) didn't know was that the world actually *was* revolving around him—he had vertigo.

We didn't discover this until he was five and could finally tell us.

During those five years, we followed his lead. The road to uncovering and defining his complex sensory sensitivities was, at times, confusing and circuitous. Along the way, we had to find out what drives him, what motivates his reactions, what stirs him and soothes him in order to begin to know him in tiny increments every day. This, I thought intellectually, was the easy part. After all, as his mother, I loved the minutiae of his existence, reveled in his perfect beauty, even as I stared with drunken love at his crossed eyes and pimply face a mere four weeks after our first glimpse of each other.

I was prepared to love him with all my heart.

What blindsided me was my fear.

He cried inconsolably, and I felt my own helplessness. He wailed, and I felt his disapproval. He couldn't sleep, and I felt forsaken and fragile. As he grew, I spent more than a few nights blinking in the darkness, wondering if I had chosen the right school or teacher or therapy or doctor or response.

It was all about me. And yet, it was not about me at all.

It hit me. How could I respond to him with sensitivity, taking his needs and feelings seriously, without taking them personally? How could I get out of the way enough to parent in the moment, allowing him—and me—to flourish as mother and child, so that both of us are organically changed in the process?

I realized, in those moments, that intuitive, conscious, attached parenting requires something that none of us learns on the playground, in the classroom, or on the job: *grace.*

The only way I got a taste of its delicacy was through my own painful rites of passage. Those times, as a mother, when I've had the whistle blown on my own pretense and defense. I now know that a baby is wise and forthright enough to smoke a parent out of her hiding places. The same goes for that same baby standing tall enough to reach my collarbone when he hugs me.

I need my maternal radar more now than I ever did. He needs me to move away—closer. His space is sacred. And yet, he needs to share that space. He needs my sensitivity to his changing moods, perceived overreactions, and quirky preferences.

But more than my understanding, he needs my authentic presence.

Responding to him is no longer about meeting basic needs, but about recognizing individual, deeply personal ones—and respecting them, in spite of my fear.

I have learned to respond to what's invisible. Because I want to see him with my heart, not my eyes.

Lu Hanessian
Author of *Let the Baby Drive*

Appendix to Chapter Four: Additional Research and Resource Recommendations

Additional Research

Adults who received abundant emotional support from their parents during childhood are likely to have relatively good health as adults.[23]

Babies cry less when the mother (or primary caregiver) keeps the baby physically close and responds quickly. (M. Ainsworth et al) A longitudinal study of twenty-six infant-mother pairs shows that consistency and promptness of maternal response is associated with decline in frequency and duration of infant crying.

Bell, Silvia M. and Ainsworth, Mary D. Salter. Infant Crying and Maternal Responsiveness. Child Development, 1972, 43, 1171-1190.

Mothers who accurately perceived the urgency of their infants' cries consequently responded appropriately. The benefit to infants in the study proved to be higher cognitive development and language-acquisition scores. The mothers who responded to their infants' cries inconsistently were found to have lower self-esteem and lack of social supports.[24]

Mothers of securely attached infants tend to be more sensitive, reliable, and accepting of their infants.[25]

The synchrony, or dysynchrony, of interactions between parent and infant have been found to determine security of attachment. Mothers

---

23　Shaw, "Emotional support from parents early in life, aging, and health," *Psychology and Aging.*

24　Lester et al., "Developmental outcome as a function of the goodness of fit between the infant's cry characteristics and the mother's perception of her infant's cry," *Pediatrics.*

25　De Wolff and van Ijzendoorn, "Sensitivity and attachment: A meta-analysis on parental antecedents of attachment," *Child Development.*

who were found to be inconsistent, intrusive, and overstimulating were more likely to have insecure attachments with their babies.[26]

Toddlers who had insecure attachments with their mothers and were inhibited in their behavior exhibited higher cortisol levels in stressful situations.[27]

Parental warmth and positive expressiveness with children was strongly correlated with children's development of empathy and social functioning, especially in older children.[28]

Mothers whose behavior toward their preschool children is responsive, nonpunitive, and nonauthoritarian are more likely to have children who exhibit prosocial behavior.[29]

If a child's need for comfort is not met by an emotionally responsive adult, the child's nervous system can, over time, remain in a hyperaroused state.[30]

Uncomforted stress can lead to a host of physical ailments later in life, including eating and digestive disorders, poor sleep, panic attacks, headaches, and chronic fatigue.[31]

If left to cry alone in childhood without therapy in later life, the higher-

---

26   Isabella and Belsky, "Interactional synchrony and the origins of infant-mother attachment: A replication study," *Child Development*.

27   Nachmias et al., "Behavioral inhibition and stress reactivity: The moderating role of attachment security," *Child Development*.

28   Zhou et al., "The relations of parental warmth and positive expressiveness to children's empathy-related responding and social functioning: A longitudinal study," *Child Development*.

29   Zahn-Waxler et al., "Child rearing and children's prosocial initiations toward victims of distress," *Child Development*.

30   Graham et al., "The effects of neonatal stress on brain development: Implications for psychopathology," *Development and Psychopathology*.

31   Field, "The effects of mothers' physical and emotional unavailability on emotion regulation," *Monographs of the Society for Research in Child Development*.

level brain functions that regulate antianxiety chemicals in the brain are impaired. This may result in clinical depression.[32]

Recommended Reading

A Parent's Guide to Autism by Charles Hart.

Effective Parenting Plans: A Developmental Approach for Lawyers and Divorce Professionals by John Hartson, PhD, and Brenda Payne, PhD.

Gifts: Mothers Reflect on How Children with Down Syndrome Enrich Their Lives by Kathryn Lynard Soper with forward by Martha Sears, RN.

Giving the Love that Heals: A Guide for Parents by Harville Hendrix, PhD, and Helen Hunt, PhD.

Hold On to Your Kids: Why Parents Need to Matter More Than Peers by Gordon Neufeld, PhD, and Gabor Maté, MD.

Kangaroo Care: The Best You Can Do to Care for Your Preterm Infant by Susan Luddington-Hoe, PhD.

Let the Baby Drive: Navigating the Road of New Motherhood by Lu Hanessian.

Mothering Multiples by Karen Gromada.

Parenting from Your Heart: Sharing the Gifts of Compassion, Connection, and Choice by Inbal Kashtan.

Parenting through Crisis: Helping Kids in Times of Loss, Grief, and Change by Barbara Coloroso.

Playful Parenting by Lawrence Cohen, PhD.

Special Children, Challenged Parents by Robert Naseef.

The A.D.D. Book by William Sears, MD, and Lynda Thompson.

The Crying Baby by Sheila Kitzinger.

The Fussy Baby Book: How to Bring Out the Best in Your High-Need Child by William Sears, MD, and Martha Sears, RN.

The Fussy Baby Book: Parenting Your High Need Child from Birth to Age Five by William Sears, MD, and Martha Sears, RN.

The Happiest Baby on the Block by Harvey Karp, MD.

---

32   Hariri et al., "Modulating emotional responses: Effects of a neocortical network on the limbic system," *NeuroReport*.

The Hidden Feelings of Motherhood: Coping with Stress, Depression, and Burnout by Kathleen Kendall-Tackett, PhD.

The Men They Will Become: The Nature and Nurture of Male Character by Eli Newberger, MD.

The Natural Child: Parenting from the Heart by Jan Hunt.

The Premature Baby Book by William Sears, MD, Robert Sears, MD, James Sears, MD, and Martha Sears, RN.

The Science of Parenting by Margot Sunderland.

The Sears Children's Library: *What Baby Needs, Baby on the Way, You Can Go to the Potty*, and *Eat Healthy, Feel Great* (all of these children's books are authored by William Sears, MD, Martha Sears, RN, Christy Watts Kelly, and Renee Adriani).

Why Love Matters: How Affection Shapes a Baby's Brain by Sue Gerhardt.

Recommended DVDs

The Happiest Baby on the Block by Harvey Karp, MD.

Recommended CDs for playful moments

Baby Beluga by Raffi
Dream Big by Roger Day
Ready to Fly by Roger Day
Singable Songs for the Very Young by Raffi

Useful Web Sites

www.attachmentparenting.org: Web site of Attachment Parenting International.

www.askdrsears.com: Web site for Dr. William and Martha Sears and Drs. Jim and Bob Sears, providing advice and information on numerous topics in childrearing.

www.bringingbabyhome.com: Web site of the John Gottman Research Institute.

www.childtrauma.org: Web site of the Child Trauma Academy, founded by Bruce Perry, PhD, MD.

www.cnvc.org: Web site of the Center for Nonviolent Communication.

www.drjaygordon.com: Web site of Jay Gordon, MD.

www.gordonneufeld.com: Web site of Gordon Neufeld, PhD.

www.letthebabydrive.com: Web site of Lu Hanessian.

www.naturalchild.com: Web site of the Natural Child Project, founded by Jan Hunt.

www.playfulparenting.com: Web site for Lawrence Cohen's program *Playful Parenting*.

www.thehappiestbabyontheblock.com: Web site of Harvey Karp, MD.

Chapter Five

Principle 4
Use Nurturing Touch:
The Healing Power of Physical Closeness

Use Nurturing Touch: The Healing Power of Physical Closeness

It is through our hands that we speak to the child, that we communicate.

Touching is the primary language.

The newborn baby's skin has an intelligence, a sensitivity that we can only begin to imagine.

How, then, ought we to touch—to handle—a newborn baby?

Very simply: by remembering what this infant has just left behind. By never forgetting that everything new and unknown might terrify and that everything recognizable and familiar is reassurance.

To calm the infant in this strange, incomprehensible world into which it just emerged, it is necessary—and enough—that the hands holding him should speak in the language of the womb.[1]

Frederick Leboyer, MD
Birth without Violence

For infants, touch is as vital as the air they breathe and the milk they drink. From Ashley Montagu, we learn that touch is the foundation upon which all senses are based, the "mother of the senses," and the earliest sensory system to become functional in all species. It is the one sense that we cannot live without, as has been tragically demonstrated in orphanages and hospitals where untouched babies used to die of a strange disease called "hospitalism" or "marasmus," known today as "failure to thrive." Dr. Montagu reported that as late as the 1950s, the death rate of infants under one year of age in various United States

---

1   Leboyer, *Birth without Violence*, 59–60.

institutions for abandoned children was nearly 100 percent. These babies were only touched during routine examinations or when they needed a bottle or a diaper change.[2]

Touch: A Matter of Life and Death

Dr. Fritz Talbot of Boston was one doctor who decided to try something different. He remembered a trip he made to Düsseldorf, Germany, before World War I, where he toured a children's clinic. As he was shown about the wards, he noticed a large old woman who was carrying a very sick infant. When he inquired who the woman was, the attending physician said, "Oh, that is Old Anna. When we have done everything we can medically for a baby, and it is still not doing well, we turn it over to Old Anna, and she is always successful." So what was Old Anna's secret? It was what we would call tender, loving care as she rocked and held these fragile babies. Dr. Talbot introduced this kind of care when he returned to Boston, and his methods spread. In 1938, Bellevue Hospital in New York established the rule that every baby should be picked up and "mothered" on the pediatric wards; that year their death rate fell from 35 percent to less than 10 percent.[3]

Today we have new policies that dictate how child therapists can deal with traumatized and abused children. Naturally, we want to protect our children from abuse and unhealthy touch, but blanket policies such as the ones described below are not the answer. Dr. Bruce Perry, senior fellow of the Child Trauma Academy, writes:

> I certainly don't have all the answers, but I do know
> that many of our current childcare practices are hurting
> our children. For example, in California, at a large
> center serving three- to five-year-olds, staff members
> are not allowed to touch the children. If they want to
> be hugged or held, the adults are supposed to push
> them away! This is a classic example of how a seemingly
> good idea—wanting to protect children from sexual
> predators—can have serious negative consequences.

---

2   Montagu, *Touching*, 97–99.
3   Ibid.

> Children need healthy touch. As we've seen, infants can literally die without it. It's part of our biology.
>
> Unfortunately, we've become so afraid of unhealthy touch that we may actually make it more likely by failing to meet the needs of children for healthy physical affection. This can make them more vulnerable to pedophiles, not less, as children will tend to seek out those who appear affectionate towards them.[4]

The Oxford English dictionary defines touching as "the action or an act of touching (with the hand, finger, or other part of the body)" and "exercise of the faculty of *feeling* upon a material object." The word *feeling* has an interesting double meaning here, because the tactile faculty we refer to as "feeling" is directly related to the complex language of our entire range of emotions. This double meaning is no accident—feeling and emotion are interrelated and stem from our earliest relationship to touch. Each neural or muscular stimulation and its related emotion make an indelible imprint on the developing brain.

Nurturing touch begins in the womb. Even before an embryo develops eyes or ears, his skin is highly developed. Research has shown that a fetus as young as nine weeks will bend his fingers as if to grip something if his palm is touched. The amniotic environment is a soothing, rocking, gentle environment, and the baby's skin is like an external nervous system, the medium by which the external world is perceived.

When we observe the behavior of our closest mammalian mothers, their inborn behavior after a relatively short labor is to stimulate their babies through licking. This is nature's way of ensuring that a baby's urinary, gastrointestinal, and respiratory systems are activated. The purpose of a human mother's much longer labor is to massage the human baby in utero, stimulating the baby's systems so that the mother can concentrate on giving her baby a different kind of postlabor experience. A reciprocal process begins immediately after birth—the mother's gentle touch as she holds and caresses her baby begins the all-important bonding and attachment process; the baby's suckling helps to expel the mother's placenta.

---

4   Perry et al., *The Boy Who Was Raised as a Dog*, 235.

During the birth process, mother and infant have had a somewhat trying time. At birth, each clearly requires the reassurance of the other's presence. The reassurance for the mother lies in the sight of her baby, its first cry, and in its closeness to her body. For the baby, it consists of the contact with and warmth of the mother's body, the support in her cradled arms, the caressing, the cutaneous [skin] stimulation it receives, and the suckling at her breast, the welcome into "the bosom of the family." These are words, but they refer to very real psycho-physiological conditions.[5]

Human Babies—Cache or Carry?

Anthropology also teaches us a great deal about what human babies are designed to expect from their caregivers, based on very real biological needs. Mammalian maternal behavior is divided into two distinct behavioral norms: "cache" mammals and "carry" mammals. The *cache* mammals are those that leave their babies in hiding for long periods of time so the mother can hunt for food. These mothers have milk high in fat and protein, allowing their babies to sleep for long periods of time in order not to attract a predator with their cries. The *carry* species are those mammals whose babies are relatively immature and must be on their mother's bodies or in very close proximity. These mothers produce milk that is low in fat and protein, which digests quickly, guaranteeing that the baby will be hungry more frequently. This forces the mother to stay close by, ideally having the baby on her body so they can move together quickly if needed to escape a dangerous situation. Human babies are by far the most immature babies born, needing constant care, including feeding, holding, rocking, and other soothing behaviors. Unfortunately, Western culture has traditionally treated human babies as if they were more like cache animals, trying to invent ways to keep them quiet and alone for as long as possible,

---

5   Montagu, *Touching*, 73.

especially at night. This can force babies to go against their biology and, in some cases, lead to failure to thrive.

Researchers in the United States and England have found that on average, babies in these countries are only touched or held for approximately 25 percent of their daytime hours. By nine months of age, the touch time goes down to 16 percent. Even young infants in a model day care center were only touched 14 percent of the day. In contrast, studies done with the *!Kung San* tribe in Africa found that infants are in touch with their mothers for approximately 70 percent of the day and in someone else's arms the rest of the time. These babies cry much less than Western babies.[6]

Attachment parenting encourages parents to find a happy balance in their ability to keep their babies physically close. Seventy percent may seem overwhelming for some parents, especially if they have a physical challenge to holding their babies that much, but being aware of the biological needs for babies to be held and soothed encourages us to find creative ways to meet these needs.

Why Is Touch So Important?

Nurturing touch has so many advantages; for instance, it stimulates growth-promoting hormones. Growth hormone emanates from the hypothalamus, and touch is what sends a message to the pituitary gland to release this hormone. A Duke University researcher discovered that when baby rats were not licked by their mothers, it took only forty-five minutes before growth hormone was suppressed.[7] As Dr. Tiffany Field, the director of the Touch Research Institute at the University of Miami, explains, "Our fingertips contain an incredible pharmacy. Slide them across the trunks of preterm infants and the pressure stimulates a branch of a cranial nerve called the vegetative vagus, which, in turn, stimulates the gastrointestinal tract, releasing hormones like glucose and insulin [which aids in gastrointestinal food absorption, thus enhancing digestion]." They also found that premature infants who were gently stroked produced more immunoglobulin, which protects against respiratory infections. More research tells us that nurturing touch improves intellectual and

---

6   Heller, *The Vital Touch*, 119–120.
7   Ibid., 37.

motor development immediately from birth. It also helps regulate babies' temperature, heart rate, and sleep-wake patterns, especially when the baby is held skin-to-skin. These babies not only gain weight faster, but they also nurse better, are calmer, and are able to be more quickly soothed when they cry. [8] [9] [10] Parents also benefit from practicing nurturing touch. As discussed in chapter 3, the hormone oxytocin (the "mother love" hormone) is released through loving touch, so babies, mothers, and fathers all benefit from massage, hugs, and snuggle time. The calming effects of skin-to-skin contact help parents get to know their babies better, strengthening the emotional bonds between parent and child. Additionally, an inverse relationship exists between nurturing touch and adult physical violence. Cultures that rate high in physical affection, touch, holding, or carrying rate low in adult physical violence. Those cultures rating low in physical touch have high rates of adult physical violence.[11]

Kangaroo Care

Doctors in Bogotá, Colombia, discovered an amazing solution to their lack of funding for incubators for premature babies: their mothers' bodies! They called this type of care "kangaroo care," or "K-care" for short, which creatively describes how a baby is held skin-to-skin on the mother's chest. Babies who were able to breathe on their own were placed between their mothers' breasts for warmth, and the mothers were encouraged to let their babies

---

8   Schanberg and Field, "Sensory deprivation stress and supplemental stimulation in the rat pup and preterm human neonate," *Child Development.*

9   Gray et al., "Skin-to-skin contact is analgesic in healthy newborns," *Pediatrics.*

10   St. James-Roberts et al., "Supplementary carrying compared with advice to increase responsive parenting as interventions to prevent persistent infant crying," *Pediatrics.*

11   Heller, *The Vital Touch,* 71.

suckle as frequently as they could. The nurses soon realized that these babies grew faster, gained significantly more weight, slept better, and their heart rates and temperatures stabilized more quickly. Fathers were also given the opportunity to hold their babies, and the results were remarkably beneficial for the babies. Many of the infants were able to leave the hospital sooner, and the mothers and fathers felt much more confident about their abilities to care for their babies once they returned home.[12] More recent research has shown that if a K-care baby's body temperature cools down, the mother's body warms up, and if the baby's temperature gets too warm, the mother's body cools down.

Dr. Nils Bergman first introduced K-care to hospitals in South Africa in 1995. His website, www.kangaroobabycare.com, has excellent information and research, with significant contributions by his colleague Susan Ludington-Hoe. They provide a lot of research that demonstrates the profound physiological and attachment benefits to premature and full-term babies and their parents especially when done within the first hour after birth.

Now many hospitals practice K-care around the world, and if you deliver a premie, be sure and ask whether you can practice K-care with your baby. More benefits to K-care are discussed in the Additional Research section at the end of this chapter.

How You Can Provide Nurturing Touch

Parents can meet their children's need for loving contact in many ways. Skin-to-skin holding in the form of kangaroo care is beneficial for all newborn babies and helps them transition peacefully to the outside world. Part of your birth plan could include instructions on how you would like your baby cared for directly after birth. Many hospital nursery nurses are directed to scrub the baby, sometimes with rough wash clothes, but you may request that the baby stay with you and if possible, that Mother or Father give him his first gentle bath with warm water and a gentle approach.

Breastfeeding provides an excellent opportunity for a mother to snuggle with her undressed infant. If a mother or other caregiver

---

12   Ruiz-Peláez et al., "Kangaroo mother care: An example to follow from developing countries," *British Medical Journal.*

is bottle-feeding, the baby can still be held skin to skin to give the baby that important touch time. For instance, the baby's clothing can be removed and the mother can hold the baby in the same feeding position as a nursing mother, as discussed in chapter 3. Bath time is another opportunity for skin contact. The calming effects of nurturing touch are increased with the warmth of the bath water, and studies have shown that this simple technique can foster more secure attachments with baby.[13] Many parents find that it is safer and easier to bathe with their infants, rather than bathe the baby in a sink or other hard surface; this, too, increases opportunities for nurturing touch.

Infant Massage

Massage is perhaps the best way to provide nurturing touch to infants, and the benefits continue as children get older. Massage can soothe a colicky baby, help a child unwind before bedtime, and provide playful interaction between parent and child. While all parents can use massage as a special way to connect with their babies, it is a particularly wonderful tool for fathers to nurture their attachment relationships. Vimala McClure, the founder of the International Association of Infant Massage, writes:

> The bonds of trust and love, the lessons of
> compassion, warmth, openness, and respect that
> are inherent in the massage routine will be carried
> by your child into adulthood. Especially if your
> parenting practices reflect the same values of infant
> massage, your child will be more likely to respond
> to others with empathy and warmth, to respond to
> social problems with compassion and altruism, and to
> experience life as a joyful adventure in which he has
> the opportunity to love and be loved—to help others
> and extend himself in genuine service to humanity.[14]

---

13 Saunder, "Co-bathing as a gentle solution for attachment difficulties," *British Journal of Midwifery.*

14 McClure, *Infant Massage: A Handbook for Loving Parents,* 13.

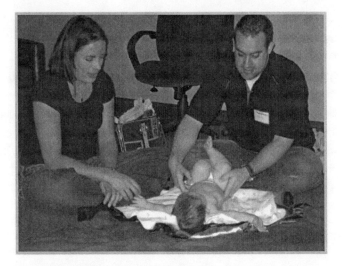

Parents who practice infant massage report many benefits, including some that they never would have associated with nurturing touch. Recently, writer Jennifer Mahal shared this story in the *San Diego Union-Tribune* when she interviewed parents who were taking a baby massage class in a San Diego elementary school:

> Itzel Serrano used to hate being put into her car seat.
> The five-month-old would fuss and kick when her
> father, George Serrano, strapped her in. That was
> before George and his wife, Aracely, took a class in
> infant massage offered by the Kids on Track pilot
> project in the Chula Vista Elementary School District.
> "Before, I would pick her up and put her in the car
> seat, but now I tell her. I show her the car seat. I tell
> her we're going for a ride," George said, watching
> Itzel, his first child.… "She responds much better."
>
> Communication and bonding between parent and
> child is what the five-week class is all about, instructor
> Elaine Lopez said. "It's not about the strokes, it's
> more the bonding and attachment," said Lopez, who
> teaches a group of five to seven parents to massage
> their babies by demonstrating on a doll named Lucy.

"How a baby is viewed influences how a baby is cared for," said Suzanne P. Reese, an international instructor with Infant Massage USA who trained … Lopez. Infant massage works as a way to create greater understanding between children and adults because it is all about nurturing, she said. "It's simple and effective and you don't need the electronic tools and gizmos and gadgets…. It's the love from your heart to your hands."

Studies done by the Touch Research Institute at the University of Miami School of Medicine show that infant massage can help preterm babies grow and develop, can help preschoolers behave better, and has positive effects on the parent-child relationship. Enriquez, who brings her three-year-old son, Gael Ontiveros, with her to the weekly sessions, said learning how to massage Valeria has helped her discover her daughter's likes and dislikes. "She loves to have her toes rubbed," Enriquez said in Spanish. "She'll put her foot on me and wait very still."

Parents are taught to ask their babies' permission before starting massage. They warm drops of oil in their hands, making a swishing noise that acts as a cue to the baby. Martha Hernandez said her five-month-old, Edwin, is antsy before she starts. He calms "the minute I do the massage," she said.

The class cycles through a series of massage strokes with names such as water wheel, open book, sun and moon, and Indian milking. Although Lopez teaches the massage strokes as a series, going from hands and feet to the stomach and the back, she tells the parents to pay attention to what their child wants and follow the little one's lead. "This is really child-led, it really truly is, because it's all about the baby," said

Lopez, a mother of three. That means if a child needs to eat during class, they eat. If they want their back rubbed instead of their front, so be it. "Sometimes [Itzel] doesn't want to be massaged," George said. "Sometimes she just wants to play."

No fancy lotions or salves are used. Parents learn that babies can be massaged with 100 percent cold-pressed olive oil. "They can use what they use in a salad," Butler said, noting that babies often like to suck their fingers and toes. "We want them to be able to do it and not have to buy costly products."

Parents are encouraged to incorporate massage time into their family's lives. Many families add it to their child's bedtime or bathing routines. Lorena Lopez sets aside time for her nine-month-old, Raul Grajeda, and her four year old, Rene Grajeda. She said doing massage has allowed her to connect with both sons. "Rene has his time and Raul has his time," Lopez said through an interpreter. "It's important to be able to do this, with our lives being so hectic."

The commitment of the parents coming to the class has impressed the instructors. "These moms are so dedicated. They have a million things on their plate—cooking, cleaning, taking care of their husbands—but they're taking this hour and a half," instructor Elaine Lopez said. The instructors said during the last session, one mother walked several miles to the class because her car broke down and she didn't want to miss it.

"I think those babies are experiencing a lot of love," Lopez said. [15]

Jennifer K. Mahal
San Diego freelance writer

15   Mahal, "Massaging baby induces bonding," *San Diego Union Tribune.*

Benefits of Infant Massage[16]

- Promotes bonding
- Encourages relaxation
- Makes baby feel loved
- Promotes better sleep
- Facilitates body awareness
- Boosts immune system
- Promotes sensory stimulation
- Improves skin condition
- Improves blood circulation
- Aids digestion and waste elimination
- Balances respiration
- Helps parents learn to read baby's cues and better respond to their needs
- Helps build parents' and baby's self-esteem

Infant massage classes are now available in most communities. Although this practice has been used in many cultures around the world for centuries, it is relatively new to parents in Western cultures. As research catches up with the miraculous benefits to babies and parents, the practice is now being promoted by hospitals and infant development experts around the world. Resources for classes are available at the end of this chapter.

---

16   Frequently asked questions," Infant Massage USA Web site.

"Babywearing"

In 1990, a study was published by Dr. Elizabeth Anisfeld and her team of researchers at Columbia University, who wanted to determine if close physical contact would increase infants' security of attachment.[17] The mothers who participated in the study were low income, inner-city mothers, married and single, who had just delivered in an inner-city hospital. One group of moms was given soft baby carriers (called "Snuglies"), and the other group was given plastic infant seats to use to carry their babies. The researchers wanted to determine if this one factor alone would correlate to the security of

attachment of these babies to their mothers at thirteen months of age. By three months of age they observed a marked difference in the degree of responsiveness and sensitivity from the mothers using the soft carriers. At

thirteen months, using the Strange Situation, they found an astounding **83 percent of the infants who were carried in the soft carriers were securely attached**, whereas only **38 percent of the infants carried in plastic infant seats were securely attached**. They concluded that the close physical contact alone was related to the secure attachment of baby and mother.

All over the world, mothers have found this simple tool to be the greatest mothering technique ever invented. In Western culture, it is a relatively new practice and is common-

---

17　Anisfeld et al., "Does infant carrying promote attachment? An experimental study of the effects of increased physical contact on the development of attachment," *Child Development*.

ly referred to as "babywearing." This refers to carrying a baby in a sling or other soft carrier and provides the same benefits as carrying the baby in arms. Carried babies cry less and are more calm and content.[18] Many pediatricians are concerned about a new phenomenon they are seeing in their practices of babies with "flat-head syndrome," or plagiocephaly, caused by babies spending too much time lying on their backs.[19] Babies who are carried rather than spending all their time in plastic seats or car seats do not have this

problem. Another advantage is that infants who are carried can see the world at their parents' level but can also snuggle in when feeling overwhelmed or overstimulated. Babywearing also meets a baby's need for physical contact, comfort, security, stimulation, and movement, all of which encourage neurological development. Many parents find babywearing extremely effective for meeting a child's need for nurturing touch while on the go or doing everyday tasks around the house.

---

18   Heller, *The Vital Touch*, 199.

19   Littlefield, "Car seats, infant carriers, and swings: Their role in deformational plagio-
      cephaly," *Journal of Prosthetics and Orthotics*.

My Baby Doesn't Seem to Like a Sling—Help!

Q. I recently received a baby sling as a gift, but my baby doesn't seem to like it. When I put him in it, he starts to fuss. He is three months old, and I've carried him in arms a lot up to this point. Is there anything I can do to get him to accept being in the sling? If not, can I still be an Attachment Parent without using a sling?

A. Using a baby sling or other soft baby carrier is a great way to ensure that your baby gets lots of holding and carrying as you move through your busy life. The hands-free aspect makes it easy for you to get other things done at the same time you are meeting your baby's needs for touch, closeness, movement, and your presence. Up to now, you may have been meeting these needs by holding your baby in arms. It is certainly possible to be an Attachment Parent without using a sling by continuing to carry him in arms and finding other high touch ways to stay connected, like infant massage. But don't give up on the sling just yet! Slings are convenient and make it easier to hold your baby longer.

Here are some suggestions that may help:

The Attachment Parenting Book by Dr. William Sears and Martha Sears has an excellent chapter on babywearing. The authors point out that using a sling can take a little practice and might feel awkward at first, but will become second nature after a while. One of their suggestions is to put on the sling in the morning when you're getting dressed. Then you already have it on and can put baby in it whenever you'd like during the day instead of first putting him down, which isn't always convenient to do. That is a good way to get used to wearing the sling and will make it easier for you to try it with your baby.

- Babies can often sense when you are stressed or upset and become upset, too, so try to stay calm and patient as you introduce the sling.
- Double check to be sure that you are wearing the sling correctly and that you know how to position

your baby in it comfortably. Your sling probably came with detailed instructions and maybe even an instructional video, which you may want to review.

- You may find it helpful to talk to another parent you know who is experienced in wearing a baby. She or he can help you make sure that there is nothing you overlooked, and give you tips on adjusting the sling to fit you and your baby comfortably.

- Every baby is different, so you may need to experiment to see what works best for yours. You can try putting him in the sling at different times—when he is sleepy or wide-awake, calm or fussy, et cetera, to see when your baby is most agreeable to being in it.

- You may also want to try different positions. From three months or a little older, many babies like facing forward in the sling; if possible, get an experienced babywearing parent to assist you.

- If you are breastfeeding, you can nurse your baby while using the sling, and it may be a good way to get your baby to stay interested in staying in the sling longer.

- Some parents find that a little distraction helps as they get their baby settled into the sling. When you first put your baby in it, try walking around, patting, and talking to him reassuringly. Movement is usually calming, so this may help him get used to the sling without starting to fuss. Another idea for distraction is to have your partner or someone else talk to him for a little while or show him a toy to engage him for a few moments when you first put him in the sling.

- Don't put a time limit on getting your baby to accept being carried in the sling. Keep in mind that you are making a change in his routine, and it may take a little while for him to get used to this new way of being held.[20]

---

20   Silver, "Slings and attachment parenting," *Attachment Parenting: The Journal of API*.

Many creative and fashionable baby and child carriers are available and are used across the world. Various types of carriers can distribute the weight load of the child across the caregiver's body differently and allow the child to be positioned in several ways. Try multiple carriers and positions to determine what is most comfortable for parent and child, recognizing that carrier needs may change as the child grows. Some API support groups offer a "sling library" to give parents the opportunity to try on and experiment with different slings or carriers. It is now easy to buy carriers at most baby retail outlets and of course on many Web sites.

Most soft baby carriers can be used for discrete breastfeeding. This helps mothers who are uncomfortable breastfeeding in public—or those whose babies nurse frequently due to growth spurts or teething—to nurse their babies on cue while going about their daily business. Soft carriers may offer more comfort and protection for babies who are otherwise easily distracted from nursing.

Gentle movement may be helpful as a child acclimates to a new carrier. Walking or swaying with the baby in the carrier may approximate the baby's experience in the womb and make the carrier feel more familiar and comfortable. Parents can also support the baby with their hand(s) until both parent and child feel comfortable that the carrier is secure.

As children grow, they continue to need nurturing touch for comfort and connectedness. Babywearing can continue for as long as is comfortable for both parent and child. Many carriers can accommodate growing toddlers. Soft carriers provide special security to the older child in busy and crowded locations and keep busy hands from the temptation of touching breakable objects! An overwhelmed toddler may be comforted by the familiar security of being carried. Be assured that carrying a baby into toddlerhood and beyond will not "spoil" the baby. Parents can follow the child's lead and try not to make him feel bad about still wanting to feel the closeness that carrying provides. If you find your child is too heavy to hold comfortably, take a few minutes out, if possible, to provide attention or comfort in your lap.

Many devices can be used to hold a baby or young child independently that, if overused, do not promote attachment (swings, jumpers, plastic carriers, strollers, or car seats when not being used for safety reasons). Parents using these devices should be sensitive to the baby's behavior and body language, and they must be conscious to avoid the overuse of these products. If using a stroller or baby carriage, use a brand that allows the baby to face the parent rather than looking away. Some children like the security of seeing their parents, especially since very young babies don't yet understand where their parents have gone when they are out of sight.

Nurturing Touch and the Older Child

Frequent hugs, snuggling, back rubs, and massage all meet the older child's need for touch, as does more physical play such as wrestling and tickling. Use playfulness and games to encourage physical closeness in a child who is resistant, and remember that touch is an ongoing need throughout life.

Children need various types of play, from rough-and-tumble wrestling to imagination games. Many girls and boys, even sometimes as babies, enjoy some rough-and-tumble play, and it can strengthen attachment. Often parents find themselves specializing in only one type of play and may even be uncomfortable with other types, especially if they were not touched very much in their own childhood. This can be especially true for play that on the surface seems harsh or mean, but may in reality only be wrestling on the floor or a child enjoying a ride on Daddy's back. These types of play serve an important purpose for children who are working through emotions, processing the images they see in the media, and exploring their own ability to control aggression. Children benefit immensely when each parent can actively engage in all types of play, including those that require parents to challenge their own comfort levels. It is important, however, for parents to respect the child's boundaries. Sometimes eye contact, a wink, or a smile is enough to connect with an older child, and wrestling or tickling should never be forced or overdone.

Parents should also remember to use nurturing touch with partners and other loved ones! We all know how much we appreciate a hug, a neck massage, or even a warm handshake when we interact with family, co-workers, and friends. All humans thrive on touch and the reconnection it provides. We share Sharon Heller's vision as she concludes her book, *The Vital Touch*:

> I can't deny that this book is a call to arms and that
> the victory parade I envisage will be a march through
> the malls with more babies strapped on our hips, our
> backs, our fronts, or our shoulders. I believe this will
> be good for all babies—and especially those content
> only when held. Each tender touch buys love stock
> kept in a permanent reserve, always there to be drawn
> from. What better security could parents offer?[21]

---

21 Heller, *The Vital Touch*, 234.

Appendix to Chapter Five: Additional Research and Resource Recommendations

Additional Research
Bowling Alone

In 1995, Robert Putman, a professor of international affairs at Harvard University, released an article that caught the attention of the U.S. government and became the subject of widespread response and social concern. The article, entitled "Bowling Alone," spoke of the decline of what Putman called "social capital," which refers to an individual's network of social connections. He noted with statistical evidence that while individually centered activities (such as bowling alone, computer games, and Virtual Reality) are on the rise, participation in community-based activities such as bowling leagues, PTA meetings, religious groups, Boy Scouts, … and voting are seriously declining. He quoted a poll in which Americans were asked if they could trust most people. In 1960, 58 percent of Americans said that they did, whereas in 1993, only 38 percent responded in favor of trust…. A touch-starved nation very quickly becomes a trust-starved nation.[22]

Studies in Uganda have shown that babies who are carried in upright positions are quicker to walk and develop faster in other areas too: the upright position heightens a baby's visual alertness while developing muscles in the back and neck. Carried around all day, babies become familiar with their worlds as they watch from their secure vantage point. Because they're held close and upright, they stay calmer—studies show that they even cry less than babies who aren't carried regularly.[23]

Studies of premature babies using techniques similar to those taught [in Infant Massage] have demonstrated that daily massage is of tremendous benefit. Research projects at the University of Miami Medical Center,

---

22 Caplan, *To Touch Is to Live*, 18–19.
23 Ibid., 54.

headed up by the Touch Research Institute's founder, Dr. Tiffany Field, have shown remarkable results. In one study, twenty premature babies were massaged three times a day for fifteen minutes each. They averaged 47 percent greater weight gain a day, were more active and alert, and showed more mature neurological development than infants who did not receive massage. In addition, their hospital stay averaged six days less.[24,25]

Urs Hunziker and Ronald Barr of McGill University Faculty of Medicine in Canada asked mothers to carry their three-week-olds in their arms or in a soft body carrier for at least three hours a day until the babies were three months old. The babies who received more carrying—four and a half hours compared to a little over two and a half for the control group—cried 43 percent less than the control group. And they cried 51 percent less in the early evening when babies are presumed most fussy. Furthermore ... they found that infant crying did not peak at six weeks of age in the infants who were held more [as found by an earlier study conducted in 1962 by T. Berry Brazelton]. At six weeks ... the babies cried for a little over an hour a day, less than the just over two hours a day that infants in the control group cried and less than Brazelton's figure of three hours as the average amount of daily crying for the Western infant.[26]

One of the University of Miami Touch Institute's discoveries in the early 1990s was that the benefits of touch therapy are mutual. So vibrant is the power of touch that the massage giver enjoys as many significant health benefits as the massage recipient. For one study, the Institute recruited retiree "grandparent" volunteers and trained them to massage premature, drug-exposed, "failure-to-thrive" newborns, orphans, and abused children. After a month of massage, the infants were more active, their alertness and tracking behaviors improved, they slept better, and they were more sociable and easier to soothe. But the children were not the only beneficiaries. The retirees showed a dramatic decrease in depression, increased feelings of self-worth, improved sleep patterns, and fewer doctor visits. They reported less anxiety, drank

---

24 McClure, *Infant Massage: A Handbook for Loving Parents*, 7–8.

25 Field, "Infant Massage," *Zero to Three*.

26 Heller, *The Vital Touch*, 199.

fewer cups of coffee, and their levels of urine cortisol, a stress-related hormone, decreased. In fact, the positive effects on the "grandparents" were greater after giving a massage than after receiving one.[27]

Kangaroo Mother Care (KMC), a technique first developed in 1978 to deal with overcrowding of neonatal units in Colombia, uses mothers or fathers as incubators. Babies weighing less than two thousand grams at birth are attached to their caregivers' chests in skin-to-skin contact and kept upright twenty-four hours a day. The study showed that KMC is at least as good as traditional care with incubators, improves breastfeeding rates, and improves bonding between parent and infant. Parental confidence and sense of fulfillment are also improved. Two decades of implementation and research have made it clear that KMC is more than an alternative to incubator care and should be encouraged even in affluent settings, say the authors.[28]

Kangaroo care had a significant positive impact on the infant's perceptual-cognitive and motor development and on the parenting process. The authors speculated that K-care has both a direct impact on infant development by contributing to neurophysiological organization and an indirect effect by improving parental mood, perceptions, and interactive behavior.[29]

!Kung San infants are in constant physical contact with their mothers or other caregivers, with the smallest cry responded to within ten seconds. Researchers from McGill University found that while crying escalated in infants around the same time in both cultures, *!Kung San* infants cried only half as long.[30]

Eighty-three percent of the infants carried in soft carriers were classified

---

27 Gordon and Adderly, *Brighter Baby: Boosting Your Child's Intelligence: Health and Happiness through Infant Therapeutic Massage*, 11.

28 Ruiz-Peláez et al., "Kangaroo mother care: An example to follow from developing countries," *British Medical Journal*.

29 Feldman et al., "Comparison of skin-to-skin (kangaroo) and traditional care: Parenting outcomes and preterm infant development," *Pediatrics*.

30 Hunziker and Barr, "Increased carrying reduces infant crying: A randomized controlled trial," *Pediatrics*.

as securely attached compared to the control group where only 38 percent of the infants were securely attached. These researchers found that carrying increased responsiveness and attachment.[31]

One study showed that premature infants who received three fifteen-minute periods of massage a day for ten consecutive days experienced a 47 percent increase in weight gain. By eight months of age, these babies showed advanced weight gain and better intellectual and motor development.[32]

Skin-to-skin holding of newborn infants had many beneficial effects as an analgesic. Researchers compared differences in crying, grimacing, and heart rate of babies held skin to skin or not held during a heel lance procedure. They found that crying and grimacing were reduced by 82 percent and 65 percent, respectively. They noted it prevented the explosive rise in heart rate that normally accompanies heel lance.[33]

Full-term babies nurse more frequently when they are carried by their mothers.[34]

Premature babies who were held skin to skin with their caregivers had less severe infections, less time in the hospital, and breastfed longer than the control group.[35]

Premature babies who were touched and held gained weight faster and were healthier than the control group.[36]

---

31 Anisfeld et al., "Does infant carrying promote attachment? An experimental study of the effects of increased physical contact on the development of attachment," *Child Development.*

32 Schanberg and Field, "Sensory deprivation stress and supplemental stimulation in the rat pup and preterm human neonate," *Child Development.*

33 Gray et al., "Skin-to-skin contact is analgesic in healthy newborns," *Pediatrics.*

34 St. James-Roberts et al., "Supplementary carrying compared with advice to increase responsive parenting as interventions to prevent persistent infant crying," *Pediatrics.*

35 Rey and Martinez, "Manejo racional del niño prematuro [Rational management of the premature infant]," In: *Curso de medicina fetal y neonatal,* 137–151.

36 Conde-Agudelo et al., "Kangaroo mother care to reduce morbidity and mortality in low birthweight infants," *Cochrane Database of Systematic Reviews.*

Recommended Reading

A Ride on Mother's Back by Emery Bernhard.
Babywearing: The Benefits and Beauty of This Ancient Tradition by
    Maria Blois, MD.
Birth without Violence by Frederick Leboyer, MD.
Essential Touch: Meeting the Needs of Young Children by Frances M.
    Carlson.
Infant Massage by Vimala McClure.
Kangaroo Care: The Best You Can Do to Care for Your Preterm Infant by
    Susan Luddington-Hoe, PhD.
Loving Hands by Frederick Leboyer, MD.
*Mother Nature: Maternal Instincts and How They Shape the Human
    Species* by Sarah Blaffer Hrdy, PhD.
The Science of Parenting by Margot Sunderland, PhD.
The Vital Touch by Sharon Heller, PhD.
To Touch Is to Live by Mariana Caplan, PhD.
Touching: The Human Significance of the Skin by Ashley Montagu, PhD.

Recommended DVD

BabyBaby OhBaby produced by David Stark—A video that helps
familiarize parents with the basics of infant massage which can be
purchased at www.babybabyohbaby.com.

Tummy 2 Tummy is the first non-product specific, instructional
    babywearing DVD available at www.tummy2tummy.com. It
    covers the four different types of baby carriers: Ring Slings,
    Pouches, Asian Back Carriers, and Simple Pieces of Cloth, all in
    one interactive DVD.

Useful Web Sites

www.askdrsears.com/html/5/t051100.asp: The Sears family provides
information on how to wear your baby.

www.infantmassageusa.org: Web site of Infant Massage USA.

www.KangaGuru.com: Web site for more information on KC for preterm and fullterm infants.

www.kangaroomothercare.com: Web site of Kangaroo Mother Care Promotions and the work of Dr. Nils Bergman. Promotions that provide a bibliography of skin-to- skin research.

www.mamatoto.org: General information about babywearing with "how-to" guides and videos.

www.midwiferytoday.com/articles/kangaroocare.asp: Web site article Kangaroo Care: why does it work?

www.naturalchild.org/guest/laura_simeon.html: The Natural Child Project Web site, with article on babywearing.

www.rebozoway.org: Web site dedicated to babywearing and attachment parenting practices with information about the Rebozo carrier that originated in South America.

www.thebabywearer.com: A resource for information on babywearing.

www.tummy2tummy.com: Web site for instructional information on babywearing.

www6.miami.edu/touch-research: Web site of the Touch Research Institute.

Chapter Six

Principle 5
Ensure Safe Sleep-
Physically and Emotionally:
The Critical Importance of
Nighttime Needs

Ensure Safe Sleep-Physically and Emotionally: The Critical Importance of Nighttime Needs

> *The reality is, no babies need to sleep through the night. That is completely a cultural construct. It is usually not the babies that have the sleep problems—they can sleep where and when they need—but it is the parents who have the sleep problems. These are usually induced by the notions of the baby being separate from the parent. It is not that the baby can't sleep, they just can't sleep how the parents want it, when they want it, and in a solitary environment. Biologically speaking, this is unnatural for them, and their emotions rightly tell them so.*[1]

Dr. James McKenna
Anthropologist, cosleeping researcher, and
Director of the Mother-Baby Lab at Notre Dame University

"Is your baby sleeping through the night?" is often the first question a new parent hears. For many parents, this question undermines their confidence and creates unnecessary anxiety. The truth is that most young babies do not sleep through the night. This is simply a myth that continues to be perpetuated in our modern society—a myth that Dr. McKenna calls "a cultural construct" since many cultures around the world don't have that expectation. Babies have needs at night just as they do during the day—to be fed, to be comforted, and to be protected. They may feel fear and loneliness, sadness, or feel too cold or too hot—and therefore they need the reassurance of a loving parent to help them feel secure during the night. API encourages parents to respond to their children's needs at night just as they do during the day. This requires exploring a variety of different safe sleeping arrangements and choosing the approach that best allows parents to be responsive at night. Some of these approaches are explored in this chapter.

---

1   Parker, "The greatest gifts we can give our children: An interview with Dr. Jim McKenna," *Attachment Parenting: The Journal of API.*

Understanding Infant Sleep Patterns

Many physiological and developmental reasons account for the ways babies sleep. Human infants are designed to feed frequently because mother's milk is lower in fat and digested very easily. Their immature brains are so underdeveloped that they need frequent feeding and skin-to-skin nurturing to stimulate healthy growth. Dr. William Sears explains infant sleep patterns in his book, *Nighttime Parenting*: "In the first few months, most babies sleep fourteen to eighteen hours per day without any respect for the differences between day and night. A baby's sleep pattern resembles his feeding pattern: small frequent feedings and short frequent naps." Adults and infants also sleep differently, in that adults have fewer periods of REM (rapid eye movement) sleep (also known as active sleep) and more periods of deep sleep or "quiet sleep," whereas infants have frequent periods of REM sleep and fewer periods of quiet sleep.

During REM sleep, our brains are actively dreaming, which seems to stimulate the development of higher brain functions. Sleep researchers believe that the more complex the brain, the more REM sleep is required to help in its development. From a biological perspective, infant sleep patterns appear to increase the baby's ability to survive, allowing him to feed more often and maintain close contact with the mother. The younger the human being, the more REM sleep he requires, which increases the probability of wakefulness, especially during the transitions from active sleep to quiet sleep, which tend to occur on average every ninety minutes.

As we get older, periods of REM sleep lessen greatly. Infants' sleep patterns gradually adjust to adultlike sleep patterns beginning around the ages of two and three years.[2]

---

2   Sears and Sears, *Nighttime Parenting*, 16.

Sleeping Like a Baby

When it comes to sleeping like a baby, we know the following:

- Most babies don't sleep through the night, but may wake up every one and a half to two hours to be fed.
- Babies weren't designed by nature to sleep seven to eight hours straight—in fact, some experts feel it could be dangerous for an infant to sleep that long.
- When you bring your newborn home from the hospital, it's a good idea to begin a routine of sleeping when the baby sleeps to catch up on the hours you missed during the night.
- You will feel more rested if you keep your baby close by or in bed with you, as long as you follow safe cosleeping guidelines.

What Exactly is Cosleeping?

"Cosleeping" and "bedsharing" (also referred to as "sharing sleep" or the "family bed"), are terms often incorrectly used interchangeably to describe a sleep arrangement where family members sleep in the same bed. References to these words often lead to confusion about publicized information on safe versus unsafe infant sleep practices. Cosleeping, however, is an umbrella term that is used to refer to infants and their adult caregivers sleeping in "close proximity" though not necessarily in the same bed. Bedsharing, one form of cosleeping, is sharing the same bed with an infant. Cosleeping is encouraged by API and the AAP and governed by safe practice guidelines ("Creating a Safe Sleep Environment," p. 163). Unsafe infant sleep practices, including sleeping with an infant on a couch, recliner, or other non-bed surface, are not accepted forms of cosleeping or bedsharing.

The Benefits of Cosleeping

From a purely practical standpoint, parents report that they get more sleep with fewer interruptions when they cosleep. They don't need to get up to attend to baby's needs, which keeps parents from having to wake up fully during feedings. Cosleeping improves mother's milk supply, increases the number of feedings, and increases the duration of the breastfeeding relationship. While the American Academy of Pediatrics does not support bedsharing, they do support infants sleeping in the same room as the parents (close proximity).

Babies feel warm, secure, and protected; therefore, they fret and cry less. Mothers worry less about their infants at night when they can reach out and touch the baby, and both parents develop a closer bond with the baby. In addition to these benefits, cosleeping also enhances the breastfeeding and attachment relationships. Breastfeeding is better established through frequent nursing.

From a physiologic basis, when cosleeping, the baby experiences more periods of light sleep, which stabilize heart rates and breathing patterns, and, as mentioned previously, decrease the risk of SIDS. We have had mothers over the years report to us that they believe they were able to save their child's life—some from sleep apneas, some from other unforeseen occurrences—because they were cosleeping. The following story powerfully illustrates the importance of mother-baby togetherness at night:

> I had decided to cosleep with my son for many
> reasons. I enjoyed looking at him cradled in my arms,
> nursing him at night was easier, and, as a first-time
> mother, having him right there relieved any fears that
> something may be wrong. On the night of his six-week
> appointment, by my side was the best place for him.

I was wary of having my son vaccinated because of the controversies, including their possible link to autism. Having an autistic younger brother myself made my fears seem reasonable. But, after his physician assured me that any chance of a reaction was remote, my son Angus received his DTaP along with his other shots.

We had an early appointment that morning, and we returned home to what seemed to be a normal day. Angus became grumpy later in the afternoon and had a slight fever as well as some redness around the injection site, but the nurse on call said that this was normal and to give him ibuprofen. By eight o'clock in the evening, we were both tired and he fell asleep at my breast as he had done since his birth.

At about 11 p.m., I felt something slapping against my chest. It was not hard but was repeated rapidly. I had a nightlight on and when I looked next to me, I saw my son thrashing his arms about and an expression of a silent scream on his face. He was not breathing. My reflexes took over, and I sat up and yanked him into the air and to my chest. As I raised him up, I heard him inhale deeply, and he began to scream. I called the doctor and found that he indeed had a reaction to the shots and to give him Benadryl. Within thirty minutes of that dose, he calmed down and was able to sleep again, though I could not.

I know that if Angus were not sleeping there by my side, I would have woken up to a crib death. Because of cosleeping, my son is alive. Angus is now five years old.

Lilith M.

Are There Dangers with Bedsharing?

A little historical background may help put this concern into better perspective. It's important to know that infant solitary sleep is a relatively new practice that has evolved in the Western world only within the last one hundred years. Recently, various medical and professional organizations have discouraged parents from sleeping with their children for fear that it contributes to an increase in sudden infant death syndrome (SIDS). However, new research demonstrates that sharing sleep, when practiced by informed parents, can be safe and beneficial. In fact, many cultures around the world, where millions of parents routinely sleep with their children, have reported some of the lowest SIDS rates. In some of these cultures, such as China and Japan, it is virtually nonexistent. Dr. James McKenna, one of the only cosleeping researchers, offers important advice to all parents regarding solitary sleep:

> Now we at least know that if you're going to put a
> baby alone in a crib in a room by itself, you would
> put a baby on its back, and at least that's a big step
> up in the chances of the baby surviving. But what
> we also now know is three to four studies show quite
> conclusively that putting babies to sleep in a room
> by themselves at three to six months of age *doubles*
> their chances of dying from SIDS. Indeed, when
> cosleeping is defined by the baby sleeping within
> the proximity of a responsible adult caregiver, and
> not necessarily bedsharing, the hypothesis that
> cosleeping reduces the chance of SIDS has in fact
> been confirmed.[3]

British researcher Dr. Helen Ball found that breastfeeding mothers were more likely to sleep on their side in a protective position—tucking their knees up under the baby—and arouse more quickly than bottle-

---

3   Parker, "The greatest gifts we can give our children: An interview with Dr. Jim McK-
     enna," *Attachment Parenting: The Journal of API.*

feeding mothers. For those reasons, McKenna recommends that bottle-fed babies sleep on a separate surface close to the mother.[4]

Parents often worry that they might roll over and suffocate their baby during the night, but remember that just as we are able to sleep in a bed without falling out of it, sober parents are acutely aware that a baby is in the bed. Research conducted by Dr. Miranda Barone put this worry to the test and videotaped mothers and babies sleeping together. "In more than 1,000 hours of observing forty mother-infant pairs, no mother was ever remotely close to overlying or suffocating her infant. Instead, maternal and infant behaviors were beautifully synchronized— when one moved, the other responded, without fully awakening."[5] In fact, she says that in the context of attachment

relationships, her study found that the "attachment behavioral system [such as the need to be physically close to the caregiver and other sensory needs] operates twenty-four hours per day and does not deactivate during sleep, where infants spend sixty percent of their time."[6]

America's Anti-cosleeping Campaign

In September of 1999 and again in May of 2002, the U.S. Consumer Product Safety Commission (CPSC) issued warnings about the practice of cosleeping as dangerous and life-threatening. This can be confusing for parents when in fact the American Academy of Pediatrics (AAP) is in favor of cosleeping or sleeping in close proximity. What the CPSC is really warning against is bedsharing. As a result, a nationwide campaign began in conjunction with the Juvenile Products Manufacturing Association (JPMA) that discouraged and frightened

---

4   McKenna, *Sleeping with Your Baby: A Parent's Guide to Cosleeping*, 48–49.

5   Barone, "Sleeping like a baby: How bedsharing soothes infants," *Mothering* magazine.

6   Ibid.

parents from bringing their infants to bed. Because of this confusion, parents reported sleeping on couches or recliners with their babies, which is many times more dangerous than bedsharing. Ironically if a baby's death occurs in this unsafe environment, it is reported as a "cosleeping" death. A groundswell of opposition came from other researchers, psychologists, parents, and others who protested the lack of solid science behind the campaign. They found that the data was collected anecdotally and inefficiently from newspaper clippings, coroners' reports, and death certificates with very little information from the parents. Even today, no standard interview questions or protocols are used to collect information after a baby dies at home. Additionally important is the need for what researchers call a "control group" of infants in order to make legitimate comparisons for all the factors involved in the children's sleeping environments.

In the 1990s, researchers in the United Kingdom conducted the largest case-control study ever done on infant deaths, called *The Sudden Unexpected Deaths in Infancy* (SUDI) study, carried out by the Confidential Enquiry into Stillbirths and Deaths in Infancy (CESDI). They included information from 450 sudden or unexpected infant deaths and 1,800 matched "control" infants. According to one of the researchers, Dr. Peter Fleming, a professor of infant health and developmental physiology at the University of Bristol and pediatrician at the Royal Hospital for Children in Bristol, "The CESDI study showed that for infants who shared a room with a parent, the risk of SIDS was approximately half that for infants who slept alone. In other words, putting a baby to sleep in a separate room (rather than the room in which the parents slept) *doubled* the risk of SIDS."[7]

Back in the United States in 2002, scientist Dr. Tina Kimmel reviewed the CPSC data and analyzed data from the CDC's Pregnancy Risk Assessment Monitoring System (PRAMS), which surveyed mothers with infants from two to six months of age, and included the question "How often does your new baby sleep in the same bed with you?" At the time of the report, only five states kept the data. However, from that information Dr. Kimmel was able to determine that not only was it safe to sleep with your baby, but that "it was actually less than

---

7   Fleming, "Where should babies sleep at night?" *Mothering* magazine.

half (forty-two percent) as risky, or more than twice as safe, for an infant to be in an adult bed as in a crib."[8]

With all the safety mechanisms in place to make cribs safer, still more infants die alone in cribs than in the family bed; yet, there has never been an outcry to ban cribs.

Dr. Fleming questions the logic behind this sweeping campaign:

> "No one would suggest that because sleeping in a
> crib can be hazardous under certain conditions, no
> baby should sleep in a crib. By analogy, therefore, it is
> equally illogical to suggest that because under certain
> circumstances bedsharing can be hazardous, parents
> should not bedshare with their baby. Given the near
> universality of the practice of bedsharing at some
> stage, it is far more logical to identify the conditions
> under which bedsharing is hazardous and to give
> parents information on how to avoid them."[9]

The blanket condemnation of bedsharing without any attempts to educate the public about how to do it safely is a big concern of many parents and professionals. The bottom line is that many parents are going to do it anyway at some point, so they need to be well versed in safe cosleeping guidelines. Dr. McKenna expressed his disappointment and concern about the short-sighted focus of the campaign:

> By refusing to point out that cosleeping, and cosleeping
> in the form of bedsharing, can be practiced either safely
> or unsafely, and that sleeping next to a baby is not
> inherently dangerous, especially for a breastfeeding,
> sober mother, the CPSC misses opportunities to
> educate millions of parents about how to cosleep safely.
> Its actions suggest instead that parents are neither

---

8   Kimmel, "How the stats really stack up: Cosleeping is twice as safe," *Mothering* magazine.

9   Fleming, "Where should babies sleep at night?" *Mothering* magazine.

educable nor intelligent enough to make their own decisions about how, or whether, to cosleep.[10]

Dr. Fleming agrees: "Rather than issuing broad statements, not based upon good evidence, to suggest that parents should not bedshare with their babies, I suggest that giving them accurate information, based upon careful studies of healthy babies as well as babies who have died, will allow parents to make safe and appropriate choices."[11]

Regardless of the research, some parents just don't feel comfortable or are unable to sleep with their baby in the bed. If you're one of those parents, then it's important to know that it's okay. You can still practice attachment parenting without sleeping with your baby—it's about being responsive to your baby and being in close proximity during the night. We uphold a parent's right to choose, to make informed decisions that feel right for everyone. The American Academy of Pediatrics (AAP) provides safety guidelines for the use of cribs and other separate sleeping surfaces on their Web site at www. aap.org/family/inffurn.htm.

What about Cosleeping with Nonbiological Parents?

Many adoption agencies are beginning to support cosleeping with adopted babies for a couple of very good reasons. First, many internationally adopted babies come from countries where it is the custom to sleep with the baby. Second, adopted babies seem to adjust much better and are more likely to form a secure attachment with their adopted parents sooner when the parents sleep with them.

In the case of stepparents, the biological parent will need to discuss this openly to gauge the stepparent's feelings about bedsharing. If the stepparent has a close loving relationship with the baby, has mentally and physically taken on the role of a parent, and agrees to follow the safe-sleeping guidelines, then the biological parent may decide that it would be safe to cosleep. Any parent, biological or step, who is a deep

---

10   McKenna, "An exclusive *Mothering* special report," *Mothering* magazine.

11   Fleming, "Where should babies sleep at night?" *Mothering* magazine.

sleeper should not sleep with an infant in the bed, because they are less likely to be as aware of the baby.

Some may have an unspoken fear that sleeping with a young child may stimulate sexual feelings—especially in a nonbiological parent. It's important to remember that sexual abusers are not born, but created by their own horrible experiences in childhood, and that a normal, healthy adult will not be tempted to abuse a child whether or not they share the same bed. It is, however, imperative that biological parents take time to get to know a person very well before inviting him or her into the family and the family bed. A stepparent may feel uncomfortable with the situation based on his or her personal beliefs or childhood experiences—these feelings, if that is the case, should be respected and alternative arrangements discussed.

Sharing Sleep with Multiples

It can be a little more complex to cosleep with more than one infant. Dr. McKenna recommends bedsharing with one baby at a time while the mother is breastfeeding. If the mother is single or otherwise doesn't have a father to help care for one of the babies in the family bed while she cares for the other, then she can make sure, for instance in the case of twins, that both are in front of her and she is sleeping in a protective position with her knees bent upward. Two or more babies in the family bed make it a little more difficult for everyone to be comfortable or safe. If you share the bed with twins, be aware that as they grow they will begin to move around in the bed and can fall onto the floor if the bed isn't securely protected or if the mattress isn't on the floor (read the Safe Cosleeping guidelines).

Parents of multiples can consider placing young infants in the same bassinet, crib or cosleeping device (called "cobedding") while in the same room with the parents. This practice may be frowned upon by your pediatrician or others but in his book *Sleeping With Your Baby*, Dr. McKenna writes, "Nowadays when you hear a recommendation against cobedding, it often illustrates cultural biases against cosleeping in general where medical authorities assume, without any data, that if some instances of bedsharing between an adult and a baby are dangerous, then certainly two infants of equal body size must likewise pose a mutual threat."

We recommend you read Dr. McKenna's book as well as *Mothering Multiples* by Karen Gromada.

Create a Safe Sleeping Environment

API recommends the following research-based guidelines that, when followed, allow parents and infants to share sleep in the safest way possible.

The following guidelines should be followed regardless of where baby sleeps:

1. Place your baby to sleep on her back. This helps protect your baby from Sudden Infant Death Syndrome (SIDS).
2. Choose a firm mattress, free from fluffy bedding, bumpers, and stuffed animals. Never place your baby—or fall asleep with your baby—on a couch, recliner, beanbag chair, fold-out couch, inflatable bed, or waterbed to sleep.
3. Keep baby cool. Adjust clothing and room temperature to keep baby from overheating. UNICEF recommends a temperature of between 60-64 degrees Fahrenheit for night-time sleep.
4. Use a fan in the room where baby sleeps to help circulate air and maintain a cooler environment.

If your baby sleeps with you:

1. Breastfeed your baby. Breastfeeding mothers spend more time in lighter stages of sleep, making them more aware of their baby. They also tend to sleep in a protective position (with knees bent upward) that prevents baby from moving down under the covers.
2. Place baby next to Mom, rather than between mother and father.

3. Use approved side rails or bed extenders when placing Baby in the family bed. Fill in any crevice between the bed and walls or furniture with a rolled-up baby blanket or towel. Placing the adult mattress on the floor (like a futon) creates the safest possible sleep environment.

4. Baby should not be left to sleep alone on an adult bed, even during naps. If parents do not have access to a crib or cosleeping device for naps, place a smaller mattress or futon on the floor.

5. Be mindful about sharing sleep and settle the baby safely next to Mom in a planned environment rather than falling asleep from exhaustion on the couch, a recliner, beanbag chair, or other unsafe place to share sleep.

6. Only primary caregivers should sleep with an infant. Do not allow babysitters or older siblings to sleep with baby.

If your baby sleeps in a crib:

Cribs must meet CPSC safety guidelines, including:
  □ slat spacing of less than 2 3/8"
  □ slats must not be loose or broken
  □ the headboard and footboard must not have cutout designs
  □ corner posts should be no more than 1/16" higher than other rails

When You Should Not Bedshare

Parenting and infant care should focus on both health and safety. Bedsharing with an infant is healthy and safe in most cases, but there are situations that require parents to use a bassinet or crib instead.

You should NOT share a bed with an infant if:

□ you use alcohol or drugs – Using any substances that interfere with your judgment or level of consciousness at night will interfere with your ability to be aware of your baby. These substances include over-the-counter medication such as sleep aids or cold medication.

□ you smoke – A higher risk of SIDS has been associated with parental cigarette smoking and bedsharing.

- you have a poor sleeping surface – Sharing sleep with your baby should not be done on a couch, recliner, water bed or any location where the infant could become wedged between the surface and the parent.
- your baby is premature, low birth weight, or has a high fever
- there are other children or animals in the bed – The family bed should not include older children who may not be as aware of the baby in bed.

Establishing Nighttime Routines

Regardless of which sleeping arrangement a family chooses, nighttime routines help everyone unwind from a busy day and help establish healthier sleep habits. Remember that especially for working parents, this is a "high attachment" part of the day! In the early weeks, the main routine will likely be holding, rocking, and feeding. As mentioned earlier, your baby will sleep a lot at first and will have his own routine for a while, which is sure to be very different from yours. As he becomes a little more mature, his sleep routines will become a little more predictable, but guaranteed not to stay that way. Some infants are easily overstimulated by the environment, whether that environment includes television noise, playful siblings, car travel, or the general busyness of the day.

Sometimes babies will get fussy, cry, and seem to "fight" sleep because they are overstimulated. What they may need is calming down by slowing down the home environment. A pleasant bedtime routine may include playing soft music, giving the child a warm bath or a massage, rocking, reading, or singing to the child, and reducing stimulation in the period before sleep. You'll soon learn what quiet activities your baby enjoys, and it will serve to deepen your connection. Ignore any well-intentioned advice that by doing this you will "spoil" the baby. These kinds of routines, while seemingly tedious at times, can create lasting loving memories.

The Magic of Lullabies

For many generations mothers and fathers around the world have enjoyed rocking and singing to their babies. Today's parents are relearning the lullabies long forgotten from their own mothers, or learning new ones as they listen to lullabies on CDs. Researchers have found that mothers who sing to their babies every day have babies who are more advanced in their language and early communication skills, and they found an unexpected benefit to the mother. A recent study found "a number of parents who said [that] when they'd had post-natal depression, or feelings like that after the birth of their child, [singing] not only relaxed the child but relaxed them as well."[12]

No matter what the stresses of the day have been, one of the most relaxing things you can do is rock and sing to your baby. There are obvious benefits to the baby, as he has been hearing his mother's voice in the womb for many months, and her voice has an immediate calming effect. The rocking motion is also important for the baby's vestibular system in the brain which is responsible for balance, spatial perception, movement and motor coordination. Several lullaby CDs are listed at the end of this chapter.

Developing Healthy Sleep Habits for the Older Child

Parents can experiment to find the routine that works best for their child, and remember that any bedtime routine will likely take from thirty minutes to an hour or more. Some parents find it helpful to begin quieting down the environment up to two hours before bedtime. Recommendations for older children include eliminating from their diet food or drinks with caffeine or a lot of sugar (for some children, food dyes can create hyperactivity), turning off the TV, dimming the lights, or reducing noisy activities before bedtime. If you are breastfeeding a toddler, continue to watch your diet, avoiding caffeine in drinks or chocolate and spicy or gassy foods—even foods with citric acid can be

---

12   McDonald, "Lullabies help children's language development: Study." ABCNews.com
     Web site.

a culprit. Also avoid sweeteners such as aspartame if you suspect they could be bothering your baby.

As bedtime approaches, many children calm down easily with a predictable nighttime routine; others experience a high-energy spurt just before bedtime and may need high-energy play before they can relax. Some children are relaxed by a bath, while others are excited by it. Do what works to help each individual child prepare for sleep, and remember the importance of a regular bedtime that is early enough to allow sufficient sleep—eight to ten hours—if the child must wake early for school or other activities.

A Father's Story

It may be a "different" arrangement, but I can't imagine it being any other way. I am awake and leaving the house before anyone else begins to stir. Some mornings it takes every ounce of self-restraint to keep from climbing back into bed and snuggling up to my loved ones in our big family bed. There is something surreal about sharing space, time, warmth, and listening to each other breathe in synchronicity for a moment, splinter into our own rhythms, and then find each other again.

We were already sharing a family bed when we heard about "cosleeping." Neither my wife nor I came from cosleeping families, but when our first son was born, it simply felt right to continue to have him right next to us. He had shared our bed while in utero; why should it change after he was born? Sure, we had well-meaning friends and relatives express concern when they heard about our sleeping arrangement. We read other peoples thoughts about it, both those for and against it. Even after learning more about cosleeping, continuing to have our son in our bed simply worked for us.

Our oldest son knows that there is an option to sleep in his own bed in our room or in a separate room, but the choice and the change will be one that is based on his needs. When I wake up in the morning to see my little family cuddled together, nestled in against the coldest mornings, it's just what I need to go on.

Dax L.

Keep in mind that sleep routines change as the child grows and matures. Try not to get stressed out; keep a sense of humor and remain flexible.

Bedtimes may shift earlier or later as nap schedules and sleep needs change, and the total amount of sleep that a child needs decreases as he gets older. When a child transitions out of a nap or starts school, sleep cycles can become erratic for awhile. Illness and growth spurts can also contribute to changing sleep pat-terns. Through all of these changes, parents can help the child learn to trust his body and recognize the signs of tiredness without forc-ing him to go to sleep when he is not tired or keep him awake when he needs sleep, just for the sake of a routine. Parents can be proactive in teaching their child ways to calm down to prepare his mind and body for sleep.

Transitioning out of the Family Bed

When the time comes for a child to transition to his own bed, parents need to make sure that the transition is gentle and respectful of any feelings of fear or upset experienced by the child. This is especially true when a child is transitioning due to the birth of a sibling, as the child may already have some anxiety related to the birth. Young children who have their own bed often go to sleep more willingly when parents lie down with them in their bed until they are very drowsy or until they go to sleep—usually after reading a few stories. Children outgrow this need when they are developmentally ready and will happily go to sleep on their own, although older children may still enjoy a brief snuggle time with parents before bed.

Communicating with Your Partner

Since no set rules govern nighttime parenting, considering the needs of each family member will help make the best choice for the family. Some parents do not feel comfortable with the idea of having a baby sleep in their bed, or one parent may want to cosleep and the other might not. It's not unusual for fathers to be a little more reluctant and resistant to cosleeping, but in her research, Dr. Ball found that fathers reported that they found bedsharing "more enjoyable than disruptive." She further suggests that bedsharing helps fathers feel more quickly bonded to their babies.[13]

It's important to discuss individual feelings and to resolve any concerns in a way that is respectful to each parent while still meeting the baby's nighttime needs. When considering the different possible sleeping arrangements, some parents are concerned about how cosleeping will impact intimacy with their partner. Neither parenthood nor cosleeping has to put a damper on intimacy; a little creativity and preplanning can ensure that intimacy doesn't wither on the vine. (Read chapter 9 for more about keeping intimacy and balance in your relationship.)

Parents need to discuss the idea of bedsharing as soon as possible—if not before the baby is born, then shortly afterward to prevent any

---

13   McKenna, *Sleeping with Your Baby: A Parent's Guide to Cosleeping*, 52.

misunderstandings. For the family bed to work best, both parents need to be on board with the decision. If the mother is planning on nursing, she will find that bedsharing, or having the baby within arms' reach, will help her sleep and stay rested while better facilitating the breastfeeding relationship. If Mom is breastfeeding, it usually works out well for Dad, because he doesn't have to get up to get the baby.

The main priority is that both parents be on the same page, so that the family bed doesn't create a wedge in the relationship. Frank, open communication is key in any relationship, so if problems arise, talk about them. If you don't know the answers, find information that can help you. An endless amount of information can be found on the Internet and in books. You can feel confident about any information that you find through API's Web site.

Night Waking

As they grow, many babies will go through a phase where they sleep for longer periods of time, only to begin waking at night during different developmental stages. They may wake during nightmares (some actually experience "night terrors"), teething, illness, growth spurts, or during times of family stress or transition in their lives. Babies are very sensitive to their parents' stress, or when they are simply trying to steal a few minutes of time to do something else, all of which can affect their sleep-wake patterns. It's possible that occasionally some babies may be overstimulated by sleeping with the parents. The only way to know is to try having Baby sleep on a separate surface near the adult bed. The key is tuning in to what the baby is trying to communicate and finding the sleep arrangement that works best for the family and where everyone gets the best sleep. Recent research indicates that some babies do better if their sleep arrangements are consistently in the same place, whether bedsharing or sleeping separately. Just about any parent can tell you that babies seem to have built-in radar for when Mom and Dad want time to themselves. Don't take it personally! Baby is just trying to keep his connection with Mommy.

After thirty years of caring for children and counseling parents, Dr. Sears found that most infants wake up several times during the night. He reassures parents that it is not because of anything they have done.

"Every baby is different, and sleep behavior has more to do with inborn temperament than with any 'bad habits' caused by Mom and Dad," says Dr. Sears.[14]

Gentle Ways to Get Your Baby to Sleep

Dr. Jay Gordon is a pediatrician and coauthor of *Good Nights: The Happy Parent's Guide to a Good Night's Sleep* and *Listen To Your Baby*. He knows firsthand from working with hundreds of families that sleep deprivation can become a big issue for many parents. He describes himself as one the strongest proponents of attachment parenting and the family bed, but he understands that when parents become unhappy with the arrangement, largely due to frequent nursings and night-wakings, then it is time to make some changes. However, Dr. Gordon is adamant that both parents be in agreement and feel good about the decision to gently change their child's sleep habits. He first warns parents:

> I don't recommend any forced sleep changes during
> the first year of life. Probably the only exception
> to this would be an emergency involving a nursing
> mom's health. There are many suggestions in books
> and magazines for pushing "sleeping through the
> night" during a baby's early months or during the
> first year. I don't think this is the best thing to do,
> and I am quite sure that the earlier a baby gets "non-
> response" from parents, the more likely he is to close
> down at least a little.[15]

In his books and on his Web site, Dr. Gordon provides parents with gentle, sensitive ways of teaching toddlers to sleep without nursing. He feels that parents are the best judges as to whether his techniques work, and he encourages them to follow their instincts.

Other pediatricians, such as Dr. Paul Fleiss, raise concerns about the crying-it-out method of sleep training. He warns parents:

---

14   Sears and Sears, *The Attachment Parenting Book*, 90.

15   Gordon J, "Changing the sleep pattern in the family bed," Dr. Jay Gordon's Web site.

Don't ignore your children's cries. After all, they may be
sick, in danger, or in pain. Babies and young children
are emotional rather than rational creatures. They
can't comprehend why their cries for help are being
ignored. Even with the best of intentions, ignoring
children leads them to feel abandoned. The result will
be insecure, unhappy children. You cannot "spoil"
children by responding to their cries. "Spoiled" children
are those who don't know what to expect from their
parents. They are often alternately punished or praised
for the same activity at different times.[16]

The Problem with Sleep Training

Parents who are frustrated by frequent night-waking or who are
sleep deprived may be tempted to try sleep training techniques that
recommend letting a baby "cry it out." It was once believed to be
healthy to teach a baby to "self-soothe." New research suggests that
these techniques can have detrimental physiological effects on the baby
by increasing the stress hormone cortisol in the brain.[17] The increase
in cortisol can have long-term effects on emotional regulation, sleep
patterns, and behavior. In *The Science of Parenting*, Margot Sunderland
describes the physiological processes that occur when a baby is allowed
to cry himself to sleep:

His stress levels will have gone up, not down. Studies
show that after being left to cry, babies move into a
primitive defense mode. This results in an irregularity
in breathing and heart rate, both of which can
fluctuate wildly, and high levels of cortisol.[18]

An infant is not neurologically or developmentally capable of
calming or soothing himself to sleep in ways that are healthy. The part
of the brain that allows him to begin the process of learning to regulate

---

16   Fleiss, "Pillow talk: Helping your child get a good night's sleep," *Mothering* magazine.

17   Sunderland, *The Science of Parenting*, 79.

18   Ibid., 80.

his own emotions, or self-soothe, isn't well developed until he is two and a half to three years of age. Babies and young children depend on their parents to help them calm down and learn to regulate their intense feelings—they are the child's "emotional regulators."

Parents can of course choose to ignore it [a baby's crying], but perhaps that child will ignore them when they turn 14, 15, or 16, too.[19]

> Dr. James McKenna
> *Attachment Parenting: The Journal of API*

Sleep training involves placing the baby alone in a crib before he is fully asleep. When the baby cries, parents are taught to comfort the child verbally or with pats on his back only after waiting increasing periods of time to respond and then leaving the room. The child finally falls asleep from exhaustion. After a few nights of this, some children will learn to fall asleep quickly and without crying.

While sleep training has become extremely popular in Western cultures, it is not without controversy because no evidence has shown that it is really beneficial in the long term, and, in fact, it may be detrimental to emotional and psychological development. Why is it so popular? In an effort to help parents get more sleep, this kind of advice is dispensed in popular parenting books, by pediatricians and sleep researchers who most often have little knowledge of children's normal emotional, cognitive, or neurological development. Such advice is often based on the premise that infants are neurologically ready to be "taught" when to go to sleep at night and that they should be able to sleep throughout the night, uninterrupted.

---

19 Parker, "The greatest gifts we can give our children: An interview with Dr. Jim McKenna," *Attachment Parenting: The Journal of API*.

Leaving infants to cry it out in order to learn to sleep on their own, Dr. McKenna has observed, deprives babies of oxygen and creates a situation where the baby must redirect his energies away from growing and fighting disease. He states that "the baby is burning energy and calories needlessly that could have been put into other more beneficial processes."

McKenna offers powerful advice to parents regarding sleep training:

> I think sometimes parents are under the mistaken
> impression that if they don't sleep train their babies,
> somehow some developmental or social skill or
> competency later in life will be kept from them or
> that their babies will never exhibit good sleep patterns
> later in life.
>
> If they think this, then they really ought to know
> that there has never been a scientific study anywhere
> that has shown any benefit for babies whatsoever in
> sleeping through the night at young ages, or even
> sleeping through the night at any particular time.
> What is important is the nature of social relationships
> and support within which babies develop all kinds of
> skills pertaining to independence.
>
> One of the most important things I am hoping to do
> is remind parents that no one can tell them what they
> should do with their babies. They have to learn to
> trust their own judgment, look at the research that is
> now available on these issues of sleep behavior, and see
> that there are major critiques about this solitary sleep-
> training model.[20]

It's very likely that your baby's pediatrician will discourage you from bedsharing, but he or she should be supportive of the baby sleeping in close proximity in accordance with the AAP guidelines, which state, "A separate but proximate sleeping environment is recommended: The risk of SIDS has been shown to be reduced when the infant sleeps in the same

---

20   Ibid.

room as the mother."[21] You are *not* obligated to share information about your child's sleeping arrangements with your pediatrician, but you are obligated to be informed and to provide a safe sleeping environment wherever your child sleeps. For that reason API has launched the Safe Sleep Campaign to help educate parents and professionals about how to create a safe environment. A brochure titled Safe Infant Sleep Guidelines is available for free at www.attachmentparenting.org/safeinfantsleep/campaign.php. This brochure can be downloaded and used by any parent, professional and agency. Be discriminate of any advice that goes against your instincts, and listen to your baby! As the parent, you have the right to make informed decisions for your child; when it comes to sleeping, keep it safe!

---

21 American Academy of Pediatrics Task Force on Sudden Infant Death Syndrome, "The changing concept of sudden infant death syndrome: diagnostic coding shifts, controversies regarding the sleeping environment, and new variables to consider in reducing risk," *Pediatrics.*

Appendix to Chapter Six: Additional Research and Resource Recommendations

Additional Research

Mothers tend to be more responsive when cosleeping, which may be a protective behavior.[22,23]

Mother-infant breastfeeding pairs showed that babies were largely responsible for positioning themselves during the night and spent most of their sleep on their sides or back, just inches away from the mother's face. Mothers reported that they got better quality of sleep when their babies slept nearby.[24]

Breastfeeding episodes triple during the night [compared to nights when not cosleeping], which increases milk supply and in turn affects hormone levels and can prevent ovulation, thus helping to prevent another pregnancy.[25]

Cosleeping infants spend less time awake and cry less frequently.[26]

Risk factors found to be related to infant deaths in an adult bed are a smoking parent, prone sleeping position, parents affected by alcohol or

---

22 Mosko et al., "Parent-infant cosleeping: The appropriate context for the study of infant sleep and implications for sudden infant death syndrome (SIDS) research," *Journal of Behavioral Medicine*.

23 Mosko et al., "Infant arousals during mother-infant bed sharing: Implications for infant sleep and sudden infant death syndrome research," *Pediatrics*.

24 McKenna et al., "Infant-parent cosleeping in an evolutionary perspective: Implications for understanding infant sleep development and the sudden infant death syndrome," *American Sleep Disorders Association and Sleep Research Society*.

25 McKenna, "Babies need their mothers beside them!" *World Health*.

26 Ibid.

drugs, use of heavy comforters or blankets that can cause overheating, and inappropriate sleep locations such as a couch or waterbed.[27]

Bedsharing is associated with family nurturance, less use of transitional objects, flexibility in family structure, and parental reports of higher adaptive functioning on the part of the children.[28]

Bedsharing was found not to be related to behavior problems in children.[29]

In military families, bedsharing was associated with parental reports of better adaptive functioning and less psychiatric treatment.[30]

Recommended Reading

Good Nights: The Happy Parents' Guide to the Family Bed (and a Peaceful Night's Sleep!) by Jay Gordon, MD, and Maria Goodavage.

Mothering Multiples: Breastfeeding and Caring for Twins or More! by Karen Kerkhoff Gromada.

Nighttime Parenting: How to Get Your Baby and Child to Sleep by William Sears, MD.

Sleeping with Your Baby: A Parent's Guide to Lullabies for Sleepy Eyes by Susie Tallman.

Lullabies for Sleepy Eyes by Susie Tallman.

Guide to a Good Night's Rest for the Whole Family by William Sears, MD, Martha Sears, RN, Robert Sears, MD, and James Sears, MD.

The Family Bed by Tine Thevenin.

---

27 McKenna et al., "Infant-parent cosleeping in an evolutionary perspective: Implications for understanding infant sleep development and the sudden infant death syndrome," *American Sleep Disorders Association and Sleep Research Society.*

28 Witman-Flann, "Parent-child cosleeping: The impact on family relationships," *Dissertation Abstracts International.*

29 Mandansky and Edelbrock, "Cosleeping in a community sample of 2- and 3-year-old children," *Pediatrics.*

30 Forbes et al., "The cosleeping habits of military children," *Military Medicine.*

The No-Cry Sleep Solution by Elizabeth Pantley.
The Science of Parenting by Margot Sunderland.
Three in a Bed: The Benefits of Sharing Your Bed with Your Baby by
Deborah Jackson.

Recommended DVDs

The Benefits of Bedsharing (2005)
Platypus Media, www.platypusmedia.com
Written by: Dr. Helen Ball, Sally Inch, and Marion Copeland

Recommended CDs

Good Night, Sleep Tight by Marylee and Nancy.
Lullabies for Sleepy Eyes by Susie Tallman.
More from Pooh Corner by Kenny Loggins.
Quiet Time by Raffi.
Return to Pooh Corner by Kenny Loggins.
The Happiest Baby on the Block New "Super Soothing" Calming Sounds
by Harvey Karp, MD.
Traditional Lullabies by Growing Minds With Music.
Welcome Home My Child: Songs for a Mother's Journey by Lu
Hanessian.

Useful Web Sites

www.attachmentparenting.org: Web site of Attachment Parenting
International.

www.attachmentparenting.org/safesleep/campaign.php

**www.attachmentparenting.org/pdfs/API_Safe_Infant_Sleep_
brochure.pdf**

www.askdrsears.com: Web site of the Sears family.

www.babyfriendly.org.uk/pdfs/sharingbedleaflet.pdf: UNICEF U.K. Baby Friendly Initiative leaflet on bedsharing.

www.bfmed.org: Web site of the Academy of Breastfeeding Medicine.

www.dur.ac.uk/sleep.lab: Durham University Parent-Infant Sleep Laboratory (U.K.); director Dr. Helen Ball.

www.ilca.org: Web site of the International Lactation Consultant Association, including information on cosleeping and breastfeeding.

www.llli.org: Web site of La Leche League International.

www.nd.edu/~jmckenn1/lab: Web site of the Mother-Baby Behavioral Sleep Laboratory at the University of Notre Dame; director: Dr. James McKenna.

www.usbreastfeeding.org: Web site of the United States Breastfeeding Committee.

Chapter Seven

Principle 6
Provide Consistent, Loving Care:
Keeping Your Attachment with Baby Secure

Provide Consistent, Loving Care: Keeping Your Attachment with Baby Secure

> *The notion that relationships are essential for regulating*
> *our behavior and moods and feelings as well as for*
> *intellectual development is one that needs greater emphasis*
> *as we think about the kinds of settings and priorities we*
> *want for our children. The interactions that are necessary*
> *can take place in full measure only with a loving caregiver*
> *who has lots of time to devote to a child.*[1]
> T. Berry Brazelton, MD, and Stanley I. Greenspan, MD
> *The Irreducible Needs of Children*

Perhaps the most critical decision parents face in their parenting journey is who will be the primary caregiver of their cherished and vulnerable new baby. For most parents over the centuries, this has been the role of the biological mother, but in the last fifty years, we have seen a huge cultural shift in the United States, with a larger percentage of mothers reentering the workforce with very young children. In 2006, 62 percent of mothers with children under the age of six were employed outside the home (in comparison to 11.9 percent in 1950).[2]

This chapter is about giving parents information about their baby's need for consistent, loving care, why this is so important to a baby's development, and resources and creative solutions to help make this happen. We begin with the premise that all parents love their children and want what is best for their physical, emotional, and spiritual development, and, when given the facts, parents can then make better decisions and come up with wonderfully resourceful ideas for their child's care. An important note to this chapter: When studies refer to "nonmaternal care," they are referring to care other than the baby's primary attachment figure, which is not necessarily always the mother. A growing number of fathers are taking on the role of the primary caregiver for their young children. When we speak of the primary caregiver, it can

---

1   Brazelton and Greenspan, *The Irreducible Needs of Children*, 5–8.

2   U.S. Department of Labor, Bureau of Labor Statistics, Women in the Labor Force: A Databook, 16.

refer to the mother, the father, or any person who is the primary person caring for the baby or child during their waking hours and to whom the baby has the most secure attachment. This could also be a grandparent, adult sibling, other extended family members, or a nanny.

Dr. Stanley Greenspan, Clinical Professor of Psychiatry and Pediatrics at George Washington University Medical School, and T. Berry Brazelton, Clinical Professor of Pediatrics Emeritus at Harvard Medical School, have written movingly about the critical necessity for a stable loving caregiver in the early years of a child's life. In their book *The Irreducible Needs of Children*, they advocate for parents to understand their essential roles in protecting the precious attachment process, which is the foundation of their child's future psychological, intellectual, and moral well-being.

Dr. Greenspan, one of the world's foremost authorities on infants and young children with developmental and emotional problems, conveys some of his ideas for childcare in his book, *The Four-Thirds Solution*. First, he gives parents insight about the critical emotional needs in a child's first three years: "Our society doesn't tell parents that the most important gift they can give their children is not a good education, elaborate educational toys, or summer camps, but time—*regular, substantial chunks of it*—spent together doing things that are emotionally and developmentally meaningful for the child."[3] The book describes how different families have adjusted their work schedules to make it possible for each parent to spend at least two-thirds of the day with the baby, not necessarily at the same time, giving a "four-thirds" solution for the child's care. This is one of many ideas for parents to consider if one parent cannot be the primary caregiver in the early years.

Attachment theory has been described in chapter 1 of this book, and reviewing this introductory chapter lays an excellent foundation for understanding the attachment needs of a baby and young child. Exciting research in the field of neurobiology (the mechanisms by which human relationships shape brain structure and function) is confirming what attachment theorists have been seeing for over fifty years: a baby's brain and even his DNA is shaped by relationships. This was a stunning discovery only made possible with the modern technology of brain imaging and the mapping of the genetic code.

---

3   Greenspan, *The Four-Thirds Solution: Solving the Child-Care Crisis in America Today*, 89–90.

How Stress Affects a Baby's Brain

Cortisol is a stress hormone that is released by the adrenal glands when we are in a state of fear. Babies who are left to cry for long periods or who are afraid in a strange situation release massive amounts of cortisol, potentially creating a dangerous level in the brain. If released at toxic levels, it can damage key structures in the brain. Elevated cortisol levels are seen in the brains of depressed people and those with post-traumatic stress disorder:

> [R]esearchers at the National Institutes of Health
> have found a link between depression and traumas
> experienced in early childhood. Studies have shown
> that abused, neglected, or otherwise unnurtured infants
> and children are more likely to be depressed as adults,
> and now we have a way to understand the link between
> experience and the biology. It all relates to something
> called the hypothalamic-pituitary-adrenal axis.[4]

In other words, a baby who is stressed produces hormones that make the synapses and neurons more vulnerable to an injury. The longer they remain elevated, the more likely it is that the functioning of many emotional and biological systems is affected. Even in very young babies, the amount of stress has a profound effect on what is called the baby's "intrinsic memory." We cannot consciously recall events stored in our intrinsic memory; these memories are deeply encoded, creating generalizations from experience. The processing of these memories and emotional reactions takes place in the amygdala, which is an almond-shaped group of neurons located deep within the medial temporal lobes of the brain. This exciting research is where attachment theory and biology intersect. Dr. Daniel Siegel describes it this way:

> An infant who has a healthy, secure attachment has
> had the repeated experience of nurturing, perceptive,
> sensitive, and predictable caregiving responses, ...
> which have been encoded implicitly in her brain. She

---

4   Pert, *Molecules of Emotion*, 269.

has developed a generalized representation of that
relationship—a mental model of attachment—which
helps her know what to expect…. Given that these
repeated experiences have been predictable, and that
when there have been disruptions in mother-infant
communication, the mother has been relatively quick
and effective at repairing the ruptures, this fortunate
infant has been able to develop a secure, organized
model of their emotional relationship.[5]

Now more than ever before, we understand the vital role the
parent-child relationship plays in shaping the template of the baby's
emotional, intellectual, and biological life. It is critical that parents do
everything they can to ensure that the primary caregiver in their baby's
life be nurturing, predictable, and responsive.

Studies on Childcare

Studies done on the long-term effects of nonmaternal care of
infants and young children have been controversial and confusing, with
mixed conclusions. However, emerging data clearly sound warnings to
parents. Some concerning research indicates that babies under the age
of one year who spend more than thirty hours in daycare (some studies
say twenty hours) may develop behavioral problems as they get older,
such as excessively aggressive behavior. Boys seem to be particularly
vulnerable to long hours in daycare.[6]

Center care, in and of itself, adversely increased the
likelihood of infants developing insecure attachment
to their mothers, compared with infants who were
in maternal care, individual non-parental care with
a relative, individual non-parental care with a paid
caregiver, or family daycare. The results suggest

---

5   Siegel, *The Developing Mind*, 32.
6   Belsky and Rovine, "Non-maternal care in the first year of life and the security of
infant attachment," *Child Development*.

that it is the poor quality of center care and the high infant-caregiver ratio that accounted for this increased level of attachment insecurity among center-care infants.[7]

Another key factor that emerges from this research is the importance of continuity of care in the early months and years of a child's life. Until the child is old enough to verbalize his needs to his caregiver, it is critical for the caregiver to be in attunement with the baby so that his needs are met consistently and sensitively. Try to imagine what it must be like for a baby who is crying to be fed or picked up when the caregiver is overwhelmed with several babies needing the same thing. A mother of triplets, or especially quadruplets, is given tremendous sympathy and often offered help in caring for her babies, yet in the best daycare situation, a four-to-one ratio is considered a manageable standard. Adding to this the low salaries daycare providers typically earn, is it any wonder that daycare employees have one of the highest turnover rates of any occupation? Dr. Isabelle Fox, in her book, *Being There: The Benefits of a Stay-at-Home Parent*, coined the phrase "caregiver roulette" to describe the high turnover rate of care providers in American daycare facilities. When a baby adjusts to the smells and voice of one care provider and then a new person comes in, he has no frame of reference and no comprehension of this new person, the new smells, or the new voices. When an infant experiences the frequent loss of caregivers, especially in the preverbal years, it can be emotionally devastating and as a result he may become insecurely attached or learn not to attach to anyone.

The stress of caring for several babies all day long takes a tremendous toll, especially when the caregiver is not emotionally invested in the babies. Dr. Greenspan has found that even the most dedicated childcare providers often "hold back" emotionally because separating from their tiny charges would be otherwise "too emotionally wrenching."[8] He

---

7   Sagi et al., "Shedding further light on the effects of various types and quality of early childcare on infant-mother attachment relationship: The Haifa study of early child care," *Child Development*.

8   Greenspan, *The Four-Thirds Solution: Solving the Child-Care Crisis in America Today*, 43.

warns that even in the best centers, the ratio for infants to caregiver is four to one, and the toddler ratios can rise as high as ten to one.[9]

> We are expecting [the daycare system] to operate the way very well-functioning families do.... As a result, children aren't getting the consistent one-on-one nurturing with the same caregiver ... that almost all of us who study and work with children agree they need. Furthermore, many highly motivated caregivers don't receive the training, support, and pay they need to work with children on a sustained basis.[10]

Academic Warns Childcare Can Lead to Aggression

Professor Jay Belsky, director of the Institute for the Study of Children, Families, and Social Issues at Birkbeck University, revealed that U.S. research showed children who spent long periods of time in daycare were more likely to have poor behavior. Researchers found that 17 percent of the children who were in care for more than thirty hours a week were regarded by teachers, mothers, and caregivers as being aggressive toward other children. That compared with 6 percent for the group of children in childcare for less than ten hours a week.[11]

Working and Alternate Caregivers

Mothers who plan to return to work shortly after the birth of their baby sometimes tell their doctors or friends that they are afraid to get "too attached" to their babies. They are worried that this will make separation too painful when they must return to work. However, it is detrimental for parents to distance themselves emotionally from their babies, because it can permanently impact their growing relationships

---

9   Ibid., 5–6.
10   Ibid., 5–6.
11   Associated Press, "Study: Child aggression linked to hours in daycare," CNN Web site.

with their children. Instead, parents should treasure those early weeks of bonding with Baby and get to know his personality, feeding patterns, and what makes him unique. This will help a mother make better decisions about her baby's care and create better communication with the caregiver. Pediatrician and author T. Barry Brazelton made this observation over twenty years ago at a public talk in Denver, Colorado:

> I've had young [pregnant] women sitting in my office and they ... don't want to get into the subject (of their babies) in depth anymore. I began to realize that what they were saying to me, when they were not willing to share the deeper emotional feelings about the turmoil of pregnancy or not wanting to talk about nursing, was that they had to return to work too soon. They were already guarding themselves, in pregnancy, from too deep an attachment. Now, that scares the hell out of me.... These young women are grieving for what they might have had at a time when they ought to be investing themselves so emotionally and passionately that, of course, it is going to hurt to leave.... If you can guard yourself like that, then what kind of a nurturing person are you going to be?[12]

Dr. Brazelton is one of many professionals who continually challenge parents to take very seriously their children's needs for consistent care. Parents in the United States must face the reality of the challenges of the childcare situation and, if both parents must work (or in the case of a single parent), creative strategies can be used. Find out if employers offer a leave of absence; a parent may be able to return to work after

---

12 Magid and McKelvey, *High Risk: Children without a Conscience,* 17.

a year or two without sacrificing their career path. Parents can explore a variety of economic and work-arrangement options that permit their children to be cared for by one or both parents at all times. For example, a family can consider ideas for cutting expenses, or they may be able to use financial assets they already have so that one parent can be home. Today's workplace is increasingly flexible and family-friendly, providing employees with the opportunity to explore different work situations that best fit their families' needs. Some places of employment are getting creative and helping new parents with on-site daycare, or even allowing the baby to stay with Mom or Dad at their workstation. Recently, an article in *USA Today* reported that an advertising firm in Austin, Texas, allows its employees to bring their babies to work until old enough to crawl. The article went on to say that the Parenting in the Workplace Institute in Framingham, Massachusetts, reports that the number of companies allowing children at work on an occasional basis climbed to 29 percent last year, up from 22 percent in 2006, according to the Society for Human Resource Management. Some of these progressive companies include Marriott International, Microsoft, and JCPenney.[13]

The Parenting in the Workplace Institute (parentingatwork.org) promotes baby-friendly workplace programs, and they have identified more than eighty organizations (and they say this number is probably very low) in which employees can bring their babies to work every day. They have found that babies at work tend to be overwhelmingly content, primarily because their needs are met quickly and they are held much of the time by parents and coworkers. Mothers who take their babies to work are more likely to continue breastfeeding, and nursing on cue also keeps the babies happy and healthy. The Institute is devoted to expanding the adoption of these baby programs as well as explaining and promoting the attachment care principles that lead to success for businesses and for babies.

Some parents are now telecommuting, or working from home; this can allow both parents to interact with baby during the day. Some employers allow parents to bring the baby to the workplace for breastfeeding or checking in. Working part-time, working as a consultant, working on limited projects, or participating in a job share can all allow parents more access to their infant during the critical first year of life and beyond.

---

13   Armour, "Day care's new frontier: Your baby at your desk," *USA Today* Web site.

Parents who attend API support groups often share their solutions for how they found ways for one parent to be the primary caregiver. Here is one family's story:

> When I had my first baby, my husband was a struggling musician playing five nights a week at a nightclub, and I was teaching school. We decided to try to make it on one salary, but soon realized that we could not pay our bills and were faced with me going back to teaching and putting the baby in daycare. When we started looking at the costs, it almost didn't seem worth going back, so we got creative. We got a loan from the Teacher's Union to help us when money got short each month. I learned how to get very frugal with money, like clipping coupons and going to yard sales. In fact, my friends and I made a game of bargain hunting, and we helped each other when we saw a good sale or found a new recipe. We got by with one car, and I learned I was able to qualify for supplemental food through the WIC program in our community. When I look back on those years, I have no regrets about the sacrifices we made as a family—it was so worth it to be with my baby and not have the worry

of whether he was crying and needing to be picked up, or was taking his first step and one of us was not there for him. I went back to teaching school when he was a toddler and my husband and his mother were able to share childcare duties with him during the day, so it was amazing what a little creativity and determination did to help us find a plan that worked for us.

Making the Transition to Work

Parents whose work situation does not lend itself to this type of flexibility have even more reason to practice attachment parenting. Being sensitive and responsive to the child's needs and feelings, holding, and cuddling can help parents and babies reconnect after being apart. For instance, parents that share sleep with their baby can have the extra touch time that they missed out on during the day. Infant massage is another way to reconnect in the evenings, and breastfeeding mothers find that pumping their milk while separated keeps up their supply so they can continue the nursing relationship when they are together in the evenings and on weekends.

It is also important to realize that the caregiver will be an incredibly important attachment figure in the child's life, and the parents may experience some jealousy. Keeping the lines of communication open is critical, and finding ways to keep the connection strong with your child while sharing this attachment with another caregiver is important to the health of your child and the success of this arrangement.

Here are some helpful tips when a parent is returning to work:

- It is extremely important to have continuity of care with a consistent, loving caregiver. The parent needs to make sure the caregiver is someone who makes the baby's needs the top priority. Ideally, the caregiver will be someone who already understands the importance of attachment-promoting practices. When possible, choosing a family member, close friend, or someone with whom parents have an ongoing relationship will reduce the incidence of caregiver turnover. In the case of a paid nanny, offer incentives up front to keep her for at least the first three years if possible—perhaps a raise each year or other perks. Ideally the care will take place in the baby's home environment.

- Parents should expect and encourage their child to form an attachment to the caregiver. They may consider introducing the caregiver to the eight principles of parenting and explaining to the caregiver how they want the baby to be responded to and cared for. Parents may want to consider providing the caregiver with a sling to carry the baby.

- Ideally, the parent will give the child time to get to know a new caregiver in the parent's presence. Parents should begin the transition well in advance of any separation so that it is a gradual process and is comfortable for the child.

- Avoid "caregiver roulette." Frequent turnover of caregivers can be very damaging to the attachment process, so if you are looking at daycare arrangements, try to find a program where the caregivers are stable and move up with the babies as they progress to the next age group.

- Minimize the number of hours in nonparental care as much as possible to provide the best opportunity for a child to build secure attachments with parents.

- Parents can find ways to reconnect with their children when separated because of employment. Try to spend some quiet time with your child at the end of the day rather than rushing to fix dinner or shopping. Planning ahead, perhaps cooking meals and freezing them, may give you more "down time" with your child at the end of the day. Parents can include a child in day-to-day tasks, and babies enjoy being in a sling and watching Mom or Dad do tasks around the house.

The books listed at the end of this chapter go into much detail about the pros and cons of substitute care, how to find and interview a potential caregiver, and how parents can find creative solutions to staying home, working part-time, or splitting care with parents and caregivers.

Overcoming the Politics of the Daycare Discussion

> Some parents may see any criticism about childcare as an attack on their particular decisions... The assumption is that critics of daycare are really advocating a return to an era when women stayed at home and cared for children instead of pursuing careers.
>
> These agendas... are preventing us from having a coherent discussion about the actual quality of daycare today.... If we clear away the smoke... this is what we see: Much of the childcare available for infants and toddlers in this country simply isn't good for them.[14]
>
> Stanley Greenspan
> *The Four-Thirds Solution: Solving the Child-Care Crisis in America Today*

---

14   Greenspan, *The Four-Thirds Solution: Solving the Child-Care Crisis in America Today*, 25–26.

Separations due to Shared Custody

Some families find themselves in a difficult situation because of work schedules, divorce, or shared custody. In their book, *The Unexpected Legacy of Divorce: A 25 Year Landmark Study*, Judith Wallerstein, Julia Lewis, and Sandra Blakeslee give guidance to parents, attorneys, and judges in considering the attachment needs of babies and very young children:

> When a baby doesn't see her primary caregiver for several days, the child suffers a lot because she is likely to assume that the caregiver has disappeared and that she's been abandoned. But our knowledge about how much absence the infant can tolerate without severe suffering is still insufficient to build regular disappearances of a parent into the child's schedule. Putting the child's best interests forward and honoring what is best for the child is extremely hard to do.... It requires parents to stand apart from their raw, hurt, jealous, competitive feelings and take an objective, compassionate look at what life will be like for their child.... surely the job of the court is to give priority to the helpless child over the demands of the parent.[15]

The United States court system obviously has an enormous need to receive education on the attachment needs of children whose parents are going through a separation or divorce. Of particular importance are custody decisions that are based on the developmental needs of the child. Usually a schedule based on a baby's gradual abilities to tolerate longer separations from his primary caregiver is the ideal. Information on providing consistent and loving care during these difficult situations is available through resources listed on the API Web site, www.attachmentparenting.org.

---

15   Wallerstein et al., *The Unexpected Legacy of Divorce: A 25 Year Landmark Study*, 216–217.

The Three Important P's

Infants best survive and have the capacity to develop into secure and loving individuals when they experience three important behaviors from their parents or primary caregivers. In most cases, nature has ingeniously programmed mothers and fathers to provide these three critical responses to rear healthy children.

The first is to provide *protection* from danger, predators, abuse, or neglect. Almost all species protect their newborn and attempt to keep them from harm's way.

The second is to provide *proximity* to facilitate protection as well as timely responses to hunger, stimulation, and bodily care. Cosleeping, babywearing, and physically "being there" are behaviors that keep the infants close, and, as a result, their needs are more likely to be met promptly.

The third is *predictability* of responsive nurturing: to provide the infant with a familiar set of arms, smell, voice, and patterns of response. Unfortunately, in contemporary society, when parents are absent a good part of the baby's waking hours, the frequent changing of substitute caregivers places the infant under unusual stress. The predictability of his or her world is shaken. Infants or toddlers without language or intellectual ability can't understand why, suddenly, a stranger is feeding, holding, bathing, talking, and comforting them. Trust that their world is predictable and safe is undermined. For millions of infants and toddlers in daycare, "Caregiver Roulette" has become the norm. (The infant never knows into whose arms he or she will land.) Such caregiver roulette occurs when caregivers change frequently, often every few months, and continuity of care is broken and trust is undermined. This can produce long-range negative consequences.

Studies have shown that providing proximity, protection, and predictability of care in the earliest years is the best investment parents can make to create secure, successful, and loving adults.

Isabelle Fox, PhD
Author of *Being There: The Benefits of a Stay-at-Home Parent*

Short-term Childcare Choices

The first few weeks and months of parenting, your newborn will quickly teach you what flexibility and "going with the flow" truly mean. Instead of trying to fit a new baby into the existing pre-baby schedule, parents can come up with creative ways to design new routines that include the baby. This may mean taking a sleeping newborn out on date night, getting exercise by taking walks with baby in a sling, or working with employers to customize a schedule that maximizes parents' time with their children. Parents can take a trusted caregiver with them if they go out for a long evening or special event; many babies are happy to stroll around a restaurant or other interesting environment with a caregiver, allowing parents some time to be alone. This technique also works well for family vacations or business trips.

Being together as a family in the first months of a baby's life allows parents to solidify parenting views and ensure that the baby is receiving consistent care. A baby thrives when he knows what to expect and when his needs are met in a responsive and loving manner by caregivers (again the reminder that babies love predictability). In the early months, a baby's natural attachment-promoting behaviors along with a parent's instinctual drive for caregiving work together to develop a strong bond. Families can support the breastfeeding relationship of mother and baby by helping them to stay close during infancy, thus making breastfeeding success more likely.

Practical Tips for Short Separations

Although having one or both parents providing consistent, loving care at all times is certainly the ideal, it is not always possible. If parents need to be separated from an infant or young child for a short time, the following tips may help minimize stress and fear:

- Leave the child with a trusted care provider to whom the child is attached and who is familiar with, supportive of, and willing to use attachment parenting principles. A good option is family members or friends with whom your child has developed a trusting relationship.

- Respect the child's feelings and follow his lead about his readiness to separate. Being empathic, understanding, and patient allows the child to adjust to separations according to his own timetable.

- Talk to older children about the separation. Parents should let the child know they are leaving, call to check in, and let them know when they can expect to see their parents again.

- Accept that even older children have occasional difficulties with separation from one or both parents. Toddlers and older children naturally like to be with their parents, and some level of separation anxiety is perfectly normal and age appropriate. Parents know their child better than anyone and can judge when his anxiety is unusually problematic. If this is the case, it is necessary to evaluate other factors in the child's life that need special attention.

- Use creativity to help avoid unnecessary anxiety-producing experiences. For example, some parents have found that it is easier for a young child to separate if the child is picked up for an outing with a caregiver rather than the parent(s) leaving the child at the caregiver's home.

When the child becomes verbal, she will be better able to handle separation, especially if she has a solidly attached relationship with her parents as a foundation. She will be better able to communicate her feelings, signaling her parents that she is ready for short separations, and also allowing parents to check in with her during those separations.

A Mother's Story: An Unexpected Evening Out with Our Five Year Old

You never know when a precious family memory will start out as a seeming disaster! Many years ago, my husband and I had been planning a special evening out with his boss. I bought a new dress and carefully arranged childcare with a trusted family friend. The plan was that I would drop our boys off (ages seven, five, and two), come home, and have a leisurely bath, so we'd have plenty of time to get ready. For some reason, our five-year-old son did not want to be left that night—he worried about it all day, but I kept reassuring him that he'd have so much fun, we'd only be gone a few hours, and that Mommy and Daddy would spend some special time with him the next day. I finally got them all in the car, but as I was pulling away from the curb, I looked back to see that he was still very distressed and begged me to let him stay home. Impulsively, he ran back into the house and I followed, asking my husband to talk to him, as I had no choice but to take the other boys to the sitter. I dreaded the scene when I returned home, thinking that they would both be upset and my husband would be stressed about what to do. We were going to a very exclusive restaurant that did not cater to children, so I wondered if we'd have to cancel.

I will never forget the joy on my son's face when I came back in the house. My husband had dressed him in his Sunday best suit, and they were both looking so handsome. They had talked through the problem and decided that if it was this traumatic to be left, and if he was willing to go to a grown-up event and sit quietly in the restaurant, we would let him go with us. Of course, he was an angel that night and all the guests couldn't get over his maturity and sweetness. I remember how it felt so right to listen to him and find a positive solution that kept all of our dignity intact. And I will always be grateful to my husband for trusting that our son's needs came above a dinner out with the boss!

Barbara N.

Parents must avoid using shame, fear, threats, or intimidation to force the separation or to attempt to prevent children from crying about it. This can prolong and exacerbate a child's fears of separation. Be especially aware of the preverbal child's reaction and behavior both when the parent leaves and when parent and child are reunited. The child may cry, be extremely clingy, or may suddenly revert to a less mature behavior. Parents must take into account their child's personality and developmental stage in assessing whether the separation or childcare situation is causing anxiety or stress.

Some children seem to accept separations that are not their choice, only to later display negative behavior or sadness caused by the stress they have experienced. Therefore, it is important to be aware of the child's reactions and sensitive to his feelings. Parents may acknowledge a child's feelings by articulating what he must be feeling: "You feel sad because Mommy left, don't you?" Long separations can cause a baby to go through feelings of grief and loss and can affect his attachment to his parents. Therefore, it is critically important that parents who are separated from their children spend focused and intentional time reconnecting with their child after separation.

Children are ready for separation at different ages, and sensitive parents will know what their child's tolerance levels are, depending on whom the caregiver is and the length of time they will be away. Being in attunement with your child will give you the knowledge and insight as to what is best for keeping strong the security of attachment you have nurtured.

Appendix to Chapter Seven: Additional Research and Resource Recommendations

Additional Research

Poor quality care can result in:

- Substantial amounts of unoccupied time spent tuned out and unengaged in social interactions.
- Delays in cognitive and language development, prereading skills, and other age-appropriate behaviors.
- Insecure attachment to caregivers.
- More frequent displays of aggression towards other children and adults.[16]

In families where both parents work, the Families and Work Institute found that among parents of children under age six, 41 percent use full- or part-day childcare for their children, and 64 percent of parents say they coordinate work schedules to be able to access established childcare hours.[17]

A four-state survey of 100 randomly chosen childcare centers found that the vast majority of children who spend their days in childcare centers were receiving less-than-adequate care.... Most troubling was the lower quality of care for very young children, where only 10 percent of the facilities were considered to be of high quality. "Babies in poor-quality rooms are vulnerable to more illness because their basic sanitary conditions were not met for diapering and feeding; are endangered because of safety problems that exist in the room; miss warm, supportive relationships with adults; and lose out on learning because they lack

---

16 Phillips, Testimony before the U.S. Senate Committee on Labor and Human Resources, March 1, 1995.

17 Bond et al., *When Work Works: A Summary of Families and Work Institute Research Findings*, 7.

the books and toys required for physical and intellectual growth," the study said.[18]

A 1997 study showed that infants were less likely to be secure when low maternal sensitivity/responsiveness was combined with poor quality childcare, more than minimal amounts of childcare, or more than one childcare arrangement.[19]

Significant effects from maternal responsiveness and sensitivity correlated with insecure attachment especially when combined with poor quality childcare, more than one childcare arrangement, or many hours in childcare.[20]

Children who spent more time in nonmaternal childcare during the first four-and-a-half years of life scored lower on social competence and higher on externalizing behaviors, including caregiver-child conflicts as rated by caregivers. Spending more time in childcare also predicted more externalizing behaviors of children in kindergarten as reported by mothers and teachers. The quantity of time spent in nonmaternal childcare was a stronger predictor of child outcomes than childcare quality, type, instability, and exposure to peers. The highest level of positive caregiving was provided by in-home caregivers, including fathers and grandparents caring for only one child, closely followed by home-based arrangements with relatively few children with each adult.[21]

An earlier study found that infants exposed to twenty or more hours a week of daycare were more likely to be classified as insecurely attached than those in maternal or paternal care. Boys in particular showed

---

18 Greenspan, *The Four-Thirds Solution: Solving the Child-Care Crisis in America Today,* 27–29.

19 Ibid., 36–37.

20 Belsky, "Quantity of nonmaternal care and boys' problem behavior/adjustment at ages 3 and 5: Exploring the mediating role of parenting," *Psychiatry: Interpersonal and Biological Processes.*

21 National Institute of Child Health and Human Development, "Does amount of time in child care predict socioemotional adjustment?" *Child Development.*

vulnerability in attachment to both parents when in daycare more than thirty-five hours a week.[22]

Babies and young children need time to develop trust with others and to feel comfortable in their new environment.[23]

The data from several studies suggest that repeated overnight separations present a greater challenge to the development of organized primary attachments than do daytime separations. Furthermore, it is known that, especially in high-conflict separations, frequent transitions can exacerbate interparental conflict.[24,25,26,27]

Recommended Reading

A Secure Base by John Bowlby, MD.
Being There: The Benefits of a Stay-at-Home Parent by Isabelle Fox, PhD.
Molecules of Emotion by Candace Pert, PhD.
Effective Parenting Plans: A Developmental Approach for Lawyers and Divorce Professionals by John Hartson, PhD, and Brenda Payne, PhD.
Of Cradles and Careers: A Guide to Reshaping Your Job to Include a Baby in Your Life by Kaye Lowman.
The Developing Mind by Daniel Siegel, MD.
The Four-Thirds Solution: Solving the Child-Care Crisis in America Today by Dr. Stanley Greenspan, MD.

---

22 Belsky and Rovine, "Non-maternal care in the first year of life and the security of infant attachment," *Child Development.*

23 Stein and Call, "Extraordinary changes in behavior in an infant after a brief separation," *Journal of Developmental and Behavioral Pediatrics.*

24 Amato and Rezac, "Contact with non-residential parents interparental conflict, and children's behavior," *Journal of Family Issues.*

25 Emery, "Interparental conflict and the children of divorce and discord," *Psychological Bulletin.*

26 Hess and Camera, "Post-divorce family relationships as mediating factors in the consequences of divorce for children," *Journal of Social Issues.*

27 Johnston et al., "Ongoing postdivorce conflict: Effects on children of joint custody and frequent access," *American Journal of Orthopsychiatry.*

The Milk Memos: How Real Moms Learned to Mix Business with Babies and How You Can, Too by Cate Colburn-Smith and Andrea Serrette.

The Science of Parenting by Margot Sunderland.

The Stay-At-Home Dad Handbook by Peter Baylies and Jessica Toonkel.

The Unexpected Legacy of Divorce: A 25 Year Landmark Study by Judith Wallerstein, PhD, Julia M. Lewis, and Sandra Blakeslee.

What about the Children? by Judith Wallerstein, PhD.

Why Love Matters: How Affection Shapes a Baby's Brain by Sue Gerhardt.

Useful Web Sites

www.babiesatwork.org: Information for parents and businesses who want to implement a policy for bringing baby to the workplace.

www.familyandhomc.org: Resources and support for stay-at-home parents.

www.ncfr.org: provides an educational forum for family researchers, educators, and practitioners to share in the development and dissemination of knowledge about families and family relationships, establishes professional standards, and works to promote family well-being.

www.parentingatwork.org: Dedicated to promote, educate, and provide resources for successful implementation of parenting-in-the-workplace structures.

Chapter Eight

Principle 7
Practice Positive Discipline:
Be the Change You Wish to See

Practice Positive Discipline: Be the Change You Wish to See

When we use punishment, our children are robbed of the opportunity to develop their own inner discipline—the ability to act with integrity, wisdom, compassion, and mercy when there is no external force holding them accountable for what they do.[1]

Barbara Coloroso
Kids Are Worth It!

From the attachment parenting perspective, positive discipline embodies the "golden rule" of parenting; in other words, treat children the way you would want to be treated if you were the child. Positive discipline is an overarching concept based in the understanding that when a child is treated respectfully within loving, age-appropriate boundaries, he will develop a conscience guided by his own internal discipline and empathy for others. Positive discipline is rooted in a secure, trusting, and loving relationship between parent and child. With a strong foundation of trust, positive discipline incorporates empathic and respectful strategies that over time will strengthen the connection between parent and child, while harsh or overly punitive discipline weakens the connection.

A New Way of Seeing Children

The concept of positive discipline is very different from what is generally practiced in Western cultures and calls for nothing less than a paradigm shift in the way we view and treat children. Adults have a tendency to project their own perspectives or reasons to explain a child's behavior, often to justify spanking or other harsh punishment: "She's doing that just to make me mad!"; "If I don't stop my two year old from talking back to me now, just wait until she's a teenager!" These responses generally reflect the parents' lack of understanding of appropriate child development or a repetition of what they learned from their own early childhood experiences. Without a conscious effort to be open to new

---

1   Coloroso, *Kids Are Worth It!*, 78.

information and a willingness to change, we are destined to parent the way we were parented, which, in many cases, continues to perpetuate myths and misunderstandings about children.

Becoming a Conscious Parent

In their book, *Giving the Love that Heals*, Harville Hendrix and Helen Hunt describe conscious parenting this way:

> The conscious parent meets the needs of the child by providing safety, support, and structure for the child as she moves through each developmental stage. He is attuned to the unique personality and temperament of his child and able to see what his child needs as she grows and changes. He is educated about the developmental stages of children and is able to stay alert and flexible in interactions with her.
>
> He is intentional in his interactions with this child, rather than reactive.... He has tools for dealing with his child's frustrations, anger, and regressions that turn these potentially disruptive emotional responses into occasions for strengthening the child's wholeness and maintaining her connection to her parents, her immediate environment, and the larger world. And he has ways of promoting laughter, creative expression, spiritual depth, and moral character as his child begins to express the journey through life.[2]

Every day new child development and neuroscience research provides deeper insights about children, how they think, and why their behavior changes during childhood. So much of their behavior corresponds to brain development. For instance, brain researchers have found that the part of the brain that controls impulsive behavior, called the prefrontal cortex, is the last part of a child's brain to develop; this occurs during the fourth to fifth year of life. The prefrontal cortex, located in the forehead

---

2   Hendrix and Hunt, *Giving the Love That Heals*, 38.

above the eyes, is considered to be the seat of the conscience where the capacities of empathy and compassion are developed. Through the use of new brain imaging techniques, researchers have found that the brain of a child who was abused and neglected is considerably smaller, with an underdeveloped prefrontal cortex, than the brain of a healthy child. If the prefrontal cortex is damaged, these children are less likely to be able to develop a conscience and will not be able to feel empathy for anyone. Scientists call this "adaptive behavior," which the child develops for his own survival. Brain research is providing amazing new information about babies and children that helps us understand them more fully, especially in the realm of prevention and how we can encourage healthy development. If you are interested in brain research findings, we strongly recommend books and materials written by Drs. Bruce Perry, Dan Siegel, and Allen Schore.

Your empathic care will create the "hardwiring" in your baby's brain and allow for the healthy development of the baby's capacities for trust, empathy, and affection, which are the building blocks for your child's growing conscience.

> The simple and unavoidable conclusion of these neurodevelopmental principles is that the organizing, sensitive brain of an infant or young child is more malleable to experience than a mature brain. While experience may alter the behavior of an adult, experience literally provides the organizing framework for an infant and child. Because the brain is most plastic (receptive to environmental input) in early childhood, the child is most vulnerable to variance of experience during this time.[3]
>
> Neuroscientist Bruce Perry, MD, PhD

While principles of attachment parenting encourage parents to trust their own instincts, many lack confidence and feel the need to rely on science to validate and substantiate what they already know on an intuitive level, if only to quiet the doubts of family or friends.

---

3   Perry, "Childhood experience and the expression of genetic potential: What childhood neglect tells us about nature and nurture," *Brain and Mind*.

What is Positive Discipline, and Why is it Important?

At the heart of positive discipline is a secure attachment relationship with your child. Gordon Neufeld and Gabor Maté write in their book *Hold On to Your Kids* that "for purposes of childrearing, the crowning achievement of a working attachment is to instill in a child the desire to be good." In other words, they say when a child feels secure in his connection (attachment) to his mother and father, he will want to be good, and he will be a child who is easy to parent.[4]

The word "discipline" is derived from the word "disciple," meaning one who follows another's teachings. Children learn by example, so it's important that parents strive to model positive actions and relationships within a family and with others—strive to be the kind of adults you would like your children to be.

If you consider that the act of disciplining is actually teaching through modeling behavior and keeping your connection strong, then the very first lessons of inner discipline begin with consistently responding with empathy for your baby's feelings and needs.

Your presence and responsiveness, as discussed in chapter 6, are critical components for forming a trusting bond. As babies learn to communicate their needs more effectively, and as parents begin to develop their intuitive sense of interpreting their babies' signals, babies learn that their needs will be met, and soon a reciprocal relationship of attunement is formed. This strong bond, if maintained, will continue to fulfill the child's innate needs for trust, safety, and protection while fostering his capacities for trust, empathy, and affection.

Positive discipline involves creating a positive home environment that not only allows but also encourages children to learn and explore. Does that mean putting away breakable items for a while? Absolutely! The more relaxed, safe, and secure a child feels in his own environment, the more he will explore and learn. After all, child's play is learning. An environment that is more child-friendly helps minimize stress for you, too.

---

4   Neufeld and Maté, *Hold On to Your Kids,* 70.

[T]he crowning achievement of a working attachment is to instill in a child the desire to be good…. What we don't see is that it's the child's attachment to the adult that fosters that goodness.[5]

Gordon Neufeld, PhD, and Gabor Maté, MD
Hold On to Your Kids

Positive discipline requires a shift in thinking and a new understanding about children. Seeing the world through the eyes of your child will enhance both you and your child's empathy skills. This is where it is critical that you learn as much as you can about child development through books and other resources. Once you learn what the cognitive and behavioral expectations are for different ages and phases, it is much easier to be patient and respond appropriately to redirect and guide the child's behavior. One of the primary factors that contributes to parents' overreacting or becoming abusive to their children is inappropriate developmental expectations.[6] When you see your child in this way, respect, understanding, and compassion, rather than yelling, threatening, and the use of physical punishment, will come naturally. In this process, you will begin to uncover his unmet needs (and sometimes your own). For example, when your toddler has an emotional meltdown, you can learn not to take his behavior personally and recognize that it could possibly be due to lack of sleep, hunger, feeling sick, or the need for one-on-one time. Positive discipline involves positive communication and, with older children, crafting solutions together while keeping everyone's dignity intact.

---

5   Ibid.

6   Bavolek and Keene, *Adult-Adolescent Parenting Inventory AAPI-2:Administration and Development Handbook*, 6.

The Goal of Positive Discipline

The goal of positive discipline is to help your child develop his own conscience and self-discipline. In doing so, we hope to raise cooperative, happy, joyful, and compassionate children who not only care about others but who also do what is right because it is the right thing to do, rather than because they are afraid of punishment.

What does positive discipline look like in day-to-day life? Some see it as proactive—using strategies to prevent unnecessary problems or challenges with children. Such preventive strategies include anticipating and preparing for foreseeable problems in order to eliminate stress, frustration, and tantrums. Strategies include substituting a toy or object rather than forcing a toddler to share when they don't yet understand the concept of sharing or using redirection to gently guide toddlers and young children away from harm by getting them interested in something else.

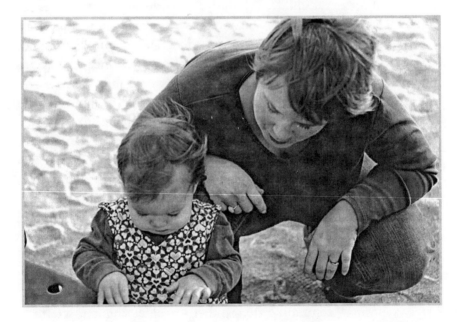

Parents are instrumental in helping their children explore safely by seeing the world through their children's eyes, modeling respect and empathy, and, when appropriate, allowing children to experience the natural consequences of their actions. For example, when your baby is crawling around and decides to touch something you don't want him to touch, recognize that he is fulfilling his need to explore and learn. Quickly move the object or get his attention, then redirect him toward something else. As he gets older, you can use words to explain what you want him to do rather than getting in the habit of saying, "No," or, "Because I said so!" Few of us would like anyone to talk to us that way. We want to model respect to our children so they in turn will learn respect for us. Parents who practice positive discipline have a general understanding of developmentally appropriate behavior and tailor loving guidance to the capabilities, needs, and temperaments of their children.

Learning to practice positive discipline takes time and a lot of trial and error, so don't be discouraged when you make mistakes. Most people weren't raised with positive discipline; it can be very hard to change old ways of thinking. We live in a culture where this type of parenting goes against the cultural norm, so it's very important that parents surround themselves with other parents who share the same values, if at all possible. If that isn't possible, parents can support each other and use books, Web sites, and parenting chat lists for resources.

Most parents wish they could handle every situation perfectly, but no parents are perfect; we were trained on the job like everyone else. At times, tempers will flare and patience will be lost. When parents react in a way that creates tension, anger, or hurt feelings, they can help repair any damage to the parent-child relationship by taking time to reconnect, talk about what happened, and apologize after everyone has calmed down. Think about how it happened and what you can do the next time a similar situation occurs. Having a mental plan will help redirect your anger and frustration. Try using these three reflective questions to help guide you in how you determine your course of action:

1. Am I treating my child the way I would want to be treated?
2. Will my words or actions strengthen my connection with my child?
3. Will my actions give my child an opportunity to learn from this experience?

Adults teach children in three important ways: The first is by example, the second is by example, the third is by example.

Albert Schweitzer

Establishing Boundaries

The big question in every parent's mind is, "What about boundaries?" Every healthy family has clear guidelines for acceptable and unacceptable behavior. For instance, some families make it clear that "in our house, we do not hit." As we mentioned earlier, children have an intrinsic need for predictability, which, as the child grows, takes the form of structure, routine, and learning the boundaries of others. Part of that structure involves understanding your personal limitations and values and the limitations within the household that incorporate the needs, feelings, and values of other family members.

Your developing connection and knowledge of child development will help guide you in establishing boundaries. There is nothing wrong with explaining to your child why he can't do a certain activity or why he has to do something he really doesn't want to do. Some will say that children should be obedient regardless and that adults shouldn't have to explain anything to children. However, research has found that children who were more empathic and able to avoid conflict had parents, particularly mothers, who were more empathic themselves, were not critical of the child, and took the time to explain the consequences of their child's actions and offered suggestions for how to effectively deal with the situation or person.[7] Again, it goes back to simply treating your children the way you would want to be treated.

---

7   Patterson et al., "A developmental perspective in antisocial behavior," *American Psychologist*.

On the other hand, know when to "pick your battles." Too often, we adults become rigid in our thinking and can become unreasonable in our expectations. The key to parenting (and life) is being flexible (within reason). Make sure your expectations and boundaries are developmentally appropriate by referencing trusted resources such as books or Web sites.

The Dangers of Traditional Discipline

Using shame, humiliation, guilt, manipulation, coercion, or physical forms of discipline can interfere with the connection between parent and child. Instilling fear in children serves no purpose and creates feelings of shame and humiliation. Dr. Neufeld strongly warns against using these tactics for getting children to behave: "We must never intentionally make a child feel bad, guilty, or ashamed in order to get him to be good. Abusing the attachment conscience evokes deep insecurities in the child and may reduce him to shut it down for fear of being hurt. The consequences are not worth any short-term gains in behavioral goals."[8]

Physical forms of discipline have been shown to lead to an increased risk of future antisocial behavior, including crime and substance abuse.[9,10] Children raised with the fear of being hurt learn to behave positively because they are in sight of their parents or another authority figure. They may fear punishment, or they may fear a loss of parental love and affection. Although physical discipline and fear may change behavior in the short term, it will not have the desired effects in the long term.

---

8 Neufeld and Maté, *Hold On to Your Kids*, 71.

9 Straus et al., "Spanking by parents and subsequent antisocial behavior of children," *Archives of Pediatric and Adolescent Medicine.*

10 Weiss et al., "Some consequences of early harsh discipline: Child aggression and mal-adaptive social information processing style," *Child Development.*

In 2002, research scientist Elizabeth Thompson Gershoff, PhD, working at Columbia University's National Center for Children in Poverty, conducted a meta-analysis on the use of corporal punishment that covered over three hundred studies and spanned sixty-two years.

She found that ten of the eleven studies in the meta-analysis indicate parental corporal punishment is associated with the following undesirable behaviors and experiences:

- Decreased moral internalization
- Increased child aggression
- Increased child delinquent and antisocial behavior
- Decreased quality of relationship between parent and child
- Decreased child mental health
- Increased risk of being a victim of physical abuse
- Increased adult aggression
- Increased adult criminal and antisocial behavior
- Decreased adult mental health
- Increased risk of abusing own child or spouse

Corporal punishment was associated with only one desirable behavior, namely, increased immediate compliance.

Gershoff summarizes: "For one, corporal punishment on its own does not teach children right from wrong. Secondly, although it makes children afraid to disobey when parents are present, when parents are not present to administer the punishment, those same children will misbehave."[11]

---

11   Gershoff, "Corporal punishment by parents and associated child behaviors and experiences: A meta-analytic and theoretical review," *Psychological Bulletin*.

Likewise, spanking a child or using other physical discipline techniques may temporarily stop a behavior, but it does not teach the child appropriate self-discipline. Instead, studies show that it can create ongoing behavioral and emotional problems.[12] Harsh, physical discipline teaches children that violence is the only way to solve problems. Controlling or manipulative discipline compromises the trust between parent and child and harms the attachment bond.

In *Beating the Devil Out of Them*, researcher Dr. Murray Straus writes of our culture's "conspiracy of silence" on the subject of corporal punishment:

> The universal and chronic use of corporal punishment
> and its potentially harmful effects on children is the
> best-kept secret of American child psychology. It
> is almost as though there is a conspiracy of silence
> among those who do research on children or write
> about childrearing. The discrepancy is so glaring that
> it is worth considering some of the reasons for the
> silence.[13]

---

12   American Academy of Pediatrics, "Guidance for effective discipline," *Pediatrics*.

13   Straus, *Beating the Devil Out of Them*, 10.

Why Spanking Doesn't Work

- It increases the risk for abuse by parents[14]
- It increases impulsive behavior in children[15]
- It increases aggression and antisocial behavior[16]
- It is a risk factor for depression, suicide, and violent behavior later in life[17]

What about "Spare the Rod and Spoil the Child?"

While we strongly believe that attachment parenting practices are fully compatible with the beliefs of most major religions, we realize that the beliefs of some readers may conflict. We want to briefly touch on a couple of points that have helped families feel comfortable practicing positive discipline. Dr. William and Martha Sears wrote *The Complete Book of Christian Parenting and Child Care*, which goes into much more depth about the applications of Christian teachings to attachment parenting. Here is some information from their Web site, AskDrSears.com:

---

14   Straus and Mouradian, "Impulsive corporal punishment by mothers and antisocial behavior and impulsiveness of children," *Behavioral Sciences and the Law*.

15   Straus et al., "Spanking by parents and subsequent antisocial behavior of children," *Archives of Pediatric and Adolescent Medicine*.

16   Weiss et al., "Some consequences of early harsh discipline: Child aggression and maladaptive social information processing style," *Child Development*.

17   Straus, *Beating the Devil Out of Them*, 165.

Some believe that it is the duty of a God-fearing parent to spank, citing specific "rod verses" to support this belief. "Spare the rod and spoil the child" is a misquote of "he who spares the rod hates his son, but he who loves him is careful to discipline him" (Prov 13:24).

At first glance, these rod verses may sound pro-spanking. But we ask you to consider a different interpretation of these teachings. "Rod" (shebet) can mean several different things. The Hebrew dictionary gives this word various meanings: a stick (for punishment, writing, fighting, ruling, walking, etc.). While the rod could be used for hitting, it was more frequently used for guiding wandering sheep. Shepherds didn't use the rod to beat their sheep—and children are certainly more valuable than sheep. As shepherd-author Philip Keller teaches so well in *A Shepherd Looks at Psalm 23*, the shepherd's rod was used to fight off prey, and the staff was used to gently guide sheep along the right path. ("Your rod and your staff, they comfort me." – Psalm 23:4).

The book of Proverbs is one of poetry. It is logical that the writer would have used a well-known tool to form an image of authority. We believe that this is the point that God makes about the rod in the Bible—parents take charge of your children.

When you re-read the "rod verses," use the concept of parental authority when you come to the word "rod," rather than the concept of beating or spanking. It rings true in every instance.[18]

In *Spare the Child: The Religious Roots of Punishment and the Psychological Impact of Physical Abuse*, author Philip Greven found the term "spare the rod, spoil the child" cannot be attributed to the Bible.

---

18   Sears and Sears, "Discipline and behavior: Spanking." AskDrSears.com Web site.

The origin of the phrase came from a poem by Samuel Butler written in 1664 titled, "Hudibras."[19]

A Look at Discipline through the World's Religions

When talking to parents from many different religious backgrounds, it has been affirming to learn that we have more in common than not, especially when it comes to the core teaching of their religion. All the major world religions have what has been called "The Golden Rule" for guiding humanity in how to treat our fellow human beings. It is also the guiding principle of attachment parenting philosophy as it applies to children. Here are some quotations from several of the major religious texts:

- Christianity: "And as ye would that men should do to you, do ye also to them likewise" (Luke 6:31, King James Version of the Bible).
- Islam: "None of you [truly] believes until he wishes for his brother what he wishes for himself." Number 13 of Imam "Al-Nawawi's Forty Hadiths."
- Hinduism: "This is the sum of Dharma [duty]: Do naught unto others which would cause you pain if done to you" (Mahābhārata 5:1517).
- Judaism: "[T]hou shalt love thy neighbor as thyself" (Leviticus 19:18).
- Buddhism: "Hurt not others in ways that you yourself would find hurtful" (*Udana-Varga* 5:18).
- Bahaí'i Faith: "Blessed is he who preferreth his brother before himself" (*Tablets of Bahá'u'lláh*, p.71).
- Confucianism: "Do not do to others what you do not want them to do to you" (Analects 15:23).

Every one of these statements is an excellent expression of the word "empathy." If one word could encapsulate the parenting philosophy

---

19   Greven, *Spare the Child*, 48.

described in this book, empathy would be that word. All over the world, people have been taught to love and treat their neighbors as they love themselves, yet we struggle with this teaching when it comes to our children. If we truly put ourselves in their place, if we imagine what our needs were as an infant or as a teenager, we have the most profound parenting strategy ever given. However, we must remember an important part of this philosophy: we must first learn to love and understand ourselves to be able to love our children. Reflecting on our own childhood histories, taking care of our own emotional, physical, and spiritual needs, and filling our own "love tank" gives us the ability to care for others. Just like the analogy of the flight attendant's instructions to "put your oxygen mask on first" and then tend to your little ones, it is critical that we take time every day to love and nurture ourselves.

Rewards and Punishments

Rewards and punishments are other ways that we as parents manipulate and coerce our children. This is likely a topic that will stimulate much discussion and doubt, but remember that the main focus of positive discipline is connection and cooperation. You may be thinking that taking away rewards and punishments leaves you no tools for effectively disciplining your children, but many alternatives exist. We have listed our top twenty-five tips for positive discipline in this chapter, as well as some of our favorite resources at the end of this chapter. Our intent is to change the consciousness of childrearing attitudes; this means looking at the root causes behind the behavior and working on the attachment relationship rather than reacting to the behavior itself. We realize that change is gradual, and even in our own families we have had to adjust our thinking and strategies over the years. Many wonderful resources available today offer parents a variety of ways to begin this change and communicate more effectively.

Alfie Kohn, father, educator, and author, sheds new light on the use of rewards in his book, *Unconditional Parenting: Moving from Rewards and Punishments to Love and Reason.*

> The first thing to understand is that rewards are remarkably ineffective at improving the quality of people's work or learning. A considerable number of studies have found that children and adults alike are less successful at many tasks when they're offered a reward for doing them—or doing them well. In fact, the first scientists to discover this result were caught off-guard. They expected that some sort of incentive for high achievement would motivate people to do better, but they kept finding that the opposite was true.[20]

Gordon Neufeld and Gabor Maté agree that the use of rewards and punishments can "destroy the precious internal motivation to be good," and then it becomes necessary to use them in order control a child's behavior.[21] They strongly advise parents to carefully nurture a child's desire to be good and protect their connection, warning parents, "It is a violation of the relationship not to believe in the child's desire

---

20   Kohn, *Unconditional Parenting: Moving from Rewards and Punishments to Love and Reason*, 32.

21   Neufeld and Maté, *Hold On to Your Kids*, 72.

when it actually exists, for example, to accuse the child of harboring ill intentions when we disapprove of behavior. Such accusations can easily trigger defenses in the child, harm the relationship, and make her feel like being bad." For instance, a one-year-old child is not developmentally capable of understanding the concept of sharing. Often when young children are together playing with toys and another child decides he wants the very toy that the other child is playing with, it leads to frustration, hitting, and tears. Rather than understanding the child's intent of fulfilling his natural drive for curiosity, exploration, and play, parents sometimes assume their child's intent is selfishness because they don't understand his emotional and cognitive abilities. Rather than punishing the child, it's so much easier and healthier to quickly intervene, using a soft, kind voice, offering another attractive toy. If that doesn't work, then the parent of the child with the toy can try to interest him in another toy and make an exchange. These strategies work much of the time, but, barring those, changing the child's environment altogether will provide a major distraction while using empathy and a caring voice to redirect his attention.

As your children grow older, many teachable moments can be used to help guide behavior that promotes the development of your child's conscience in healthy ways. When a child feels remorse for something she has done, this is a good sign and provides the opportunity to talk to your child about the feelings of others (empathy) and to discuss ways to make amends for the behavior, if it seems appropriate. Feelings of remorse are indications of a healthy developing conscience and, as most of us have experienced, we are usually quite harsh with ourselves when we feel this way. However, when parents disregard a child's remorse and use harsh punishments (spanking, grounding, removal of favorite toys, etc.) then the child's remorse turns to anger toward the parent, and he becomes motivated to misbehave. Over time, children learn not to care anymore—they can become detached from the pain of spankings, detached from their possessions and caring about others. Their behavior becomes driven by external rather than internal factors; they behave out of fear of punishment rather than a moral sense of what is right and wrong. Rewarding a child's behavior is just as detrimental as punishing; it may temporarily stop the behavior, but in the long run it denies children opportunities to develop desirable intrinsically motivated qualities and behavior.

Parenting promises intense and challenging moments, despite our best intentions to develop and maintain a strongly connected relationship. Parents who want to practice positive discipline may sometimes have difficulty communicating with, understanding, or feeling empathy toward their child. In the "perfect storm" of fatigue, stress, and frustration, some parents will react harshly or feel like hitting their child. This is not uncommon, and it is important that parents realize that anyone can snap under the "right" circumstances. It is a sign of strength and personal growth for a parent to examine his or her own childhood experiences, to explore how these may negatively influence parenting, and to seek professional help if needed. When your connection with your child breaks, always take the time to repair it, whether that means apologizing or making amends to your child. By doing so, you are modeling the very behavior you want to instill in your child.

The Words We Say

There once was a little boy who had a bad temper. His father gave him a bag of nails and told him that every time he lost his temper, he must hammer a nail into the back of the fence.

The first day the boy had driven thirty-seven nails into the fence. Over the next few weeks, as he learned to control his anger, the number of nails hammered daily gradually dwindled. Eventually he discovered it was easier to hold his temper than to drive those nails into the fence.

Finally, the day came when the boy didn't lose his temper at all. He told his father about it and the father suggested that the boy now pull out one nail for each day that he was able to hold his temper. The days passed and the young boy was finally able to tell his father that all the nails were gone.

The father took his son by the hand and led him to the fence. He said, "You have done well, my son, but look at the holes in the fence. The fence will never be the same. When you say things in anger, they leave a scar just like this one. You can put a knife in a man and draw it out. It won't matter how many times you say I'm sorry, the wound is still there."

The little boy then understood how powerful his words were. He looked up at his father and said, "I hope you can forgive me father for the holes I put in you."

"Of course I can," said the father.

Author unknown

Who of us hasn't hurt others with our words out of ignorance, anger, or frustration? Who of us hasn't been hurt by harsh words or felt like we weren't being heard by others? In all human relationships, the ability to communicate effectively and compassionately is one of the most important skills we can learn. The words we use, the way in which we speak to others (especially our children), and our ability to listen have profound, lasting effects. We live in a world where we commonly use our words as weapons to manipulate others, to get our needs met, or to express our emotions, and we learn them from the day we are born. Along with compassionate communication, empathic listening is a skill that must be taught. We live in such a fast-paced culture that it's "normal" to be only partially tuned-in to what the other person is saying. Often our minds are zoning out on other matters or racing ahead, thinking about what we want to say next. We have never learned how to be conscious in our conversations with others, and this has led to misunderstandings, misperceptions, hurt feelings, anger, frustration, the break-up of relationships, and war. Just like parenting, we learn to communicate from our parents and other adults. It takes a conscious effort to let go of old habits and learn new ways, but it is definitely possible and, in a real sense, necessary to help develop strong emotional connections and strengthen relationships, whether with your child or your spouse. Teaching your children how to communicate compassionately becomes an opportunity for you to learn new ways of communicating with other adults.

Marshall Rosenberg, the developer of a program called Nonviolent Communication (NVC), believes that we humans are not very good at identifying or expressing our needs to others, nor are we very good at listening empathically to the needs of others. The NVC program is so effective that Dr. Rosenberg has been asked to use it in foreign political peace negotiations and warring tribes, with great success. A primary goal of NVC is to "create human connections that empower compassionate giving and receiving." NVC fits hand-in-glove with the principles of attachment parenting because of its focus on respecting the needs of adults and children while developing empathy and creating emotional connections.

> This approach to communication emphasizes compassion as the motivation for action rather than fear, guilt, shame, blame, coercion, threat, or justification for punishment. In other words, it is about getting what you want for reasons you will not regret later. NVC is *not* about getting people to do what we want. It is about creating a quality of connection that gets everyone's needs met through compassionate giving.[22]

Learning to Express Our Needs

The NVC program offers many resources through its Web site, including on-site trainings, CDs, and DVDs. The four basic steps in following NVC are stating our observations, feelings, needs, and requests.

---

22 "Nonviolent communication is…" From the PuddleDancer Press website www.Non-violentCommunication.com.

- **Step 1—Observations:** Descriptions of what is seen or heard without added interpretations. For example, instead of "She's having a temper tantrum," say "She is lying on the floor crying and kicking."

- **Step 2—Feelings:** Our emotions rather than our story or thoughts about what others are doing. For example, instead of "I feel like you're irresponsible," which includes an interpretation of another's behavior, say "I feel worried."

- **Step 3—Needs:** Feelings are caused by needs, which are universal and ongoing and not dependent on the actions of particular individuals. State your need rather than the other person's actions as the cause; for example, "I feel annoyed because I need support" rather than "I feel annoyed because you didn't do the dishes."

- **Step 4—Requests:** Doable, immediate, and stated in positive action language (what you want instead of what you don't want); for example, "Would you be willing to come back tonight at the time we've agreed?" rather than "Would you make sure not to be late again?" By definition, when we make requests we are open to hearing a "No," taking it as an opportunity for further dialogue.[23]

Our Top Twenty-five Tips for Practicing Positive Discipline

The following tips are a compilation of ideas from a variety of sources, many of which fall closely in line with the NVC model of communication. No one-size-fits-all approach can cover discipline; positive discipline takes into consideration the child's age, personality, and temperament. We strongly encourage you to continue to educate yourself about alternatives to harsh discipline and seek support from like-minded friends or an API support group. This area of childrearing can be the most difficult due to one's own lack of experience and the lack of support from our culture. Additional resources can be found in the appendix at the end of this chapter.

---

23   Ibid.

1. **Maintain a positive relationship.** Refrain from projecting your own perceptions of your child's intentions. Dr. Neufeld warns, "It is a violation of the relationship not to believe in the child's desire [to be good] when it actually exists," and accusing a child of bad intentions when they didn't exist can harm your relationship and actually create within the child the desire to be bad.[24] Resolve to maintain a positive relationship with the child, even in the most difficult situations. Stay focused on identifying needs and exploring solutions. Through all stages of development, children are observing their parents and internalizing parental behaviors as appropriate. It is important for parents to model the kind of adult they would like their child to become.

2. **Use empathy and respect.** Be empathetic and respectful by acknowledging a child's feelings; keeping his needs, abilities, and developmental level in mind; and using a win-win attitude that seeks to meet as many needs as possible.

3. **Research positive discipline.** Read books or watch DVDs that focus on positive communication and discipline, and talk to like-minded parents with children of similar ages. These resources offer reassurance and helpful parenting suggestions.

4. **Seek to understand the unmet need.** What is your child trying to communicate? Children often communicate their feelings through their behavior. By looking at the world through their eyes, parents model the first lesson of empathy. Helping the child think about and understand what others are feeling also fosters this empathy. Recognize and meet the child's need for nutrition, rest, and comfort. When children are cranky and not behaving their best, it's often because they are hungry, tired, or feeling a lack of connection, and they need their "emotional tank" to be refilled.

---

24   Neufeld and Maté, *Hold On to Your Kids*, 72.

There are six triggers for bad behavior: tiredness and hunger; an immature brain; unmet psychological needs; intense emotions; parental stress; and a parenting style that activates the alarm systems in a child's lower brain.[25]

Margot Sunderland
The Science of Parenting

5. **Work out a solution together.** Propose a solution, or ask an older child to propose one. Be open to creative solutions that meet both the parent's and the child's needs. This negotiation of simple conflicts teaches the child valuable conflict-resolution skills.

6. **Be proactive.** Try to monitor the child and watch for the early signs of a problem or unmet need. Get involved quickly before major issues arise. It only takes a second for a situation to get out of control. It's much easier to avoid a situation than it is to deal with it after the fact.

7. **Understand your child's developmental abilities.** Preverbal children often cannot understand concepts such as sharing, and developmentally they have little or no impulse control. Therefore, creating lots of rules and restrictions is likely to be an exercise in frustration for both parent and child. Use redirection to guide babies or toddlers away from dangerous areas or to divert their attention to something else. Understand basic child development and develop appropriate expectations based on the child's age and abilities.

---

25 Sunderland, *The Science of Parenting*, 133.

8. **Create a "Yes" environment.** Before saying "No," stop to think, "Why not?" If the activity is inconvenient rather than dangerous, consider allowing it. If a toddler can attempt to navigate a desired path or activity with parental assistance, provide it. If you can't jointly complete the activity safely, try substituting something similar. Rather than saying no, try telling the child what he can do instead.

9. **Teach discipline through play.** Turn power struggles into playful games. Use imaginative play to work through conflicts. If a child cannot have what he wants, help him to create an imaginary scene where he can. Find the fun in everyday tasks and transitions.

10. **Change the environment by breastfeeding, cuddling, singing, dancing, or being silly.** A change of pace can be very helpful in relieving the stress of a situation, giving parents and children a mental break, and allowing them to reconnect in a fun way without parents feeling the need to resort to more punitive discipline.

11. **State a fact rather than making a demand.** For example, saying "You are close to the edge of the stairs," or "That vase is glass and will break very easily," allows the child to internalize the danger and decide for himself what action is needed to mitigate it. For younger toddlers, or in areas where the child has no experience, tell the child exactly what is expected of him. For example, "Let Mommy help you set it on the table very slowly and softly, like this, so that it won't break."

12. **Avoid labeling children** and focus instead on the behavior and the need that it is not meeting. For example, instead of calling a child "aggressive" or "clumsy," describe and demonstrate the preferred behavior for the child to understand. "This is how we pet the kitty so he

feels safe," or "Hold the cup with both hands, like this, and it won't spill."

13. **Use affirmative language.** Make requests in the affirmative: "You're standing in the chair. I need to feel you are safe. Sit on the chair, please," rather than the negative, "Don't stand on the chair!" Provide a need-based reason whenever possible. Tell your child what you want him to do rather than what you don't want him to do.

14. **Allow your child to experience some natural consequences.** Natural consequences can be excellent teachers. Parents should intervene if a natural consequence would be harmful, too scary, or if the child is cognitively unable to connect the action and the consequence. Parents should also be prepared to assist when a natural consequence occurs, especially when that consequence is not one the child expected. For example, if a child goes out without a coat, bring one along for when he realizes that he is cold. Empathize with the child about his feelings (that he's cold) rather than saying, "I told you so!"

15. **Be sensitive to strong emotions.** Be sensitive to crying and tantrums, which can be a child's way of communicating or releasing strong emotions. Keeping the child safe (which may require relocating the child) while being calm and empathic to the child's immediate needs communicates unconditional understanding, love, and acceptance. It may not be helpful to try to stop the crying or tantrum if the child is working through strong feelings. A parent's empathic presence may be all that is needed. It may help the child if an adult can help him put his feelings into words or fantasize with him about what he wished had happened

Distress tantrums happen because essential brain pathways between a child's higher brain and his lower brain haven't developed yet. These brain pathways are necessary to enable a child to manage his big feelings. As a parent, your role is to soothe your child while he experiences the huge hormonal storms in his brain and body. If you get angry with a child for having a distress tantrum, he may stop crying, but this may mean that the *fear* system in his brain has triggered, overriding his *separation distress* system. Or he may simply have shifted into silent crying, which means his level of the stress chemical cortisol will remain sky-high…. Uncomforted distress can leave a child with toxic levels of stress hormones washing over his brain.[26]

How to Handle Distress Tantrums[27]

- Use simple, calm actions
- Distraction is wonderful
- Hold your child tenderly
- Sit down calmly next to him
- Avoid using time-out
- Remind yourself that a child's distress is genuine

16. **Redefine "time-out."** Time-out is a term used to describe a variety of discipline techniques. One popular version involves putting a child on a chair or in a room, separated from his parent, for a given amount of time. We would like to take back this term, remembering its original intention: stopping the activity, taking a break, and coming back with renewed perspective. Keeping this in mind helps parents work on their relationship with their child, rather than focusing on the child's behavior, and make efforts that strengthen the parent-child connection. Positive discipline replaces the punitive use of time-out with another version of the technique. Some

26 Ibid., 122.
27 Ibid., 125–126.

parents prefer to use the term "time in" and some choose not to use these terms at all. Time-out or time in then becomes an opportunity to reconnect and work through the underlying problem that your child is having. In order to help an older toddler or child regain composure and perspective, explain to the child that both of you need to take some time away from the activity. If he is ready and willing, you can sit with your child and discuss his emotions and needs in a calm, compassionate way. In some cases, snuggle time without talking may be all that a child needs. When both you and your child are calm and ready, he can return to the activity.

Consider implementing a "meeting-on-the-couch" policy, where any member of the family (including the child) can call a "time-out" when tensions begin to arise, or when he feels the need for a period of reconnection.

A Mother's Story: Meeting on the Couch

In our family, we use a tool called "meeting on the couch." We started this when Sophia was about two, and we were finding that our attempts to negotiate solutions to disagreements ... were ending in a lot of frustration. We needed a way to stop the action and talk about it.

The couch had always been a place of connection and snuggles for us, so this is the spot we picked for our meetings. An important component of our agreement is that *anyone* in the family can call a meeting on the couch, and then everyone must stop whatever they are doing and go to the couch. Sophia calls them at least as much as we do, and, while sometimes it's frustrating to stop and go to the couch, we always do.

First, we just snuggle. Especially if emotions are running high, we don't talk right away. Sometimes I tell Sophia that I need a few minutes to calm down, and sometimes she says she does. We take deep breaths, look at each other, and practice nurturing touch. If I'm really, really having a hard time calming down, sometimes we'll turn on the TV just for a few minutes to distract us from the emotion. We try to let Sophia talk first. When she's ready, she'll tell us why she's upset. We empathize and help her put words to her emotions. We ask questions so that we really understand why it is she feels she needs to do something. Then we try to communicate our feelings and our reasons for reacting the way we do. We set boundaries where they need to be set, in the context of which need of ours needs to be met. Then there is some negotiation—a component that has gotten more advanced as she's gotten older.

When she was a toddler, it was mostly about us offering suggestions and alternatives. Now, as she approaches age five, she often amazes us with her insight and creative suggestions. It isn't about "winning" or getting her to do anything specific. For example, if she can suggest a way to do what she wants to do while meeting the need that was causing us to say no, then we're open to that. Sometimes the negotiation takes two minutes, sometimes it takes twenty. Once we come to an agreement, we "shake on it" and give hugs. Then we go back to what we were doing. If the same issue comes up again, we can often just say, "Remember our agreement!" (Or sometimes she says it to us!) If anyone in the family is having a hard time keeping the agreement, then we call another meeting on the couch and try again to come up with a solution to which everyone can agree. Sometimes it's the same solution, just reaffirmed.

When we come to an agreement, it isn't a rule imposed by us on her; it is something we've discussed and agreed to together. It's a relationship. It's touching when Sophia calls "meeting on the couch" with her dolls or tries to call them with the cat (which doesn't always go over so well!). We believe we are teaching her to approach conflict by seeking [to solve it through] connection and understanding, rather than ... coercion or bullying, and we think that's a wonderful thing she will carry with her throughout her life.

Pam S.

---

17. **Parent's "time-out"** is also an effective way for parents to regain composure and perspective. Parents can explain to the child that they are going to sit quietly for a bit and think. They can use this time to examine their expectations both of themselves and their child. If a child resists the parent taking a time-out or the child is too young to be out of the sight of the parent, the parent can sit calmly in the same room, close her eyes, take a few deep breaths, and have an internal "time-out."

If parents feel at risk for harming a child, they must take the steps necessary to ensure the child is in a safe location and separate themselves rather than reaching the breaking point—don't hesitate to call a friend or neighbor for help. For more information on how to deal with anger toward a child, see www.stophitting.com.

The process of discipline does four things that the act of punishment cannot do.

The steps are:[28]

    1. Show children what they have done wrong.
    2. Give them ownership of the problem.
    3. Give them options for solving the problem.
    4. Leave their dignity intact.

---

28 Coloroso, *Kids Are Worth It!*, 29.

18. **Talk to your child.** If a child is having a conflict with a peer, talk to the child before directly intervening whenever possible. In circumstances where someone could get hurt, swift action may be required to ensure everyone's safety, but many times asking the child how she's feeling and why she did a particular thing yields better results than immediately intervening. Keep in mind the age of your child; with very young children, keep language short and simple.

19. **Apologies should come from the heart.** Many parents remember being forced to apologize to another as a child, whether it was a sincere apology or not. It probably made the parents feel better, but it did nothing to make the hurt child feel better, nor did it teach the children anything about resolving conflicts in a positive way. Apologies should come from a child's heart and be a genuine expression of his feelings.

    Allow the child to apologize in his own way, understanding that if he does not verbally apologize, he has witnessed appropriate role modeling and will begin to apologize to others when he is developmentally ready and feels genuine remorse. Children raised with empathy are much more likely to feel compassion and spontaneously apologize.

20. **Comfort the hurt child first.** Although it is difficult for a parent to see their child hurt by another, it is important for parents to go immediately to their own child

when he is hurt and comfort him, letting the parents of the aggressor deal with the other child in their own way. However, note that it may be necessary to separate the hurt child from the aggressor if the aggressive child's parents are unavailable or not immediately responding to the situation. After comforting the hurt child, attention can turn to the aggressive child if this child is also in your care. Talk to the child about what happened and how it made the other child feel, and explore with him other ways of solving the conflict or expressing his feelings.

21. **Offer choices.** When offering choices, avoid masking a threat as one of the choices. If the child does not wish to complete an underlying act, state it first. "I know that you want to stay here and play, because you're having so much fun! But we must go now because we need to pick your brother up from soccer practice." Then offer two choices that would be appealing, such as, "Would you like to race me to the car, or would you prefer to ride the tricycle there?"

22. **Develop cooperation.** Cooperation comes from working together. It is possible as your children grow to enlist their help in working out solutions to any problem. For example, if a four-year old child is coloring on the wall, using the steps of NVC, the parent might say, "I see you are coloring on the wall. I feel frustrated because I need your help in keeping the wall clean. Would you help mommy by coloring on the paper?" If the child insists on coloring on the wall, it's a good time to take time out together to explore potential solutions- restate the problem, find out why the child has a need to color on the wall, express your needs and discuss how to solve this together and be open to creativity from the child. When children contribute to the solution they are more likely to follow it. Needless to say it won't necessarily work if parent and child are upset with each other. Wait until you both are calm and feeling connected. What about "logical consequences?" This is a term that has been used for

decades that refers to the parents imposing a consequence for a behavior of the child. For example taking privileges away if a child breaks a rule or acts inappropriately is what most people regard as a logical consequence. We want to redefine and clarify a more positive use of the term logical consequences that eliminates blaming, criticism, shame and punishment and instead considers using the opportunity for parents and children to craft solutions together, "What can we do to solve this problem together? The point is to create logical consequences that are not disguised as punishments. For instance you might agree that the crayons need to stay in the kitchen and ask for permission from mom or dad to use them next time.

When in doubt about a consequence, Barbara Coloroso offers a simple technique to help you determine if the logical consequences are appropriate:

R: Is it reasonable?
S: Is it simple?
V: Is it valuable as a learning tool?
P: Is it purposeful?

She says, "If it isn't all four of these, it probably won't be effective and it could be punishment disguised as a reasonable consequence."[29]

23. **Use praise conservatively.** In the last thirty years, many well-intentioned parents may have gone a bit overboard with praise and rewards to make sure their child developed healthy self-esteem. Thanking your child for helping out or doing something nice is more meaningful than just saying, "Good job." The overuse of praise, rewards, and value judgments may be experienced by a child as disingenuous or manipulative. Of course, everyone loves to be praised and acknowledged occasionally, but overdoing it can place an inappropriate value on a child's activities,

29   Ibid., 34.

interfering with the child's intrinsic motivation, decision-making skills, and his ability to self-evaluate; inadvertently encouraging the child to constantly seek approval; or stifling his motivation. As with other types of discipline, parents are in the best position to evaluate how to use praise and rewards and their effects on the child. Sharing feelings and describing what the child has accomplished with genuine enthusiasm—separate from the desire to change or shape a child's behavior—can build an authentic, straightforward relationship. For example, say, "Your toys are all in the toy bin!" in an excited voice. Consider celebrating the effort rather than the result, such as "You worked very hard on that puzzle," so that children know their efforts are worthwhile even if they don't always succeed.

24. **Use incentives creatively.** As children grow, they may recognize habits in themselves that they would like to change. Incentives are most effective when the child genuinely desires to change a behavior such as thumb sucking and has input into developing the incentive. The incentive should be something small and fun but not something that would be seen as a punishment if it were not received. This is an opportunity for the child to talk with the parent as to whether this is a strategy that she would like to try and to reevaluate if it doesn't seem to be working. In other words, this technique is not something the parent would arbitrarily use without the child's input and consent. If at any point the child chooses not to, for example, stop sucking his thumb, a parent should accept this decision without shame or humiliation.

   If, over time, the child consistently chooses not to change the behavior, then the parent should explore whether the child has an underlying unmet need and discuss the situation with the child.

Positive Discipline Leads to...

- Increased moral judgment[30]
- Increased empathic behavior[31]
- More competence[32,33]
- More positive behavior[34]
- Better grades[35,36]
- Positive attitude[37]
- Lower risk of smoking[38]
- Lower risk of drug use[39,40]
- Cooperation and respect[41]

30 Eisenberg et al., "Prosocial development: A longitudinal study," *Developmental Psychology.*

31 Eisenberg-Berg and Mussen, "Empathy and moral development in adolescence," *Developmental Psychology.*

32 Baumrind, "Parental disciplinary patterns and social competence in children," *Youth and Society.*

33 Maccoby and Martin, "Socialization in the context of the family: Parent-child interaction," In *Handbook of Child Psychology.*

34 Coombs and Landsverk, "Parenting styles and substance use during childhood and adolescence," *Journal of Marriage and the Family.*

35 Dornbusch et al., "The relation of parenting style to adolescent school performance," *Child Development.*

36 Steinberg et al., "Impact of parenting practices on adolescent achievement: Authoritative parenting, school involvement, and encouragement to succeed," *Child Development.*

37 Steinberg et al., "Authoritative parenting, psychosocial maturity, and academic success among adolescents," *Child Development.*

38 Jackson et al., "Authoritative parenting, child competencies, and initiation of cigarette smoking," *Health Education Quarterly.*

39 Baumrind, "The influence of parenting style on adolescent competence and substance use," *Journal of Early Adolescence.*

40 Jackson and Foshee, "Violence-related behaviors of adolescents: Relations with responsive and demanding parenting," *Journal of Adolescent Research.*

41 Baumrind, "Parental disciplinary patterns and social competence in children," *Youth and Society.*

25. Consider carefully before forcing your will on your child.
Remember your goal is not to break a young child's will, but
to help instill the desire to be "good" and develop his own
will to make good decisions. This will mean that he can feel
good about having some control in his life that can lead to
better cooperation. First, make reasonable attempts to find
an agreeable solution that will satisfy both your needs, such as
your need to leave and his need to play. You might try to use
playfulness such as turning a task into a game, offer a couple
of choices-not too many, or with a toddler redirect the child
to another activity. If nothing works, lovingly intervene in
a way that acknowledges and demonstrates respect for your
child's feelings and desires.

Taking the First Steps

Learning to use positive discipline may not come easily for many
parents, especially if they were raised in a more traditional, authoritarian
environment. The intent of this chapter is to open hearts and minds to a
new way of thinking about training children: to seek out and try positive
alternatives. Some will embrace this information without question, while
others will need time and small steps of change. Some will have skepticism
and doubt because they have never known a person who wasn't raised
without being spanked, and it can be very unnerving to think that it is
even possible. Many of us were spanked as children and feel that we turned
out okay; we may have turned out okay in spite of the spankings or because
of the unconditional love of others. That's why it's so important to attend
API support group meetings to talk with other parents. Many resources are
available in books and on the Internet, such as parent forums on the API
Web site, to provide the support you may need.

We need to be patient with ourselves as we learn new ways of
thinking and behaving with children—it isn't easy! Alfie Kohn reminds
us in a light-hearted way of the challenges we face as parents:

> The bottom line is that raising kids is not for wimps. My
> wife says it's a test of your capacity to deal with disorder
> and unpredictability—a test you can't study for, and one

whose results aren't always reassuring. Forget "rocket
science" or "brain surgery": When we want to make
the point that something isn't really all that difficult, we
ought to say, "Hey, it's not parenting."[42]

Alfie Kohn
Unconditional Parenting

In 1978, Astrid Lindgren received the German Book Trade Peace
Prize for her literacy contributions. In acceptance, she told the
following story.

Never Violence

When I was about twenty years old, I met an old pastor's wife
who told me that when she was young and had her first child, she
didn't believe in striking children, although spanking kids with a
switch pulled from a tree was standard punishment at the time.
But one day when her son was four or five, he did something
that she felt warranted a spanking—the first in his life. And she
told him that he would have to go outside and find a switch for
her to hit him with. The boy was gone a long time. And when he
came back in, he was crying. He said to her, "Mama, I couldn't
find a switch, but here's a rock that you can throw at me." All of
a sudden the mother understood how the situation felt from the
child's point of view: that if my mother wants to hurt me, then it
makes no difference what she does it with; she might as well do
it with a stone. The mother took the boy onto her lap and they
both cried. Then she laid the rock on a shelf in the kitchen to
remind herself forever: never violence. Because violence begins in
the nursery—one can raise children into violence.[43]

Astrid Lindgren
Author of *Pippi Longstocking*

---

42 Kohn, *Unconditional Parenting: Moving From Rewards and Punishment to Love and
    Reason*, 1.

43 *Never Violence,* From a peace prize acceptance speech given by Astrid Lindgren, 1978
    in Germany accessed from http://www.atlc.org/Resources/never_violence.php.

Appendix to Chapter Eight: Additional Research and Resource Recommendations

Additional Research

Children raised in homes dominated by punitive parenting styles are more likely to exhibit aggressive behavior.[44]

Coercive, harsh, inconsistent discipline and poor parent involvement and monitoring are predictors of children's antisocial behavior.[45,46]

The more adolescents are hit by their parents, the greater the risk for depression and suicidal thoughts.[47]

Responsive, nonpunitive, and nonauthoritarian parenting results in children with higher levels of empathy and prosocial behavior.[48]

Children who are more empathic and able to avoid conflict had parents, particularly mothers, who were more empathic themselves, were not critical of the child, and took the time to explain the consequences of their child's actions and offered suggestions for how to effectively deal with the situation or person. Teaching a child emotional self-regulation begins in infancy, as it is modeled to the child by the parent. Securely attached children learn that their negative emotions are acceptable and will be calmed by their parent or caretaker; insecurely attached children

---

44 Thomas, "Aggressive behaviour outcomes for young children: Change in parenting environment predicts change in behaviour," *Statistics Canada*.

45 Patterson et al., "A developmental perspective in antisocial behavior," *American Psychologist*.

46 Straus, *Beating the Devil Out of Them*, 165.

47 Ibid., 165.

48 Zahn-Waxler et al., "Child rearing and children's prosocial initiations toward victims of distress," *Child Development*.

learn that their negative emotions are not acceptable by their parents and are ignored, rejected, or dealt with harshly and inconsistently.[49]

Spanking children less than eighteen months of age increases the chance of physical injury, and the child is unlikely to understand the connection between the behavior and the punishment. Repeated spanking may cause agitated, aggressive behavior in the child that may lead to physical altercations between parent and child. Spanking models aggressive behavior as a solution to conflict and has been associated with increased aggression in preschool and school children. The more children are spanked, the more anger they report as adults, the more likely they are to spank their own children, the more likely they are to approve of hitting a spouse, and the more marital conflict they experience as adults. Spanking has been associated with higher rates of physical aggression, more substance abuse, and increased risk of crime and violence when used with older children and adolescents.[50]

Abusive parents have been found to have inappropriate expectations for their children. Beginning very early in an infant's life, abusive parents tend to inaccurately perceive the skills and abilities of their children.[51]

Approximately 85 percent of parents express moderate to high anger, remorse, and agitation while punishing their children. Although 93 percent of parents justify spanking, 85 percent say that they would rather not if they had an alternative in which they believed. Even controlling for baseline antisocial behavior, the more three- to six-year-old children are hit, the worse their behavior when assessed two years later.[52]

---

49 Patterson et al., "A developmental perspective in antisocial behavior," *American Psychologist*.

50 American Academy of Pediatrics, "Guidance for effective discipline," *Pediatrics*.

51 Bavolek et al., "Primary prevention of child abuse: Identification of high risk adolescents," *Child Abuse and Neglect: The International Journal*.

52 American Academy of Pediatrics, "Guidance for effective discipline," *Pediatrics*.

Recommended Reading

Beating the Devil Out of Them: Corporal Punishment in American Children by Murray Straus, PhD.

Connection Parenting: Parenting Through Connection Instead of Coercion, Through Love Instead of Fear by Pam Leo.

Giving the Love that Heals: A Guide for Parents by Harville Hendrix, PhD, and Helen Hunt, PhD.

Hold On to Your Kids: Why Parents Need to Matter More Than Peers by Gordon Neufeld, PhD, and Gabor Maté, MD.

How to Talk so Kids Listen & Listen So Kids Talk by Adele Fabor and Elaine Mazlish.

How to Really Love Your Child by Ross Campbell, MD.

Kids Are Worth It! by Barbara Coloroso.

Non-violent Communication by Marshall Rosenberg, PhD.

Playful Parenting by Lawrence Cohen, PhD.

Positive Discipline by Jane Nelsen.

Positive Discipline for Single Parents by Jane Nelsen, Cheryl Erwin, and Carol Delzer.

Raising Children Compassionately by Marshall Rosenberg, PhD.

Raising Our Children, Raising Ourselves: Transforming Parent-Child Relationships from Reaction and Struggle to Freedom, Power, and Joy by Naomi Aldort.

Respectful Parents, Respectful Kids: 7 Keys to Turn Family Conflict Into Cooperation by Sura Hart and Victoria Kindle Hodson.

Scream Free Parenting: The Revolutionary Approach to Raising Your Kids by Keeping Your Cool by Hal Runkel.

Spare the Child: The Religious Roots of Punishment and the Psychological Impact of Physical Abuse by Philip Greven, PhD.

The Discipline Book by William Sears, MD, and Martha Sears, RN.

Unconditional Parenting: Moving from Rewards and Punishments to Love and Reason by Alfie Kohn.

When Children Push Your Buttons: And What You Can Do About It by Bonnie Harris.

Useful Web Sites

www.alfiekohn.com: Web site of Alfie Kohn, author, speaker, and educator.

www.askdrsears.com: Web site of Dr. William and Martha Sears and Drs. Jim and Bob Sears.

www.childtrauma.org: Web site for Dr. Bruce Perry, neuroscientist and psychiatrist who specializes in brain development of traumatized children.

www.cnvc.com: Web site for Nonviolent Communication information.

www.empathicparenting.com: Web site for the Canadian Society for the Prevention of Cruelty to Children, founded by forensic psychiatrist Elliott Barker, MD.

www.kidsareworthit.com: Web site of Barbara Coloroso, author, speaker, and educator.

www.nospank.net: Web site for Parents and Teachers Against Violence in Education (PTAVE)

www.playfulparenting.com: Web site of Larry Cohen, psychologist, play therapist, and author.

www.positivediscipline.com: Web site of Jane Nelson, author and speaker.

www.screamfree.org: Web site of Hal Runkel's Scream Free Parenting program.

www.stophitting.com: Web site for The Center for Effective Discipline, with a great deal of information about spanking, discipline at home, and school and state laws.

www.stophitting.com/laws/legalInformation.

php#StateLawsSummary: Listing of states that still allow corporal punishment in the schools and information on how you can get involved in this issue.

Chapter Nine

Principle 8
Strive for Balance in Your Personal and Family Life:
Peace Within Creates Peace at Home

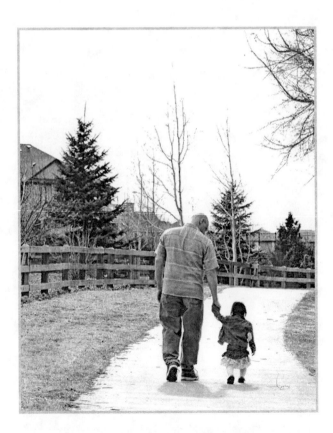

Strive for Balance in Your Personal and Family Life: Peace Within Creates Peace at Home

This style of parenting is for a short season in a marriage—or in your own personal life—and when you devote yourselves fully to that season and find the fulfillment that it brings, the season passes soon enough. You are left with no regrets over how you met the needs of your little ones and no regrets about distance between you and your partner because you didn't allow that distance to happen to the point that you couldn't reconnect.

Remember that what your kids need most is parents in a stable relationship, or in the case of a single parent home, a mother or father who is emotionally healthy. You can't give out what you don't have inside yourself, even though sometimes it feels like we have to dig awfully deep to find it. Getting a rich spiritual life, one where we are connected to God, is probably the most important thing we do as parents.[1]

Martha Sears, RN
Mother of eight and author

Balance, like the principle *responding with sensitivity,* permeates all of the eight principles of parenting. When there is balance, parents are better able to be emotionally available and responsive to their children and to others. In turn, family members feel more loving, more nurturing, and more supportive of each other.

Why would "striving for balance" be a principle? Finding balance in your personal and family life often seems as allusive as finding happiness, but it needs to be a part of your everyday routine—a principle of life. It may help to know that, like happiness, balance isn't an event but a journey that everyone struggles in on a daily basis. Balance requires focusing on nurturing all aspects of one's self—physical, emotional,

---

1   Lockard, "Mothering maven Martha Sears on balance," *Attachment Parenting: The Journal of API.*

intellectual, and spiritual—although not necessarily all at the same time. You can easily recognize when you are feeling out of balance when you are impatient, irritable, angry, tearful, anxious, or depressed.

Some people are really good at balancing their lives, but most are not, especially in our fast-paced culture. We often believe we have to fulfill the perceived expectations of our culture. Take the myth of the "supermom" as an example: the mother who can do it all—work full-time, keep a clean and organized house, have happy and well-mannered kids, *and* have enough emotional reserves to give focused attention to her husband! Another hot topic about cultural expectations concerns the overly-hyped "mommy wars" that put even more pressure on mothers to perform outside of the home as well as in the home. Whether you work outside of the home or not, balance is the key to being a happy, successful person and parent.

As a mother, it becomes that much harder to find balance when little, helpless human beings require your constant attention; it's easy to lose yourself in the care of the child. In the early weeks and months after the birth of your baby, you have to meet all of his needs, which are all-consuming most days. Remember the saying, "You can't give what you don't have"? If you deplete your emotional resources, you cannot be emotionally available to your children or your spouse.

No matter how many times you hear, "Your life is going to change when you have a baby," or "Being a parent is hard work," it doesn't really sink in until you become sleep deprived and totally exhausted. Try not to wait until you have the baby before thinking about how you will juggle the immense responsibilities of parenthood, work, and day-to-day life. During pregnancy is the optimum time to talk to your spouse or partner about what to expect; discuss how he and others can provide support to you and ways to share the workload.

At the Relationship Research Institute in Seattle, Washington, researchers John Gottman and Julie Schwartz Gottman studied couples in their transitions to parenthood and found that the secret to parents transitioning successfully has to do with learning to nurture their own relationship. According to John Gottman, "The secret to Dad's involvement with the baby is his relationship with the mother. She is able to be a better mother if he is involved with her."

We believe this principle is critical not only to your emotional health and well-being but also to your relationship with your spouse and your children. In this chapter, we will give you tips to help you find balance.

Balance is the Foundation on Which Attachment Grows

In the United States, many families live a good distance from extended family members, which is a relatively new phenomenon in the history of humankind. In generations past, new parents had grandparents, siblings, aunts, and uncles to help with the care of children and household tasks. They mentored the young family and provided much-needed support when a new baby was born. It certainly wasn't perfect, but everyone had to rely on each other for basic survival and had a deep sense of responsibility and connectedness, which is very rare today. New parents find themselves living away from their families and isolated within their own communities. Since most parents were never really prepared to be parents in the first place, it's no wonder so many families are in crisis.

I know one thing for sure: It is impossible to find one's own balance from the outside in. I now know beyond a doubt that finding—and maintaining—our balance is an inside job.[2]

Lu Hanessian
Author of *Let the Baby Drive*

---

2   Hanessian, "Chaos theory," *Attachment Parenting: The Journal of API.*

The best way to prevent the feeling of isolation is to look outward to create a support network within your local community. If you don't have an extended family nearby, you can create one from your circle of friends and other parents who share similar childrearing values. You can meet other parents through online parenting message boards, childbirth classes, breastfeeding support groups, and API parent support groups. Finding like-minded friends is critical support for meeting the challenges of the myriad decisions parents face. Your personal network can provide emotional support for its members, especially when parents don't feel supported by the greater community. Don't be afraid to ask for help once your "village" or community is established, especially if a new baby is in the family. Parents can ask friends to bring over some prepared meals, to help with household chores such as cleaning, laundry, or dishes, or to simply answer the phone or door while the exhausted new parents enjoy some solitude—resting, reading, or even taking a bath. Give a helper a grocery list and send him to the store or have him run an errand. Need to relax? Ask a friend for a shoulder or foot massage. Sometimes it can be comforting just having one good friend who is willing to help, even if that simply means listening.

Even with ample support from the outside, parents must look inward for family and individual balance. They must take into consideration the needs of *each* family member; when one person is out of balance, everyone else is affected. Certainly, the infant's needs must be a priority, as they are the most intense and immediate. Even so, he is one piece of the complete family picture that also includes the needs of the parents as individuals and as a couple, siblings, plus the family as a whole; it can be overwhelming to juggle. When you are prioritizing the tasks of the day, don't forget to make yourself a priority. We're not talking about carving out hours within a day. Start small and give yourself fifteen minutes a day. You may not be able to meet all of your needs each and every day, but start with one—whatever gives you a feeling of satisfaction, relief, or happiness. Remember that some days, all you may get to fully appreciate is the delicious peace that happens when you sit and nurse your baby or go for a stroll with baby in the evening.

If you are single or have a spouse who is away for long periods of time, creating balance will be even more challenging. In these situations, it is extremely important to seek out a support network so that you can attend to your own self-care, not just your child's. Parents should not let pride interfere with asking for help; healthy and happy parents are better able to respond to their children.

When you do get it right and have a great day, don't forget to acknowledge that to yourself. It's too easy to focus on the negative things that happen, so try to focus on the positive and make a point of expressing gratitude each day. If you write them down, you will be surprised how many positive things occur each day that are taken for granted. The end of the day is a good time to reflect on the incredible work you are doing for your child and how you as a person are growing in so many wonderful ways.

Daily Self-Assessment Checklist

"Check in" with yourself first thing each day or before you go to sleep at night. To make sure you're getting your own needs met, ask yourself these questions:

- What small thing can I do to satisfy my physical needs?
- What small thing can I do to satisfy my emotional needs?
- What small thing can I do to satisfy my spiritual needs?
- What small thing can I do to satisfy my intellectual needs?
- What small think can I do to satisfy a need of my spouse or partner?

Focus on Your Relationship

"No matter how much they love each other, no two people share the same values or feelings or have the same perspective on life, and few things highlight these personal differences as pointedly as the birth of a child," wrote Jay Belsky in *The Transition to Parenthood.*[3] Belsky and his research colleagues conducted one of the largest, most extensive studies ever done in the early 1990s on the transition to parenthood from birth through the first three years. They found that what new parents argue about most is categorized into five basic areas: [4]

- Division of labor (care of baby and household chores)
- Money
- Work
- Their relationship
- Social life

In their study, the Gottmans found that between "forty to seventy percent of couples experience stress, profound conflict, and drops in marital satisfaction during this time, all of which affect their baby's care."[5] A long-term study at the Relationship Research Institute in Seattle, Washington, showed that the level of relationship satisfaction dropped significantly in two-thirds of couples after the birth of their baby. "Conflict and hostility toward each other dramatically increased," and "their emotional intimacy deteriorated," said the researchers.[6] Fatigue and exhaustion can also lead to a significant increase in postpartum depression. On the other hand, attending parenting classes can minimize unrealistic expectations and enhance the couple's relationship. An important factor in maintaining a positive marital relationship is expressing or demonstrating appreciation to each other, "Thank you for giving the baby a bath," or "Thank you for cooking dinner and washing the dishes," and complimenting each other: "You are such a loving mother to our baby," or "You look really sexy in that shirt."

3 Belsky, *The Transition to Parenthood*, 12.
4 Ibid., 32.
5 The Gottman Institute, "Bringing baby home," The Gottman Institute Web site.
6 Gottman and Gottman, *And Baby Makes Three*, 8.

Dads especially like to feel that they are desired by their wives, and they need intimate time with them to feel connected.[7] Making time for intimacy should be a priority, and it doesn't always have to be about having sex. Having time alone and doing things together that you enjoy are ways to reconnect. You can do this in creative ways, with the realization that you now have to plan ahead, making sure the needs of your baby are being met, and schedule your time together. You can do several simple things to eliminate potential stressors that really strain relationships after a baby arrives:

- Simplify, simplify, simplify! Sit down and seriously talk about what you can do as a couple to simplify your life, to reduce everyday stressors such as cutting your commuting time by moving closer to work, buying a smaller house (or lowering your rent), or cutting out unnecessary expenses to reduce the strain of money. Eliminate unnecessary commitments to others, such as volunteer work, coaching, and meetings.

- Discuss ways in which you can divide the household chores. This takes out the guesswork and eliminates the need to be a "mind reader." Express what your needs are and how you can help each other. "I need to have a clean kitchen before I go to bed. Will you help me by making sure it's cleaned up each night?"

- In the early weeks and months, your time together will likely be moments when baby is with you, asleep in a sling or carrier, such as while taking walks in the park or around your neighborhood.

- When baby is sleeping or napping at home, it's a good time to talk, watch movies together, have a picnic dinner on the floor in front of the fireplace, or play games together.

---

7   Bringing Baby Home, "Research evaluation of the Bringing Baby Home program," Bringing Baby Home Web site.

- When you feel your baby is ready, you can introduce a "mother's helper," who can be a trusted friend, neighbor, or responsible teenager, to play with the baby so you can have time together—either in another room or part of the house.

- If you plan an evening out while your baby is still an infant-in-arms, consider having a mother's helper go with you and care for the baby out of sight, allowing Mother to be nearby and available when needed, especially if breastfeeding. Some may wonder, "Why not just ask a babysitter to feed the baby breast milk or formula in a bottle?" Remember the intention is more about maintaining the attachment relationship than it is about how the baby will be fed.

- Show appreciation and love by surprising your spouse with a special meal or dessert, a gift, or a letter expressing your love. It's the little things in life, the thoughtful gestures, that will help keep you emotionally connected.

As these studies have shown, it is critically important to consciously work on your relationship with your partner and keep communication open and honest. Yes, the first two to three years can be intense (with just one child), but realize you are investing in your child's emotional health and investing in your relationship. Be patient and understanding with each other. Know that seeking balance in your relationship and in your life is most important. If you need help, and many parents do, look for parenting classes in your area such as "Bringing Baby Home," a program developed by the Gottmans or API parent support groups.

Children Need Both Parents

Children need loving, committed parents who are willing to make their relationship a priority and help each other recognize when things get out of balance. It may help to know that mothers and fathers are wired differently; unspoken expectations of each other may create unnecessary stress. For instance, a survey found that 70 percent of fathers took weeks and months to form a strong attachment to their babies, most likely due to the other finding of the survey—fathers, on average, spend ten to fifteen minutes a day interacting with their babies. Once a baby is born, many fathers feel the need to ratchet up their work ethic because they are thrust into being the primary breadwinner for the family. When they get home, many fathers say they are ready to relax, and yet mothers are hoping the father will give them a reprieve (the "six o'clock savior"), which sets the stage for conflict. Mothers, on the other hand, spend so much time with the baby that they feel isolated, touched-out, and lonely, while fathers can feel left out, unappreciated, and unloved.

It is all too common in the transition into parenthood, but it doesn't have to be that way. The Gottmans advise couples to avoid what they call "The Four Horsemen of the Apocalypse," which their studies have found often lead to divorce:

- Criticizing each other
- Contempt (such as feeling disgusted or fed up with your spouse)
- Defensiveness (making excuses)
- Stonewalling (when one spouse shuts down emotionally)[8]

Not only do these behaviors break down relationships, but they also affect the emotional health and development of the children.

> "Our data show that children raised by parents whose marriages are characterized by criticism, defensiveness,

---

8   Gottman and DeClaire, *Raising an Emotionally Intelligent Child*, 148–154.

and contempt are much more likely to show antisocial behavior and aggression toward their playmates. They have difficulty regulating their emotions, focusing their attention, and soothing themselves when they become upset. In addition, the mothers of these children reported that the kids had an increased number of health problems such as coughs and colds. These children also seemed to be under more chronic stress, as shown by higher levels of catecholamines, which are stress-related hormones, in their urine."[9]

With all the best of intentions, sadly, many parents end up getting a divorce. If you are yourself a child of divorce, then you know all too well the lasting psychological harm it can create. At API, we hear from parents on a weekly basis about a divorce situation and how the attachment relationship with their baby or young child is being compromised. These parents have a very difficult road ahead, not only in terms of dealing with an ex-spouse who may resent the close attachment relationship, but also in terms of dealing with attorneys and judges. Most court systems are not informed about the attachment needs of children. They are overwhelmed with divorce cases and must make very tough decisions that usually don't consider the attachment needs of the child but rather the needs of the parents. You have read in chapter 7 about the detrimental effects of separation due to custody arrangements. Equally important is the degree to which both parents are able to subdue their own feelings for the best interests of their child. In the book, *The Unexpected Legacy of Divorce: A 25 Year Landmark Study,* research showed that when parents divorce, their children are "exquisitely sensitive."[10] Children may have disorganized attachments to both parents if the parents are angry and unable to cooperate with each other. This may also affect their security of attachment to others in their life as well. If, however, the parents learn to cooperate and have peaceful interactions when they exchange their child, there is a much better chance that the baby or child will thrive.

---

9   Ibid., 139.
10   Wallerstein et al., *The Unexpected Legacy of Divorce: A 25 Year Landmark Study,* 217.

When Parents Are Not Together

Whether or not their parents are married, children thrive best when both parents are involved in their lives. All children long to have a relationship with both parents, whether the parents are together or not. Barring problems such as the potential for emotional and physical abuse by a parent, every effort should be made to help children nurture relationships with both. If the father is absent from the child's life, it is important that the child be allowed to develop a loving, trusting relationship with another male role model, such as an uncle or grandfather. The same would, of course, hold true if the mother was absent in the child's life: a female role model would be needed, with whom the child could build an affectionate relationship. The characteristics and qualities that both genders provide create balanced experiences for the child that will develop a stable emotional foundation affecting all future relationships.

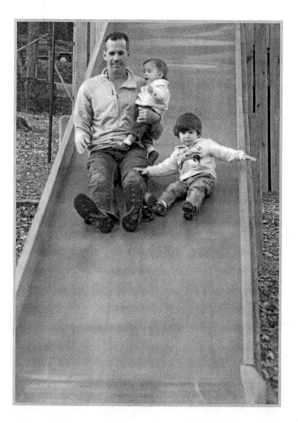

The Gottmans' research gave them very powerful information about the importance of couples being more emotionally prepared for parenthood. As a result, they developed a program called "Bringing Baby Home," integrating research into a practical preparation program for parents with striking results. They found that parents who took the program demonstrated:

• More sensitivity to their babies' signals (especially fathers)
• Better coparenting abilities
• Less hostility expressed during disagreements

They also found the following: [11]

• Fathers were more involved in parenting and felt more satisfied
• Parents in the program reported positive, stable relationships
• Fewer mothers reported anxiety and postpartum depression (22.5 percent compared to 66.5 percent of mothers who did not take the program)
• Fewer fathers reported anxiety and depression

When Parents Disagree about Parenting Practices

Parents who are having difficulties in their relationship will find parenting to be an added stressor, not necessarily the blessing that solves all their problems. One conflict that can be a great challenge is disagreement on the AP principles. Sometimes parents may only disagree on one issue, like whether or not the baby will sleep in their bed. For these problems, it's relatively easy to find a compromise solution. For instance, Mom may

---

11   Bringing Baby Home, "Research evaluation of the Bringing Baby Home program," Bringing Baby Home Web site.

have the baby sleep next to her side of the bed in a cosleeper, giving Dad plenty of room in the bed to stretch out. It is more serious when one parent disagrees with the entire AP philosophy and wants a more rigid, authoritarian approach to parenting. This is when a tremendous amount of dialogue, empathic listening, and perhaps compromises on both sides can be key in keeping the marriage intact. Relationship experts have found that one of the most influential determining factors of a parent's ideas and beliefs about discipline and childcare is their own childhood history. Couples need to take the time to discuss the deeper issues from their pasts to be able to understand and work through these conflicts. Books like *And Baby Makes Three* by Gottman and Gottman, *Giving the Love That Heals* by Hendrix and Hunt, and *Nonviolent Communication* by Rosenberg are excellent resources. These books may also give you the insight to determine if your conversations would be helped by employing a professional counselor to learn skills in communication and compromise.

In his book, *The Heart of Parenting*, Dr. John Gottman gives parents tips on what he calls "Emotion Coaching." He has found in his research that parents who learn how to build empathy into relationships with their children enhance their children's emotional intelligence. These five steps of Emotion Coaching can also be applied to adult relationships and communication:[12]

1. Be aware of the child's emotion
2. Recognize the emotion as an opportunity for intimacy and teaching
3. Listen empathetically and validate the child's feelings
4. Help the child verbally label emotions
5. Set limits while helping the child problem-solve

We would add here that in an adult relationship, step 5 could be that the couple find compromise solutions that help them both feel understood and validated.

Many parents have told us that reading parenting books and attending support group meetings have actually made their marriage relationships stronger. The same tools that they use to talk positively to their children work beautifully with adults, too! We can all use improvement in communication skills, and the parenting journey

---

12   Gottman, and DeClaire, *The Heart of Parenting*, 75.

forces us like no other form of therapy either to improve and grow or to stay stuck in the past repeating old tapes like an outdated recorder. For the most part, the loving, nurturing skills we learn through attachment parenting have a profoundly positive effect on the entire family.

Q: What can we do to help create a harmonious home life when the mother is an attachment parent and the father is not?

A: First, I would suggest being curious about the possibility that the father's lack of participation is rooted in not feeling needed and feeling criticized for not caring for the infant as well as (or the same as) Mom. I would also challenge this couple to become aware of their power struggle and the underlying dynamics surrounding other relationship issues. If these issues are unconscious, not addressed, and unresolved, they may be creating an oppositional parenting relationship.

Another idea is to listen to each other's childhood stories and memories to see if their experiences of attachment might be influencing their parenting style. An insecurely attached adult with clinging energy can use attachment parenting to compensate for her unmet childhood needs in ways that use the baby in unhealthy ways and promote hyper-dependency. Often her husband, who also grew up insecurely attached and has an avoidance attachment style, would be fostering a hyper-independence. It is easy to see how a couple, both of whom come from insecure attachments, could be fighting in the present over how they are going to parent their child, when in reality the energy of this fight is rooted in their own insecure childhood attachments. Becoming conscious of their childhood patterns could help them listen, understand each other, and co-create a joint parenting plan, providing a healthy, stable environment for their child.[13]

Rod Kochtitzky, MDiv
IMAGO Relationship Counselor

---

13 Lockard, "Back to the future: How early attachments shape your relationships," *Attachment Parenting: The Journal of API.*

Practical Tips for Maintaining Balance

Try to enjoy today by being mentally and emotionally present! Children grow up so quickly. The intense newborn stage passes in the blink of an eye; the infant stage is gone in two blinks. If you can, learn to accept—even embrace—your new unpredictable life as a parent. Simply *allowing* yourself to be flexible can often make the daily challenges easier to manage. You may have heard the warning, "After you have a baby, your life will never be the same." Some parents try to "disprove" this by attempting to maintain a lifestyle similar to life before kids but often quickly learn that it is too stressful for everyone.

No doubt about it, life changes when children join the family, and while some things may change or be on hold, you stand to gain so much more. A proactive approach to balance can help parents avoid crisis situations where they feel burned out and exhausted.

The following tips came from years of experience from many mothers and fathers. By following these tips, you will have some tools to help keep you on the right track for your own mental health and the emotional health of your family.

- **Set realistic goals.** Evaluate balance over a full day or week, not every single moment. Instead of wanting to be "the best" parent who has to do everything right, choose to be a "very good" parent who sometimes makes mistakes and learns from them. Parents have to learn "on the job" and should give themselves a break (figuratively and literally). Parenting is hard work!

- **Get organized and establish routines.** We don't mean create a rigid schedule but rather prioritize what has to be done each day. Delegate when possible, even if that means calling in reinforcements such as family members or friends. This is not the time to be independent—that strong spirit of being independent and not needing anyone contributes to isolation and burnout. Get better at asking for help and accepting help when it is offered.

- **Put people before things.** When feeling overwhelmed by household duties, parents can take a little time to reexamine and reassign chores in a more balanced way. Changing expectations around them may help also. If your sink is full of dishes, but you had a great day with your kids, you're doing okay.

- **Don't be afraid to say "No."** Unfortunately, some people perceive at-home parents as "not working." Don't be afraid to say no when asked for a favor that would compromise individual or family needs. Ask these questions before committing to any new activity: Why do I want to do this? How will it affect our family life? Is it worth it?

- **Turn "unpleasant" parental duties into enjoyable ones.** This can be done by consciously making a change of attitude and making a point to look at the positive aspects of daily tasks. For example, changing diapers can be enjoyable because it's an opportunity to look into the adoring eyes of the little person who loves you more than anyone else in the whole world. Sing songs, whistle, or hum while performing less savory duties!

- **Be creative in finding ways to spend couple's time.** Find ways to be together without compromising the needs of the infant. Try changing things around a bit. Have a candlelit dinner or a picnic in the living room. Something as simple as taking a walk together while wearing baby in a sling can be fun and can help couples reconnect or venture further abroad—many new infants can sleep through an entire dinner out in a restaurant.

- **Take time for yourself.** Each parent should try to find some time each day to do something they enjoy or that helps them relax. It is not always easy to do, but taking this time while the other parent enjoys some one-on-one time with the baby will help everyone involved.

A parent who doesn't have a partner to provide some break time might arrange for a close friend, relative, or neighbor to come over at a certain time each day (or every few days) to provide support. If possible, use this time to read, walk, meditate, take a long bath, or do something else that helps you unwind.

- **Use a "mother's helper."** Have someone that the child knows well come over to play and entertain baby while the parents have some quiet time together somewhere else in the house. This allows parents to focus on their relationship while keeping baby close by. Babies, especially newborns, are more content when they have access to their mothers.

- **Eat healthy foods.** Healthful eating is important to keep parents healthy and balanced. Prepare ahead to have good meals. Make large batches of food on the weekends, and freeze the extras for use during the week. A soft carrier allows baby to be with parents during food preparation and meals; however, safety precautions should be used when working near a hot stove.

Eating a varied, balanced, nutritious diet is important for everyone, especially busy parents. Certain foods are essential for the production of key brain chemicals, and without them, you may feel miserable and tired.[14]

Margot Sunderland
The Science of Parenting

---

14 Sunderland, *The Science of Parenting*, 252.

- **Regular exercise** also helps parents stay in balance. Include baby in your exercise routine. Walks and outings, yoga exercises with baby, and other light activity can all be done with baby along.

- **Take naps when baby sleeps during the day.** Don't be tempted to get all of your household chores done while the baby is napping. You need rest, too! Many people find they actually sleep *better* at night when they have napped or rested during the day.

- **Take care of yourself.** Get regular physicals and attend to self-care. Consider whether a physical problem could be contributing to feeling out of balance. For example, insomnia or low blood sugar can lead to feelings of fatigue and may prevent parents from achieving balance.

- **Avoid overscheduling.** As a matter of fact, with a newborn it may be wise not to schedule anything at all!

- **Look for ways to make routine tasks easier.** For instance, baby's diaper or clothes need to be changed several times a day, so choose baby clothing that is easy to put on and take off, and have changing stations and extra clothing in the most-used areas of the house (and in the diaper bag).

- **Get out of the house.** Breastfeeding makes it easier to get out of the house for couple's time, exercise, or errands since the baby's food is always packaged and ready to go. Many states have laws protecting a mother's right to breastfeed her child in public. Parents should be informed about the laws in their state so that they can rest assured that mother and baby can enjoy breastfeeding while out and about.

- **Follow your heart and listen to your baby.** Some days your mantra will be, "This too shall pass," and "I must put my baby's needs first. The house may not be clean, the dishes may be piled in the sink, but I'm putting people before things, and tomorrow is another day!"

Tips for Supporting New Mothers

If you are a spouse, professional, friend, or relative, you can support a new mother and family in many ways. A new mother can become so involved in the care of her infant that she doesn't recognize her own needs until she is in emotional or physical trouble. Mothers need frequent rest, fluids, and food just as infants do. As the mother's partner or support person, you can best help her by:

- Being patient and sensitive to her feelings and needs.
- Advocating for her need to rest and for quiet bonding time with her baby by limiting visitors.
- Saying something appreciative about each other every day: "You are such a loving mother and wife/partner," "Our baby adores you, and so do I," "I appreciate all you are doing for our family."
- Taking initiative and doing the needed chores around the house or hiring outside help.
- Asking if you aren't sure what to do.
- If reinforcements are needed, making calls to family or friends to ask them to pitch in, or being a support person for Mom.
- Being grateful. Giving her the benefit of the doubt and treating her as an ally. Imagine what it would be like to parent solo!
- Seeking to become a more empathic listener. Read *Nonviolent Communication: A Language of Life* by Marshall B. Rosenberg, PhD, or *Giving the Love that Heals* by Harville Hendrix, PhD, and Helen Hunt, PhD, for tips on how to achieve this.

Finding Balance while Parenting the Older Child

As babies grow into toddlerhood and beyond, they bring a new set of challenges. The following tips will help the family maintain balance with an older child:

- Bring a friend or mother's helper along to entertain an older baby or toddler while Mom enjoys an activity. Baby will be comforted by his mother's close proximity, and Mother will feel more relaxed knowing her baby is nearby and not feeling stressed.

- Don't overdo extracurricular activities. Allow the child some free time instead of scheduling every minute of the child's day. Children love to have time to hang around the house, read, have their friends over, talk, play games, or be creative.

- Remember to spend time together, getting to know one another and just being together. Spend time talking with each other about each family member's personal interests; this helps family members relate and improves communication. Develop family traditions together.

- Individual children need individual time with one or both parents. Parents can make a "date" on a regular basis with each of their children for special time together.

- Create family traditions with special nights, like "game night," "movie night," or "music night." Most young children look forward to special times like these and love to help with the planning.

- Parents need to nurture themselves and their relationship. As children get older and develop trusting relationships with friends and family outside of the immediate family, parents can find more opportunities to have time alone together. Parents can also develop their own hobbies, interests, or do volunteer work they may have put "on hold" when their children were younger. Set an example for the children and include them when possible.

Dealing with Parent "Burnout"

When families get out of balance, parents can feel "burned out" and "touched out" by the demands of parenting. Recognize the symptoms of burnout. Burnout is a physical, emotional, and mental response to high levels of stress. Parents may feel relentlessly fatigued, strained, and physically, emotionally, and mentally exhausted. They may also feel overworked, underappreciated, angry, resentful, powerless, hopeless, drained, frustrated, detached, antisocial, unsatisfied, resentful, like a failure, indifferent, and unmotivated. Parents who feel their emotions are taking over should get help immediately!

Regain balance and heal burnout by trying the following:

- Make regaining balance a priority *today*. It's easy to forget everything except the needs of the child, but what a child needs most of all is healthy, balanced parents. Parents should not feel guilty about taking some time for themselves to regain balance.

- Parents can take time for themselves while remaining sensitive to the needs of their children.

- Cultivate friendships with other parents who practice attachment parenting. Better yet, join (or start!) an API support group. Parents of older children can share ideas and tips, while parents of similarly aged children can empathize.

- Make time to prioritize the family's needs, and don't be afraid to simplify and let unnecessary things go. A spotless house doesn't do any good if the people who live in it are unhappy, out of touch, and out of balance.

- Every so often, take several deep breaths and slowly release them. Use yoga, meditation, visualization, or other techniques to regain calm and let go of stressful feelings.

- Professional counseling can be beneficial in helping families regain balance and in linking them to resources or other services in the community.

- When all else fails, remember those words of wisdom, "This too shall pass," and try to focus more on any positive aspects of your life's circumstances and write them down.

Lu Hanessian, mother, author, and TV show host, has intimately experienced how difficult it is to balance family and a career. She writes, "Finding balance is no cakewalk. There are the voices. People all around you are convinced about what's right for you and your children, what you should be doing with your life, your toddler, your breasts, your heart, your time, your aspirations, your groceries, your money.... A sense of balance comes naturally when we can let go of worry, not let anger fester, find ways to be proactive instead of reactive, befriend and forgive ourselves. With no boundaries, we invite resentment, over-exhaustion, depression, self-pity, self-loathing, guilt, shame, hopelessness."[15]

Perfecting the Balancing Act

In *The Hidden Feelings of Motherhood*, Dr. Kathleen Kendall-Tackett offers seven wise ways to perfect the balancing act:[16]

1. **Stop describing yourself as busy.** Your thoughts are

---

15 Hanessian, "Chaos theory," *Attachment Parenting: The Journal of API.*

16 Kendall-Tackett, "Practical steps toward achieving more balance in your life," *Attachment Parenting: The Journal of API.*

powerful. Viewing a situation as negative releases the stress hormone cortisol. This is not good for you!

2. **Guard your mind.** Be careful what you allow in your mind. Pay attention to what you watch, listen to, and read. Even art books or "films" can be excessively negative.

3. **Take care of your body.** You cannot strike a balance between your needs and the needs of your family if you are constantly run down.... Make a priority to eat well, exercise, sleep, and get regular physicals. Stop getting up early or going to bed late so you can catch up on a few extra chores.

4. **Unplug and unwind.** If you want to de-stress, it is important that you have time every day, or most days, when you are not available. That means turn off your cell phone, ignore the fax, and don't check e-mail.

5. **Practice being in the present.** It is amazing how much time we devote to thinking about the past or the future. Make a conscious effort to be present for at least a few minutes a day and see if it doesn't refresh your spirit. Practice paying attention and enjoying what's going on *now.*

6. **Plan restorative vacations.** To make vacations more enjoyable, a) stay within your budget, b) try traveling someplace closer to home, and c) gradually reenter your life, giving yourself a day or two to prepare and unpack.

7. **Be grateful for what you have.** The difficulty of the stressed lifestyle is that it keeps us looking to what we don't have, what we haven't accomplished, and what's wrong with our lives. By standing back and looking at your life, you may start to see the things that are really going well for you and that can also help you reduce stress.

A Mother's Story: The Mommy Marathon

A few weeks ago, my husband and I watched the Eco-Challenge on the Discovery Channel, a five-day, 200-mile "race" over impossible terrain. For me, parenting feels an awful lot like an endurance sport. My children require a lot from me. Their play is loud; their fights are even louder. There are no small events and even fewer quiet moments in my house.

All of this upheaval takes a serious toll on my emotional stamina. To remain present, centered, and fair in the midst of all this chaos is a Herculean task. I *want* to be their emotional anchor, but for whatever reason serenity escapes me. I either expend tremendous amounts of energy trying to keep it together amidst the storm, or I get swept up with my children in their emotional hurricane and we are all lost in it.

The only possible balance that I see for my life would be if my children were somehow "less"—less intense, less strong-willed, less, well ... loud. But *that,* unfortunately, is not an option and so it is up to me to grow and stretch FAR beyond my comfort level. I am required to go much farther than I thought I would have to, for much longer, and with much less sleep. Sometimes I hate all this growing.

There have been dark times when I surely thought my body would crack open from fatigue and grief and desperation. It is so much like labor; yet, unlike labor, I'm never sure when it will be "over." There is no monitor or measurement to tell me where I am in the process. It's like the Eco-Challenge, except there's no map, no finish line, and no emergency helicopter to get you the heck out of the race because you simply cannot take one more step. The course that I'm on has few stops and even fewer pieces of level ground. I'd love to have the space and the energy to enjoy the view, but the difficulty of my course doesn't often allow for that.

The best I can do some days is to keep focused on putting one foot in front of the other and pray for some easier road ahead.

I'm coming to understand two things: that selflessness does not mean being "without self" and that taking care of ourselves is not as simple as taking a darned bubble bath. Filling our energy reserves requires us to work on many different levels and to know that, if we want to spare our children from the screaming harpy we can become, we must do what we can to keep our reserves from running dry.

Here are a few things that, in retrospect, I wish I knew when the road was long, steep, and really, really rocky.

- **Know yourself.** It's important to understand your own temperament and the ways in which your energy gets both drained and replenished. When are you likely to get tired? Do you get drained by too many people or stimulation?

- **Recognize and identify your needs and validate your right to have them.** In order to get our needs met, we first need to know what those needs are and what we need in order to refuel. We also need to know that needing a break does not mean we're a bad or lazy parent. Don't wait until it's too late. Don't wait until the rough days to take a break. A little break each day, over time, may prevent total breakdowns because you keep your reserves from completely drying up.

- **Actively cultivate a sense of inner calm** (without falling asleep). When the world feels chaotic, we need an inner safe place, an eye of the storm. Some sense of peace can give us a place to ride it out.

- **Actively seek out a supportive community**. It really is impossible to parent without some kind of support, believe me. I tried to tough it out, and I would not

271

recommend it. Do what it takes to find others who can support you. I could go on about how I wish society would make it easier for moms to have access to the things that would help give us balance. But it's really about making our sanity and stamina a priority and doing just a little of what it takes to get it.[17]

Macall Gordon
API News

The mother's story on the previous page is an honest description of what so many of us have felt at one time or another in our parenting journey. Without support and other resources, we are taking a big risk for our children and ourselves. Margot Sunderland addresses the critical issue of stress and balance from a brain chemistry perspective in her powerful book *The Science of Parenting*. She describes the positive effects of the hormone oxytocin and its role in helping calm all human beings. We are designed to help provide emotional regulation for children and each other. When a parent is alone most of the time without other caring adults to talk to, stress hormones rise, feelings get out of balance, and irritability and anger lash out. All of us have an "emotional tank" that needs constant refueling, and it's important to be able to recognize when you are running low.

"Hugs and warm, affectionate touches with your partner trigger the release of oxytocin. This gives you a warm, calm feeling."[18] If your partner isn't available, caring friends can provide much needed relief by providing an outlet for stress through talking and empathic concern.

Research has shown that the following activities can stimulate oxytocin, an anti-stress chemical:[19]

• Meditation
• Acupuncture

---

17 Gordon, "The mommy marathon," *API News*.
18 Sunderland, *The Science of Parenting*, 268.
19 Ibid., 260.

- Massage or physical affection
- Yoga
- Having a warm bath
- Spending time in light, such as daylight or good artificial lighting

Margot Sunderland
The Science of Parenting

One of the best ways to find relief and emotional regulation is by attending parent groups. API parent-support groups have been successful because they provide the friendship, information sharing, problem solving, and empathic support that so many parents are seeking. Talking to other like-minded parents who have "been there" can provide a wealth of knowledge and relief through simple conversations. If you are new in an area and the only friend you have is two thousand miles away, she can still be a support system for you. Often the simplest of ideas can have a profound positive effect on your relationship with your child or spouse or on stress at home. As a culture, we are finally beginning to accept that we are relational beings and need each other for connection and support, whether we are parents or not. If you believe that you need more than a parent support group can provide, then by all means get professional help.

Balance begins within, and that includes not worrying so much. When you are a first-time parent, it is natural that you want to do it right; after all you are responsible for a helpless human being that you created. William and Martha Sears emphasize that attachment parenting doesn't mean that mothers must be anxious about their baby's every move nor that they have to personally respond to the baby every time, but rather involve Dad as much as possible. Don't strive for perfection, but do your best to be "good enough." Attachment parenting will give you the gift of love, empathy, and connection that will last a lifetime. "It will give you more confidence in yourself and in your ability to be not a perfect mother, but a good one."[20]

---

20   Sears and Sears, *The Attachment Parenting Book*, 118.

Appendix to Chapter Nine: Additional Research and Resource Recommendations

Additional Research

Studies have found that a happy marriage provides the strongest foundation for the first line of support.[21,22]

A primary hierarchy of needs on the part of mothers is that of spousal support, followed by social support from family of origin and friendship or community.[23,24]

Couples who provide each other with strong emotional and cognitive support are strongly predictive of parental competence in healthy full-term and preterm babies.[25]

Mothers who received support from spouses and other social support networks before giving birth tended to be more sensitive to their infants.[26]

The primary sources of stress in many families include marital/parent-child relationships, employment/financial issues, time pressures, the lack of social networks, and stress from parents' own perceptions of what is culturally expected of them.[27,28]

21 Belsky, "The determinants of parenting: A process model," *Child Development*.

22 Cox et al., "The transition to parenthood: Marital conflict and withdrawal and parent-infant interactions," In *Conflict and Cohesion in Families: Causes and Consequences*.

23 Belsky, "The determinants of parenting: A process model," *Child Development*.

24 Cox et al., "The transition to parenthood: Marital conflict and withdrawal and parent-infant interactions," In *Conflict and Cohesion in Families: Causes and Consequences*.

25 Ibid.

26 Goldstein et al., "Maternal characteristics and social support across the transition to motherhood: association with maternal behavior," *Journal of Family Psychology*.

27 Belsky, "The determinants of parenting: A process model," *Child Development*.

28 Sidebotham and the Avon Longitudinal Study of Parents and Children (ALSPAC), "Culture, stress, and the parent-child relationship: A qualitative study of parents' perceptions," *Child: Care, Health and Development*.

Mothers reported lower stress levels when they had support from the baby's father.[29]

Most parents perceive parenting as very stressful, which is exacerbated by the fact that parents feel social and cultural pressures that do not support children and families.[30]

The biggest stress reported by single mothers is that of isolation.[31] A major risk factor for child maltreatment occurs when parent isolation is combined with the lack of social networks and poor psychological well-being of the parents.[32]

Parental psychological well-being is related to the parents' own developmental histories, their individual characteristics, and general psychological and mental health.[33]

Recommended Reading

And Baby Makes Three by John Gottman, PhD, and Julie Schwartz Gottman, PhD.

Everyday Blessings: The Inner Work of Mindful Parenting by Jon Kabat-Zinn PhD and Myla Kabat-Zinn.

Getting the Love You Want by Harville Hendrix, PhD. and Helen L. Hunt, PhD.

Life Lessons for Busy Moms: 7 Essential Ingredients to Organize and Balance Your World by Dorothy K. Breininger, Debby S. Bitticks, and Lynn Benson.

Nurturing Yourself and Others by Lee Schnelby.

---

29   Tarkka, "Predictors of maternal competence by first-time mothers when the child is 8 months old: Issues and innovations in nursing practice," *Journal of Advanced Nursing.*

30   Sidebotham and the Avon Longitudinal Study of Parents and Children (ALSPAC), "Culture, stress, and the parent-child relationship: A qualitative study of parents' perceptions," *Child: Care, Health and Development.*

31   Ibid.

32   Belsky, "The determinants of parenting: A process model," *Child Development.*

33   Ibid.

Raising an Emotionally Intelligent Child by John Gottman, PhD, and
   Joan DeClaire.
Shelter for the Spirit: Create Your Own Haven in a Hectic World by
   Victoria Moran.
*The Five Love Languages: How to Express Heartfelt Commitment to Your
   Mate* by Gary Chapman.
*The Hidden Feelings of Motherhood: Coping with Stress, Depression, and
   Burnout* by Kathleen Kendall-Tackett, PhD.
*The Mother's Guide to Self-Renewal: How to Reclaim, Rejuvenate and
   Re-Balance Your Life* by Renee Peterson Trudeau.
The Science of Parenting by Margot Sunderland.
The Unexpected Legacy of Divorce: A 25 Year Landmark Study by Judith
   Wallerstein, Julia Lewis, and Sandra Blakeslee.
Transition to Parenthood by Jay Belsky, PhD.
*Wherever You Go, There You Are: Mindfulness Meditation in Everyday
   Life* by Jon Kabat-Zinn.

Useful Web Sites

www.attachmentparenting.org: Web site of Attachment Parenting
International.

www.bbhonline.org: A program that prepares new parents, developed
from the research of John Gottman and Julie Schwartz Gottman.

www.gettingtheloveyouwant.com: The website of Imago Therapy.

www.gottman.com: The Gottman Institute, information for
researching and restoring couple relationships.

www.thewellorderedlife.com: Help with organizing your home and
your life to achieve balance.

Chapter Ten

Nurturing Children
for a Compassionate World

Nurturing Children for a Compassionate World

*There is a lot of talk about world peace—peace between
nations, peace between religions, peace among races.
There are many theories about why we don't have
peace and what we can do to bring it about. We blame
other countries. We blame the president. We blame
congressional leaders. We blame the news people. We
blame this political party or that.... We think that if we
could be more politically active or influential we could
help solve the world's problems ...*

*But let's take a look at our own family. How much peace
do we have in our own homes? Do we like our children?
Do we see our spouse as our equal friend and partner?
Do our children like us and feel good about being with
us? Do our children like each other? Where is the peace in
our own families? If we can't create peace in our families,
how can we create peace in the world? Peace in our
families* is *what creates peace in the world.*[1]

David and Lee Stewart
Cofounders
The InterNational Association of Parents and Professionals
for Safe Alternatives in Childbirth (NAPSAC)

This book has been written as a guidepost, not only for parents looking
for practical parenting advice, but also for anyone with a vision for
a more compassionate world. For some parents, the eight principles
of parenting are a comfortable affirmation of how they were raised
themselves and want to parent their own children. For others, it may
be a transformative new philosophy that connects on a deep spiritual
level. We have a vision for the world that is even broader than a mere
parenting program. We hope that this book will be used as a tool for
opening the doors of empowerment for parents, that they will see that
their role is the fundamental underpinning of civilization. As stated

---

1   Stewart and Stewart, "Childrearing, the roots of violence, and the principles of peace,"
     NAPSAC News.

below, the Dalai Lama has observed that the only hope for a peaceful society is learning how to access the wisdom of our hearts:

> The question of world peace, the question of family
> peace, the question of peace between husband
> and wife, or peace between parents and children,
> everything is dependent on that feeling of love and
> warm-heartedness.[2]

We know that for some parents becoming more conscious about their parenting choices brings up many challenges. Perhaps they were not raised in a very nurturing home and are conflicted about trying a different path with their own children. Most parents in the United States were raised in families that used some form of rewards and punishment. Behavior modification is still a common tool used by classroom teachers, and it will probably be many decades before we incorporate other classroom methodologies. Unfortunately, in many states in the United States, corporal punishment is still sanctioned in the schools as a legitimate way to punish even special needs children in the classroom. In the meantime, each family has the unique opportunity to change the paradigm in its own home. You may decide to make choices in raising your children that are different than the choices your own parents made, but it does not mean you are rejecting them personally. We all try to do the best we can with the knowledge we have at the time.

Most mothers and fathers improve in their parenting from the previous generation to some degree, and healthy families recognize and hope that this will happen. If grandparents put strict conditions on their love and support, that may be a red flag of deeper issues in the family that need to be addressed; it is not necessarily a reason to doubt that what your heart is telling you is best for you and your children.

---

2   http://quote.robertgenn.com/auth_search.php?name=dalai+lama

The pressures of being a parent are equal to any
pressure on earth. To be a conscious parent, and really
look to that little being's mental and physical health,
is a responsibility which most of us, including me,
avoid most of the time because it is too hard. [3]

John Lennon

The Joys of Attachment Parenting: Being in Attunement with Your Children

A common theme that we hear from many parents is the relief, joy, and peace that comes from parenting in a more empathic and positive way. Even in the most challenging circumstances, when you have the tools to step back from the situation, assess what the child is experiencing, and act with a foundation of empathy and trust, most crises can be avoided. We hope that after reading this book, you will feel you have the guidance you need to make more positive choices in parenting your children.

The confidence that comes from seeing these solutions actually work can be thrilling, especially if we started our parenting journey with very limited strategies. We like the metaphor of "tuning in" to our children. We know that when the radio is not quite

---

3   http://www.great-quotes.com/quotes/category/Children.htm

on the station, all we hear is static. Our home life can be like that sometimes—the children are whining or fighting, and we just can't seem to figure out what's wrong. Fine-tuning the dial to get a clear, beautiful song may look like this in the home: take some deep breaths; limit the distractions; turn off the TV, computer, or telephone; and really give focused attention to the children. Then when calm returns, our family is back in attunement.

Another benefit of AP, including the support many AP parents receive from parent groups and other networking channels, is empowerment. Most of us were raised to trust authority figures such as medical professionals, government leaders, and teachers without question. When we become parents, we have a responsibility to look objectively at all our decisions and advocate for our children, many times in the process learning how to advocate for ourselves. We know from personal experience that in the process of raising our own children, we learned how to take more responsibility for many lifestyle changes in our adult lives as well. It is almost impossible to practice AP without doing a tremendous amount of soul-searching. We can't expect our children to be healthy human beings, life-long learners, and caring adults if we don't set the example.

As we stated in the introduction of this book, real change in society only happens from the "bottom up"; that is to say that all of us are the critical component in this paradigm shift to a more compassionate world. When we see even our toddlers reaching out with love and care to their friends or family members, we are witnessing the seeds of change that will blossom in future generations.

The greatest joy comes from seeing our children grow up into compassionate adults. Just as they taught us all along our journey to learn, listen, and trust, we continue to learn from them as we watch them interact with their friends, teachers, and co-workers. It would be an interesting study to follow adult children of AP families! From our experience, we know so many of these young adults are very confident to make choices based not on fear or distrust but on consideration of the facts and an empathic viewpoint. An example of this comes from a parent whose daughter was volunteering with her church in an orphanage in Russia. She knew that the care providers were overworked, but what the children needed were hugs and touch. Even though she was a teenager, she was able to set an example of loving care for the children and encouraged the workers to use infant slings rather than leave the babies alone in their cribs.

Many of us have great hope when we see our grown children taking an interest in their communities, either through volunteering in their church, making more conscious choices like recycling in their homes, or getting involved in mentoring programs or political action groups. And of course the greatest joy is seeing how they interact with children, becoming empathic parents themselves! This ripple effect will have a profound effect on entire communities and ultimately society as a whole. When we look at the challenges different nations of the world face in establishing a more democratic way of government, we can reflect on the words of Australian psychotherapist and author Robin Grille, who has written eloquently on the subject of what makes a democracy possible:

> The temperament and maturity required to be one's
> own authority, to feel the equal of all others, to be
> a responsible and active participator in public life
> and decisions, the inner strength to refuse tyranny
> or autocracy; all these qualities are second nature
> to those in whom they have been fostered from
> youth.... Individuals who have never been exposed
> to democratic notions of personal responsibility and
> egalitarianism in their upbringing cannot be expected
> to automatically immerse themselves in democratic
> living as soon as democracy is foisted upon them.
> Time and again, history teaches us that the first
> lessons in democracy must be delivered, through
> example, in the family home.[4]

In countless ways, we teach our children the values of liberty and freedom. From the first time we offer our baby solid food and trust his ability to let us know he's ready, to the most mundane choices like giving him an option in what outfit to wear to school, we are planting the seeds

---

4   Grille, "Democracy begins at home," *Empathic Parenting: Journal of the Canadian Society for the Prevention of Cruelty to Children.*

of social equality. When we give our children the opportunity to help with tasks around the house, when we include them in discussions about every day family decisions, they learn that as a family we must all help each other. When we model involved citizenship, community service, and ethical principles, our children learn our values by witnessing the best tool we have available: our example.

Challenges Parents Face

> A perfect parent is a person with excellent child-rearing theories and no actual children.
>
> Comedian Dave Barry[5]

Throughout this book, we have discussed the importance for new mothers and fathers to go into parenting with a fierce determination to meet the needs of their babies. We hope that this book has given you the confidence, information, and resources you need to begin your parenting journey. However, we also know from years of talking with and counseling parents that many challenges occur along the way. Being aware and giving this some consideration may diffuse some of these concerns and give you the assurance that these are common problems that most parents experience. None is insurmountable, and we all have the capabilities to overcome whatever curves life may bring us.

Over twenty years ago, Ashley Montagu observed that forces seemed to be conspiring to deprive parents and babies of their rights to basic human connection. Here's an example from, *Touching*:

> All through pregnancy, the mother has been elaborately prepared to minister to the dependent needs of her child.... an indispensability that ... is generally not understood by the very persons who have been elected the experts or authorities ... It is as if there was a conspiracy against both mother and child to deprive them of their ... constitutional rights to human development.[6]

---

5   http://parent-wise.org/parent/time/quotes.htm.

6   Montagu, *Touching*, 88–89.

Whether we think of these issues as a conspiracy, or merely a challenge that any conscious parent can overcome, let us always remember to look at our choices through the eyes of our babies and children, and do our best to advocate for healthy attachment. The following section provides some examples to heighten our awareness and propose some solutions.

Receiving Criticism for Parenting Choices

Attachment parenting practices are sometimes seen as a "new style of parenting," even though the basic principles of natural childbirth and breastfeeding, responsiveness, and respectful discipline have been practiced around the world since recorded history! We hear stories from some grandparents who are pleased to see parents who are going back to the "old ways" of keeping babies close and finding more natural solutions to common problems. However, parents may find that they receive criticism for practices that are unfamiliar in their own families or communities.

Mothers can be particularly vulnerable to criticism right after giving birth or adopting a newborn and adjusting to motherhood for the first time. This is where their husband or partner can be particularly indispensable in protecting the mother-baby dyad. When grandmother wants to come in and take over with the newborn for instance, Dad can gently suggest she help him with the cooking and cleaning so Mom and baby can nap together. Holidays can sometimes be a challenge when going to homes of relatives who might not approve of breastfeeding or the baby sleeping in close proximity to the parents. It's good to think ahead and rehearse some clever "comebacks." Some parents bring books with them that explain their choices in medical terms. Often, if the grandparents or other relatives know that the pediatrician recommends and encourages these methods, they are relieved and supportive.

A sense of humor is always a great way to deal with criticism, too. One family shared that if they handled any concerns with a funny anecdote, it seemed to break the ice and defuse any stress they might be feeling from relatives or friends. When a mother of a six-month-old was asked how long she was going to nurse, she laughingly said, "Oh,

I'm thinking about all the money we'll save if I keep it up until he goes to college!" Or when asked if their baby would be "too attached" or developmentally delayed from being carried in a sling, a dad replied, "I figure once he goes to kindergarten, he'll just have to learn to walk on his own!"

Your greatest advertisement for attachment parenting will be your healthy, happy babies and children. Over and over again, we have seen criticism dissolve when families and friends see the joyful, caring children that are a product of such loving care. It is very gratifying when we hear the grandparents brag to their friends about their loving grandchildren!

"Although our intellect-driven society leads us to believe the opposite, the intellect exists to serve the wisdom of the heart—not vice versa. All the drugs and technology in the world can't mend a broken heart or heal someone whose heart is no longer in the game of life. The EKG signal coming from the heart is 60 times stronger than the EEG signal from brain waves. So when there's a conflict between the intellect and the heart, the heart always wins. And the only way to heal the true discomforts of the heart is to feel them fully, have faith in a power greater than yourself, and then live your life robustly."[7]

Christiane Northrup, MD

---

7 www.drnorthrup.com/womenshealth/healthcenter/topic_details.php?topic_id=97

Handling Unwanted Advice

"Help! I'm getting so frustrated with the endless stream of advice I get from my mother-in-law and brother! No matter what I do, I'm doing it wrong. I love them both, but how do I get them to stop dispensing all this unwanted advice?" Just as your baby is an important part of your life, he is also important to others. People who care about your baby are bonded to you and your child in a special way that invites their counsel. Knowing this may give you a reason to handle the interference gently, in a way that leaves everyone's feelings intact.

Regardless of the advice, it is your baby, and, in the end, you will raise your child the way that you think best. So it's rarely worth creating a war over a well-meaning person's comments. You can respond to unwanted advice in a variety of ways:

Listen first: It's natural to be defensive if you feel that someone is judging you, but chances are you are not being criticized; rather, the other person is sharing what they feel to be valuable insight. Try to listen—you may just learn something valuable.

Disregard: If you know that there is no convincing the other person to change her mind, simply smile, nod, and make a noncommittal response, such as, "Interesting!" Then go about your own business … your way.

Agree: You might find one part of the advice that you agree with. If you can, provide wholehearted agreement on that topic.

Pick your battles: If your mother-in-law insists that Baby wear a hat on your walk to the park, go ahead and pop one on his head. This won't have any long-term effects except that of placating her. However, don't capitulate on issues that are important to you or the health or well-being of your child.

Steer clear of the topic: If your brother is pressuring you to let your baby cry to sleep, but you would never do that, then don't complain to him about your baby getting you up five times the night before. If he brings up the topic, then distraction is definitely in order, such as, "Would you like a cup of coffee?"

Educate yourself: Knowledge is power; protect yourself and your sanity by reading up on your parenting choices. Rely on the confidence that you are doing your best for your baby.

Educate the other person: If your "teacher" is imparting information that you know to be outdated or wrong, share what you've learned on the topic. You may be able to open the other person's mind. Refer to a study, book, or report that you have read. Quote a doctor: Many people accept a point of view if a professional has validated it. If your own pediatrician agrees with your position, say, "My doctor said to wait until she's at least six months before starting solids." If your own doctor doesn't back your view on that issue, then refer to another doctor—perhaps the author of a baby care book.

Be vague: You can avoid confrontation with an elusive response. For example, if your sister asks if you've started potty training yet (but you are many months away from even starting the process), you can answer with, "We're moving in that direction."

Ask for advice: Your friendly counselor is possibly an expert on a few issues that you can agree on. Search out these points and invite guidance. She'll be happy that she is helping you, and you'll be happy you have a way to avoid a showdown about topics that you don't agree on.

Memorize a standard response: Here's a comment that can be said in response to almost any piece of advice: "This may not be the right way for you, but it's the right way for me."

Be honest: Try being honest about your feelings. Pick a time free of distractions and choose your words carefully, such as, "I know how much you love Harry, and I'm glad you spend so much time with him. I know you think you're helping me when you give me advice about this, but I'm comfortable with my own approach, and I'd really appreciate if you'd understand that."

Find a mediator: If the situation is putting a strain on your relationship with the advice-giver, you may want to ask another person to step in for you.

Search out like-minded friends: Join a support group or online club with people who share your parenting philosophies. Talking with others who are raising their babies in a way that is similar to your own can give you the strength to face people who don't understand your viewpoints.[8]

Elizabeth Pantley
Gentle Baby Care

The Challenge of Consumerism

Our culture of consumerism is another enormous challenge parents face when trying to raise their children with the values of empathy and compassion. Young families are bombarded with an overwhelming array of choices—the latest cribs, strollers, swings, clothes, toys, videos, and music. Many are convinced that these are all must-haves to raise a happy, smart, and healthy child. Our media's focus on celebrity, wealth, sensational crimes, and other extreme behavior enters our homes via television, newspapers, magazines, and the Internet every day. As soon as a baby is old enough to understand language, products are being directly marketed to this age group, with child psychologists acting as consultants! As stated in chapter 9, it is all about balance. Some of the products advertised can be of help to an overwhelmed mom who may need to occasionally put the baby in a swing while she's cooking or attending to other children. Educational videos or beautiful music

---

8   Pantley, *Gentle Baby Care*, 514–519.

can of course enhance family life in ways our grandparents could have never imagined. AP parents learn to ask themselves whether or not a "convenient" device will further separate them from a strong connection with their baby or enhance their relationship with their child. We must realize that whatever our children view on the Internet or TV is like inviting a guest into your home—they look to us to protect them from inappropriate products and developmentally unsuitable programs.

The National Institute on Media and the Family reports that many children are spending most of their waking hours in front of an "ever expanding number of screens."[9] For too many children, screen time has replaced time with parents or caregivers engaging in more nurturing or educational activities like reading, imaginative play, and storytelling. Thirty-nine percent of children aged two to three have televisions in their bedrooms!

Twelve Tips to Tame the Tube

Here are ideas to give *you* control over television.[10]

1. **Avoid using TV as a babysitter.** Think of how careful you are about choosing a babysitter and daycare. Try to be just as careful about what your children watch on TV every day.

2. **Know what your kids are watching.** It is important to be aware of program content as well as the content of the daily news. The younger the child, the more impressionable he or she is, and the less experienced in evaluating content against the values of family and community. Additionally, emotional images may intrude upon and interrupt sleep.

3. **Keep TV out of kids' bedrooms.** It is difficult to

---

9   National Institute on Media and the Family, "Families become MediaWise," National Institute on Media and the Family Web site.

10   Ibid., "Tip sheet: Twelve tips to tame the tube."

monitor what your children are watching when they are watching TV in their own room. Having a TV in a child's room discourages participation in family activities and encourages him to watch TV when he could be studying, reading, or sleeping.

4. **Set some guidelines about when and what children watch.** This can be done in conversation with your children, but the final call belongs to the adults. The clearer the rules (e.g., no TV before school, or until homework is completed), the better. Setting new limits may be upsetting to your children at first, but consistency is very important.

5. **Practice "appointment" TV. Decide in advance what's good and watch it as a family.** Go through the TV guide in the paper on Sunday, and make family decisions on shows to watch for the week. Discuss reasons for the decisions with your children. If in doubt, get more information. In choosing TV shows or videos, make use of independent evaluations, such as KidScore, TV and movie guides, and articles in magazines. Discuss issues and ideas with other adults, friends, and parents of your children's playmates.

6. **Talk to your child about what he or she is watching.** Discuss what you are watching and ask specific questions. Ask what they see, as it may be very different from what you see. Ask them to tell you what things mean to them. Ask them why they watch specific shows, what characters they like and don't like. Discuss the commercials and their perception of toys, cereals, etc. and the people who sell them.

7. **Turn the TV off during meals.** Catch up with one another. Focus on each other. Share stories and activities from each family member's day.

8. **Use the VCR or DVD player to your advantage.** Record a good show and schedule a special family viewing—complete with popcorn. If a show is on at an inconvenient time such as mealtime, homework time, or family time, record it to watch later.

9. **Put the family on a TV diet.** Schedule some fun alternative activities. When you do watch television, watch it with your children.

10. **Create a TV coupon system.** Kids get coupons and turn them in when they watch a program. Unused coupons can be "cashed in" for a special family activity.

11. **Don't make the television the focal point of the room.** Make your children the focus of your attention, not the TV. Research shows that people watch less TV if it is not in the most prominent location in the room.

12. **Patronize good programs and demand more of them.** Express your opinions to TV and radio stations, network executives, and advertisers. Tell them not only what you do not like but also what you like. Addresses for networks and local stations are in your TV guide. Also, remember that your money has a voice of its own.

The Canadian Society for the Prevention of Cruelty to Children (CSPCC) has been on the forefront of this issue for decades. Their journal, *Empathic Parenting,* can be accessed on their Web site (www. empathicparenting.org), with well-researched and documented articles on the challenges parents face from a corporate culture of mass advertising to children. Dr. Elliott Barker, the founder of the CSPCC, writes:

> That happiness is to be attained through limitless
> material acquisition is denied by every religion and
> philosophy known to man but is preached incessantly
> by every American television set. Market-driven
> forces have usurped the role once assumed by family,
> home, and community. Few societies could imagine
> themselves surviving very long when one of their
> central institutions was advocating unrestrained
> greed.[11]

Children are also a captive audience at many public schools. Some school systems partner with commercial companies who give them revenue in exchange for closed circuit TV news and educational programs and (more importantly to them) the advertising of products directly to this vulnerable population. Can we swim against this tidal wave of consumer goods and protect our children from society's onslaught of materialism and unhealthy values? Parents and schools need to be vigilant about exposing their children to such blatant commercialism and create an environment conducive to learning—not only academic subjects, but more importantly, the values of living in a humane and compassionate society.

The good news is that many parents are actively seeking alternatives to such strongly negative cultural influences. When families experience the simple joys of just spending more time together, turning off the TV, reading, walking, and eating meals together, they can recapture the connection that so often becomes lost in their busy lives. These simple ideas don't cost any money either! The beauty of attachment parenting is that it encourages us to look at the most basic values in life—love, connection, and simple living.

---

11   Canadian Society for the Prevention of Cruelty to Children, "Consumerism—The world's fastest growing religion: Corporations vs. parents," CSPCC Web site.

Children and Advertising
Did you know?[12]

- The average American child may view as many as 40,000 television commercials every year.
- Children as young as age three recognize brand logos with brand loyalty influence starting at age two.
- Young children are not able to distinguish between commercials and TV programs. They do not recognize that commercials are trying to sell something.
- In 2001, teenagers, ages twelve to nineteen, spent $172 billion (an average of $104 per teen each week), up eleven percent from $155 billion in 2000.
- In 2002, children ages four to twelve [were] expected to spend an estimated $40 billion.
- In 2000, children 12 years and under, directly and indirectly, influenced the household spending of over $600 billion.
- In 1997, $1.3 billion was spent on television advertisements directed at children. Counting all media, advertising and marketing budgets aimed at children approached $12 billion.
- Children who watch a lot of television want more toys seen in advertisements and eat more advertised food than children who do not watch as much television.
- The market sales of licensed products for infants increased thirty-two percent to a record $2.5 billion in 1996.
- Thirty seconds of advertising during the [2002] Super Bowl cost $2.4 million.
- Four hours of television programming contain about 100 ads.

---

12   National Institute on Media and the Family, "Fact sheet: Children and advertising," National Institute on Media and the Family Web site.

Medical and Professional Advice

And now we come to the greatest challenge of all for many parents—to whom do we listen in the medical and professional world? This can be overwhelmingly difficult for new parents—as soon as they find out they're pregnant or wanting to adopt, they are immediately faced with so many critical decisions. If you take only one important lesson from this book, we sincerely hope it will be that you have the power, as your child's greatest advocate, to make your own choices, based on what is best for your family.

A Mother's Story of Empowerment

I am not always graceful when it comes to defending myself against criticism. The toughest situations for me are when I encounter a medical professional who is giving out perhaps well-intentioned but biased, non-AP advice. I find it frustrating when I know more than my child's health-care provider about the science behind AP, or when the doctor or nurse is too conservative or traditional to see that there are other parenting styles than those promoted in the mainstream.

Once when I was at my oldest daughter's one-year checkup at a local clinic, I encountered a doctor who advised me to start disciplining my child. As a preemie, she was only nine months developmentally and couldn't even walk. That seemed a little young to me to begin disciplining. Then the doctor informed me that he expected me to spank her so that she would learn "no." I debated this issue with him for several minutes, but after he made it clear that he wasn't going to change his mind, I decided to switch to another medical clinic in search of a doctor who would allow me, as the parent, to make my own decisions and who would be more open to AP.

I think the key to being able to thwart criticism is being confident in my parenting decisions, which comes from experience, taking the time to do a little reading on the research behind AP, and having at least one person among my family and close friends who supports AP. I also rely heavily on API.

AP parents can also empower themselves by deciding to educate their critics instead of staying silent when someone gives them unwanted advice contradicting their parenting choices. I try to educate my critics when I can, but if my words fall on deaf ears, it's okay. I know that AP is working for me and my family, and that's all that matters.

Rita B.

Doctors and other medical professionals are only human—they base their advice on not only what they learned in medical school but also, in the parenting arena, often on what they have experienced in their own homes. Remember that doctors' experience and council varies widely from one to the next, depending on their training and their ability to read and digest mountains of the latest research and methodologies. Many patients have educated their doctors in the areas of healing and childrearing! Your job as the consumer is to ask a lot of questions—do your homework by not only reading and researching but also by talking to trusted friends, relatives, and parents. Ultimately, you should listen to your own common sense and decide what seems to be a good fit for you and your family. Networking can be your greatest tool and asset when looking to find a professional in your area. One of the reasons that we founded API (maybe the most important reason!) was to give parents a way to support each other in their parenting and to create a networking opportunity for finding all kinds of resources in the community. API groups often invite speakers to give talks on a variety of subjects—from birth options, to educational options, to medical professional choices in the community.

A Legacy of Love

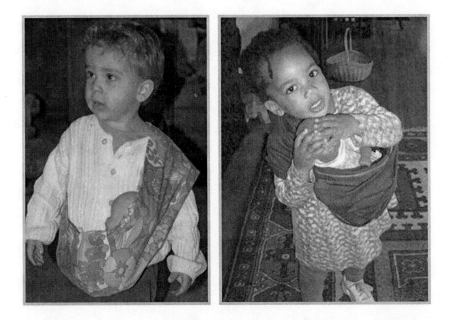

Our children are living examples of what it means to fully embrace life with joy, passion, and enthusiasm by living in the moment and finding wonder in everything. The love, empathy, and affection our children learn from us and others in their lives will carry on into their adult relationships and with their children. Our children can be *our* greatest teachers in life if we allow it—they will challenge us to grow in ways we never believed possible, and, as a result, we will become better human beings and parents.

If we can truly be "the change we wish to see in the world," then we can provide a home rich with love, safety, protection, imagination, and joy. When children are carefully and consciously raised with empathy, they will naturally be more compassionate toward others.

Our children don't care if we have money, position, fame, or beauty. To them, we are the universe, and all they ask of us is our love, our time, and our nurturance. In return, they give us their unconditional love and joy, and the promise of a lifetime of connection.

If we truly want peace in the world, let us begin by loving one another in our own families.

Mother Teresa[13]

Afterword

We have touched on so many issues in this book, and each of the eight principles deserves a volume of its own to give it the depth of coverage it deserves. Perhaps after reading this overview of the principles, you will find that one chapter is a particular "hot button" or one that you would like to research further. The API Web site has many resources, including forums and blogs where parents and professionals communicate, new books are discussed, and support groups blossom in communities all over the world. We sincerely hope that some of these resources will be of great help to you and your family.

---

13   http://parent-wise.org/parent/time/quotes.htm.

Appendix to Chapter Ten: Additional Research and Resource Recommendations

Additional Facts and Research
Intergenerational Transmission of Positive Parenting

Researchers from the University of Pennsylvania and the University of Otago and Canterbury University in New Zealand used a sample of more than 1,000 New Zealanders born in the early 1970s. The researchers focused on the 228 participants who had become parents of young children to try and tease out the intergenerational transmission of positive parenting. Information on how the parents were themselves reared when they were between the ages of three and fifteen had been obtained from repeated interviews with their mothers when they were growing up. Researchers visited the homes of the now-grown children and videotaped them interacting with their children in a variety of situations when the child was three to five years old. Their findings concluded that "if a mother was raised in a positive, nurturing environment, she was more likely to engage in a warm, sensitive, stimulating parenting style herself when raising the next generation."[14]

Recommended Reading

A Quiet Place by Peggy O'Mara.
Children, Adolescents, and the Media by Victor Strasburger and
    Barbara Wilson.
Gentle Baby Care by Elizabeth Pantley.
Parenting for a Peaceful World by Robin Grille.
*What Kids Really Want That Money Can't Buy: Tips for Parenting in a
    Commercial World* by Betsy Taylor.

---

14   Belsky et al., "Intergenerational transmission of warm-sensitive-stimulating parenting:
     A prospective study of mothers and fathers of 3-year-olds," *Child Development.*

Useful Web Sites

www.attachmentparenting.org/blog: Attachment Parenting International blogs and forums for parents.

www.childfriendly.com: CFI is a grassroots, non-profit organization dedicated to improving the lives of children. CFI members are working to transform their neighborhoods and communities into places that honor and respect children and support families.

www.empathicparenting.org: Web site of the Canadian Society for the Prevention of Cruelty to Children (CSPCC).

www.mediafamily.org: Web site of the National Institute on Media and the Family (phone 612-672-5437). Information for parents and other caregivers, organizations, and corporations to create better-quality media choices for families, so that we have healthier, less violent communities.

www.motherhoodproject.org: An mothers' movement that seeks to help mothers find balance between the values of the "money world" and the values of nurturing human beings and building healthy, caring relationships.

www.mothering.com: A magazine dedicated to natural living and conscious parenting.

www.newdream.org: Web site of the Center for a New American Dream. Includes information on parenting in a commercial culture.

www.pantley.com/elizabeth: Elizabeth Pantley's Web site.

parentingcourse.net: The online questionnaire provided by the CSPCC for new or prospective parents.

About the Authors

Barbara Nicholson received a master's degree in education from Stephen F. Austin State University and a bachelor's in education from North Texas State University, with Learning Disabilities certification from Texas Woman's University. Professionally she taught children with learning disabilities and has been a La Leche League International support group facilitator for over twenty-five years, educating and helping mothers with breastfeeding. In 1994, Barbara cofounded Attachment Parenting International (API), a nonprofit parent education organization, where she served as president of the board of directors for fifteen years. As API cofounder, she has given talks and conducted parenting workshops all over the country and internationally on attachment parenting issues. She is the mother of four grown sons and lives with her husband in Nashville, Tennessee.

Lysa Parker received her bachelor's in education and her master's degree in human development and family studies from the University of Alabama. She earned her designation of Certified Family Life Educator (CFLE) from the National Council on Family Relations in 2004. As cofounder of Attachment Parenting International (API), she served as the executive director for thirteen years, focusing on program development, public relations, and fundraising. Prior to her involvement with API, she worked as a special education teacher helping children with multiple handicaps and learning difficulties. She is the mother of two grown sons, a stepdaughter and is the grandmother of twin grandsons. Currently Lysa is a writer, speaker and parenting consultant in private practice at www.parentslifeline.com.

Attachment Parenting International (API) is a 501(c)3 nonprofit grassroots organization that offers parents and professionals education about attachment parenting and support through local support groups with trained facilitators, publications, research information, E-newsletters, Web site information, and online forums. API also functions as a clearinghouse of information on all aspects of child and family-related topics and engages in advocacy work on behalf of children and parents.

The mission of API is to support all parents in raising secure, joyful, and empathic children in order to strengthen families and create a more compassionate world. Through education, support, advocacy, and research, our principal goal is to heighten global awareness of the profound significance of secure attachment—not only to invest in our children's bright futures but also to reduce and ultimately prevent emotional and physical mistreatment of children, addiction, crime, behavioral disorders, mental illness, and other outcomes of early unhealthy attachment.

Appendix A. Myths and Facts about Attachment Parenting

Myth: Attachment parenting (AP) means never putting your child down, right?

Reality: Attachment parenting encourages the use of slings or soft carriers that give a child access to the movement and closeness of the parent's body. Advocates do not suggest that an infant should never be put down. AP is about being responsive to a child's needs for closeness, not about thwarting their natural drive toward independence. Children need a firm foundation of closeness before authentic, age-appropriate independence can occur.

Myth: Is there a problem in using baby gadgets (plastic carriers, swings, playpens, etc.)?

Reality: Babies are born with a biological need for human closeness and interaction. The more parents rely on things like swings and infant seats, the less time they spend actually holding and interacting with the baby. Gadgets can be helpful when used sparingly, but the key is to avoid overusing them when a baby really wants you.

Myth: My child will be spoiled if I always respond to his cries and hold him a lot.

Reality: Responding to a baby's cries and holding him will not spoil him. A quick, appropriate response tells the child that the parent takes his needs seriously and will help him manage his distress. Responding to a child's cries lays a critical foundation of trust and communication.

Myth: If a child sleeps in our bed, she will never leave.

Reality: The experience of many cosleeping parents has not proven this to be true. Depending on the child's temperament, most children naturally leave the parents' bed around two or three years of age. You can adapt to the changing sleep needs of family members in many ways. Some families place an infant in a cosleeping device attached to the side of the bed or have a toddler in a crib nearby in the same room. The key is being responsive to a child's need for a parent's presence and not rushing him or her into self-reliance too soon.

Myth: Bedsharing is more dangerous than sleeping in a crib.

Reality: Bedsharing has not proven to be any more dangerous to infants than sleeping alone in a crib. If parents follow specific safety guidelines, cosleeping and bedsharing can be safe and beneficial for both infant and parent. Parents should never cosleep or bedshare with their infants if they smoke, drink, or take drugs (even prescription medications that may cause drowsiness), become overly fatigued, or use a waterbed, very soft mattress, or a lot of fluffy bedding. For more information about safe cosleeping go to www.attachmentparenting.org/safeinfantsleep/campaign.php

Myth: Attachment parenting means nursing indefinitely.

Reality: AP advocates believe that when to wean is a personal decision and cooperative process between each mother and baby. Extended breastfeeding has many documented benefits, and current recommendations in the United States by the American Academy of Pediatrics are generally to breastfeed for the first twelve months and as long as is mutually desirable after that.

Myth: If you work outside of the home, you can't adopt this style of parenting.

Reality: Working parents can certainly adopt this approach to parenting. Attachment parenting principles suggest limiting the frequency and length of separations if possible when Baby is very young in order to maintain a healthy bond. Mothers can continue to breastfeed with the help of a part-time or flexible schedule and a breast pump. Both parents can still wear the baby in a soft carrier around the house and sleep near or with the baby at night. In fact, many working parents find attachment parenting an excellent way to create and maintain connections with the baby in spite of the daytime separation.

When you choose a caregiver for your baby, make sure to find a person or program that supports your philosophy. It's also important to pay attention to the rate of caregiver turnover. Frequent changes in caregivers (also known as "caregiver roulette") can cause the child to experience a continuous cycle of bonding and grieving.

Appendix B. Questions for Parental Self-Reflection[15]

1. What was it like growing up? Who was in your family?

2. How did you get along with your parents early in your childhood? How did the relationship evolve throughout your youth and up until the present time?

3. How did your relationship with your mother and father differ, and how were they similar? Are there ways in which you try to be like, or try not to be like, each of your parents?

4. Did you ever feel rejected or threatened by your parents? Were there other experiences you had that felt overwhelming or traumatizing in your life, during childhood or beyond? Do any of these experiences still feel very much alive? Do they continue to influence your life?

5. How did your parents discipline you as a child? What impact did that have on your childhood, and how do you feel it affects your role as a parent now?

6. Do you recall your earliest separations from your parents? What was it like? Did you ever have prolonged separations from your parents?

7. Did anyone significant in your life die during your childhood or later in your life? What was that like for you at the time, and how does that loss affect you now?

8. How did your parents communicate with you when you

---

15 Siegel and Hartzell, *Parenting from the Inside Out,* 113. "Questions for Parental Self-Reflection," from *Parenting from the Inside Out* by Daniel J. Siegel and Mary Hartzell, copyright © 2003 by Daniel J. Siegel and Mary Hartzell. Used by permission of Jeremy P. Tarcher, an imprint of Penguin Group (USA) Inc.

were happy and excited? Did they join with you in your enthusiasm? When you were distressed or unhappy as a child, what would happen? Did your father and mother respond differently to you during these emotional times? How?

9. Was there anyone else besides your parents in your childhood who took care of you? What was that relationship like for you? What happened to those individuals? What is it like for you when you let others take care of your child now?

10. If you had difficult times during your childhood, were there positive relationships in or outside of your home that you could depend on during those times? How do you feel those connections benefited you then, and how might they help you now?

11. How have your childhood experiences influenced your relationships with others as an adult? Do you find yourself trying not to behave in certain ways because of what happened to you as a child? Do you have patterns of behavior that you'd like to alter but have difficulty changing?

12. What impact do you think your childhood has had on your adult life in general, including the ways in which you think of yourself and the ways you relate to your children? What would you like to change about the way you understand yourself and relate to others?

Photo credits

Cover photo & Author photos: photo credit- Michael Gomez, www.gomezphotography.com

A special thank you to our beautiful cover family, Elizabeth Paris and Jay Barnet and their children, Zachary and Elysha Barnet

Chapter 1	Page	Photo credit
Title page	7	Michael Gomez
	23	Government photo-public domain
	25	Better Homes and Gardens-Used with permission from Meredith Corporation, Barb Lattin
Chapter 2		
Title page	33	Amy Gates
	38	Erin McSparron
	53	Dan Gray
	58	Michael Gomez
Chapter 3		
Title page	67, 69, 81, 83	Barb Lattin
Chapter 4		
Title page	93	Sumayyah Simone Photography of Central New Jersey; www.soomaya.com)
	98	Erin McSparron
	110	Amy Gates
	112	Rae Dyer

Bibliography

"Abuse." Dictionary.com. *Dictionary.com Unabridged (v 1.1).* Random House, Inc. http://dictionary.reference.com/browse/abuse (accessed: September 11, 2008).

Ainsworth, Mary D. Salter, Blehar, Mary C., Waters, Everett, and Wall, Sally. *Patterns of Attachment: A Psychological Study of the Strange Situation.* New York: Lawrence Erlbaum Associates. 1978.

Ainsworth, Mary D. Salter, and Silvia Bell. "Some contemporary patterns of mother-infant attachment interaction in the feeding situation." In *Stimulation in Early Infancy.* London, England: Academic Press, 1969.

Albers, Esther M., J. Marianne Riksen-Walsrven, Fred C. G. J. Sweep, and Carolina de Weerth. 2008. "Maternal behavior predicts infant cortisol recovery from a mild everyday stressor." *Journal of Child Psychology and Psychiatry* 49(1): 97–103.

Alho, Olli-Pekka, M. Koivu, M. Sorri, and P. Rantakallio. 1990. "Risk factors for recurrent acute otitis media and respiratory infection in infancy." *International Journal of Pediatric Otorhinolaryngology* 19: 151–161.

Amato, Paul R., and Sandra J. Rezac. 1994. "Contact with non-residential parents, interparental conflict, and children's behavior." *Journal of Family Issues* 15(2): 191–207.

American Academy of Pediatrics. 1998. "Guidance for effective discipline." *Pediatrics* 101: 723–728.

American Academy of Pediatrics Task Force on Circumcision. 1999. "Circumcision policy statement." *Pediatrics* 103(3): 686–693.

American Academy of Pediatrics Task Force on Sudden Infant Death Syndrome. 2005. "The changing concept of sudden infant death syndrome: Diagnostic coding shifts, controversies regarding the sleeping environment, and new variables to consider in reducing risk." *Pediatrics* 116(5): 1245–1255.

Anisfeld, Elizabeth, Virginia Casper, Molly Nozyce, and Nicholas Cunningham. 1990. "Does infant carrying promote attachment? An experimental study of the effects of increased physical contact on the development of attachment." *Child Development* 61(5): 1617–1627.

Arms, Suzanne. *Immaculate Deception*. Berkeley, CA: Celestial Arts, 1996.

Armour, Stephanie. "Day care's new frontier: Your baby at your desk." *USA Today* Web site. http://www.usatoday.com/money/workplace/2008-03-30-babies-at-work_N.htm (accessed May 12, 2008).

Arora, S., C. McJunkin, J. Wehrer, and P. Kuhn. 2000. "Major factors influencing breastfeeding rates: Mother's perception of father's attitude and milk supply." *Pediatrics* 106: e67.

Artz, Julie. 2007/2008. "Adopting a high-risk child." *Attachment Parenting: The Journal of API* 10(5): 3.

Associated Press. "Study: Child aggression linked to hours in daycare." CNN Web site. http://archives.cnn.com/2001/fyi/teachers.ednews/04/19/daycare.aggresssion.ap/index. html (accessed June 20, 2008).

Barone, Miranda. 2001. "Mother-infant sleep behaviors in solitary and bedsharing conditions." PhD Thesis. Claremont Graduate University. *Dissertation Abstracts International*.

———. 2002. "Sleeping like a baby: How bedsharing soothes infants." *Mothering* 114: 70–75.

Baumrind, Diana. 1991. "The influence of parenting style on adolescent competence and substance use." *The Journal of Early Adolescence* 11(1): 56–95.

———. 1978. "Parental disciplinary patterns and social competence in children." *Youth and Society* 9: 239–276.

Bavolek, Stephen J., and R. G. Keene. *Adult-Adolescent Parenting Inventory AAPI-2: Administration and development handbook*. Asheville, NC: Family Development, 2001.

———, Donald F. Kline, and John A. McLaughlin. 1979. "Primary prevention of child abuse: Identification of high risk adolescents." *Child Abuse and Neglect: The International Journal* 3/4: 1071–1080.

Begley, Sharon. "The nature of nurturing." *Newsweek*. March 27, 2000.

Belsky, Jay. 1984. "The determinants of parenting: A process model." *Child Development* 55: 83–96.

———. 1999. "Quantity of nonmaternal care and boys' problem behavior/adjustment at ages 3 and 5: Exploring the mediating role of parenting." *Psychiatry: Interpersonal and Biological Processes* 62: 1–3.

———. *The Transition to Parenthood.* New York, NY: Dell Books, 1994.

———, and Michael J. Rovine. 1988. "Non-maternal care in the first year of life and the security of infant attachment." *Child Development* 59(1): 157-167.

———, Judith Sligo, Sara R. Jaffee, Lianne Woodward, and Phil A. Silva. 2005. "Intergenerational transmission of warm-sensitive-stimulating parenting: A prospective study of mothers and fathers of 3-year-olds." *Child Development* 76(2): 384–396.

Blair, Peter S., Peter J. Fleming, Ian J. Smith, Martin W. Platt, Jeanine Young, Pam Nadin, P. J. Berry, and Jean Golding. 1999. "Babies sleeping with parents: Case-control study of factors influencing the risk of the sudden infant death syndrome." *British Medical Journal* 319(7223): 1457–1462.

Bond, James T., Ellen Galinsky, and E. Jeffrey Hill. *When Work Works: A Summary of Families and Work Institute Research Findings.* New York, NY: The Families and Work Institute, 2004. Available at http://familiesandwork.org/3w/research/downloads/3wes.pdf.

Brazelton, T. Berry, and Bertrand G. Cramer. *Earliest Relationship: Parents, Infants, and the Drama of Early Attachment.* Reading, MA: Addison-Wesley, 1990.

———, and Stanley I. Greenspan. *The Irreducible Needs of Children.* Cambridge, MA: Perseus Publishing, 2000.

Bretherton, Inge. 1992. "The origins of attachment theory: John Bowlby and Mary Ainsworth." *Developmental Psychology* 28(5): 759–775.

Bringing Baby Home. "Research evaluation of the Bringing Baby Home program." Bringing Baby Home Web site. http://www.bbhonline.org/research.aspx (accessed February 17, 2008).

Canadian Society for the Prevention of Cruelty to Children. "Consumerism—The world's fastest growing religion: Corporations vs. parents." CSPCC Web site. http://www.empathic parenting.org/religion/The%20Fastest%20

Growing%20Religion.htm#_Toc462053142 (accessed May 15, 2008).

Caplan, Mariana. *To Touch Is to Live*. Prescott, AZ: Hohm Press, 2002.

Mondloch, Catherine J., T. L. Lewis, D. R. Budreau, D. Maurer, J. L. Dannemiller, B. R. Stephens, and K. A. Kleiner-Gathercoal. 1999. "Face perception during early infancy." *Psychological Science* 10(5): 419–422.

Center for Nonviolent Communication. "Nonviolent communication is …" The Center for Nonviolent Communication Web site: www.NonviolentCommunication.com published by PuddleDancer Press. For more information go to www.CNVC. org or www.NonviolentCommunication.com

Child Welfare Information Gateway. "Child abuse and neglect fatalities: Statistics and interventions." Child Welfare Information Gateway Web site. http://www.childwelfare. gov/pubs/factsheets/fatality.cfm (accessed May 11, 2008).

————. "Promoting healthy families in your community." Prevent Child Abuse Web site. http://www.preventchildabuse.org/publications/cap/downloads/ CAP_2007_Packet.pdf (accessed May 11, 2008).

"Protective Factors for Promoting Healthy Families". Children's Bureau (HHS), Child Welfare Information Gateway, & FRIENDS National Resource Center for Community-Based Child Abuse Prevention (2008), http://www.childwelfare.gov/can/factors/protective.cfm (accessed Sept.9, 2008)

Childhelp. "National child abuse statistics" (2005), Childhelp Web site. http://www.childhelp. org/resources/learning-center/statistics (accessed May 11, 2008).

Children's Defense Fund. "America's cradle to prison pipeline, 2007 report." Children's Defense Fund Web site. http://www.childrensdefense.org/site/PageServer?pagename=c2pp_report2007 (accessed May 11, 2008).

Chopra, Deepak, David Simon, and Vicki Abrams. *Magical Beginnings, Enchanted Lives*. New York, NY: Three Rivers Press, 2005.

Cleeton, Elaine R. "Attitudes and beliefs about childbirth among college students: Results of an educational intervention." *Birth: Issues in Perinatal Care* 28(3): 192–201.

Coloroso, Barbara. *Kids Are Worth It!: Giving Your Child the Gift of Inner Discipline.* New York, NY: HarperCollins Publishers, 2002.

Coalition for Improving Maternity Services. "Ten steps of the mother-friendly childbirth initiative for mother-friendly hospitals, birth centers, and home birth services." Coalition for Improving Maternity Services Web site. http://www.motherfriendly.org/pdf/MFCI_english.pdf (accessed May 18, 2008).

Commission on Children at Risk. *Hardwired to Connect: The New Scientific Case for Authoritative Communities.* New York, NY: Institute for American Values, 2003.

Conde-Agudelo, A., J. Diaz-Rossello, and J. Belizan. 2003. "Kangaroo mother care to reduce morbidity and mortality in low birthweight infants." *Cochrane Database of Systematic Reviews* 2, CD002771.

Coombs, R. H., and J. Landsverk. 1988. "Parenting styles and substance use during childhood and adolescence." *Journal of Marriage and the Family* 50(2): 473–482.

Cox, M. J., B. Paley, C. C. Payne, and M. Burchinal. "The transition to parenthood: Marital conflict and withdrawal and parent-infant interactions." In *Conflict and Cohesion in Families: Causes and Consequences*, edited by M. J. Cox and J. Brooks-Gunn. Mahwah, NJ: Lawrence Erlbaum, 1999.

Cummings, E. M., and A. Wilson. "Contexts of marital conflict and children's emotional security: Exploring the distinction between constructive and destructive conflict from the children's perspective." In *Conflict and Cohesion in Families: Causes and Consequences*, edited by M. J. Cox and J. Brooks-Gunn, 87–104. Mahwah, New Jersey: Lawrence Erlbaum, 1999.

Dalai Lama, "Quotes by His Holiness the Dalai lama," http://www.rudyh.org/dalai-lama-quotes-quotations.htm.

DaSilva, N. 2008. "The AP Father." *Attachment Parenting: The Journal of API.* In Press.

Davis, M. K. 1988. "Infant feeding and childhood cancer." *The Lancet* 13;2(8607): 365–368.

De Wolff, Marianne S., and Marinus H. van Ijzendoorn. 1997. "Sensitivity and attachment: A meta-analysis on parental antecedents of attachment." *Child Development* 68(4): 571–591.

DeCasper, A. J., and W. P. Fifer. 1980. "Of human bonding: Newborns prefer their mother's voices." *Science* 208: 1174–1176.

Declercq, E. R., C. Sakala, M. P. Corry, and S. Applebaum. "Executive Summary." In *Listening to Mothers II: Report of the Second National Survey of Women's Childbearing Experiences*. New York, NY: Childbirth Connection, 2006.

Dick, G. 1976. "The etiology of multiple sclerosis." *Proceedings of the Royal Society of Medicine* 69: 611–615.

Dornbusch, Sanford M., Philip L. Ritter, P. Herbert Leiderman, Donald F. Roberts, and Michael J. Fraleigh. 1987. "The relation of parenting style to adolescent school performance." *Child Development* 58(5): 1244–1257.

Dunham, Carroll. *Mamatoto.* New York, NY: Penguin Books, 1991.

Eisenberg, Nancy, R. Lennon, and K. Roth. 1983. "Prosocial development in Childhood: A longitudinal study." *Developmental Psychology* 9(6): 846–855.

Eisenberg-Berg, Nancy, and Paul Mussen. 1978. "Empathy and moral development in adolescence." *Developmental Psychology* 14(2): 185–186.

Else-Quest, Nichole M., Janet Shibley Hyde, and Roseanne Clark. 2003. "Breastfeeding, bonding, and the mother-infant relationship." *Merrill-Palmer Quarterly* 49(4): 495–517.

Emery, Robert E. 1982. "Interparental conflict and the children of divorce and discord." *Psychological Bulletin* 92(2): 310–330.

Enkin, Murray, Marc Keirse, and I. Chalmers. *A Guide to Effective Care in Pregnancy and Childbirth.* New York, NY: Oxford University Press, 1992.

"Family structure, father closeness, and drug abuse: A report from National Fatherhood Initiative." National Fatherhood Initiative Web site. http://www.fatherhood.org/ research.asp (accessed April 19, 2008).

Feldman, Ruth, Aron Weller, Arthur I. Eidelman, and Lea Sirota. 2002. "Comparison of skin-to-skin (kangaroo) and traditional

care: Parenting outcomes and preterm infant development."
Pediatrics 110(1): 16–26.

Field, Tiffany M. 1994. "The effects of mothers' physical and emotional unavailability on emotion regulation." *Monographs of the Society for Research in Child Development* 59(2-3): 208–227.

————. 1993. "Infant massage." *Zero to Three* 14: 2.

Fleiss, Paul. 1999. "Pillow talk: Helping your child get a good night's sleep." *Mothering* 96. Available at http://www.mothering.com/articles/new_baby/sleep/ fleiss.html.

Fleming, Peter. 2002. "Where should babies sleep at night?" *Mothering* 114: 68–69.

Fonagy, Peter, Howard Steele, and Miriam Steele. 1991. "Maternal representations of attachment during pregnancy predict the organization of infant-mother attachment at one year of age." *Child Development* 62(5): 891–905.

Forbes, J. F., D. S. Weiss, and R. A. Folen. 1992. "The cosleeping habits of military children." *Military Medicine* 157: 196–200.

Ford, R. P., B. J. Taylor, E. A. Mitchell, S. A. Enright, A. W. Stewart, D. M. Becroft, R. Scragg, I. B. Hassall, D. M. Barry, and E. M. Allen. 1993. "Breastfeeding and the risk of sudden infant death syndrome." *International Journal of Epidemiology* 22: 885–890.

Fraiberg, Selma. *In Defense of Mothering: Every Child's Birthright.* New York, NY: Basic Books, 1997.

"Frequently asked questions." Infant Massage USA Web site. http://www.infantmassageusa. org/imusa/faq.shtml (accessed May 11, 2008).

Freud, Sigmund. *The Schreber Case.* New York, NY: Penguin Books, 2003.

Freudenheim, Jo L., James R. Marshall, Saxon Graham, Rosemary Laughlin, John E. Vena, Elisa Bandera, Paola Muti, Mya Swanson, and Takuma Nemoto. 1994. "Exposure to breast milk in infancy and the risk of breast cancer." *Epidemiology* 5: 324–331.

Gerhardt, Sue. *Why Love Matters: How Affection Shapes a Baby's Brain.* New York, NY: Brunner-Routledge, 2004.

Gershoff, Elizabeth T. 2002. "Corporal punishment by parents and associated child behaviors and experiences: A meta-analytic and theoretical review." *Psychological Bulletin* 128(4): 539–579.

Goldstein, Lauren H., Marissa L. Diener, and Sarah C. Mangelsdorf. 1996. "Maternal characteristics and social support across the transition to motherhood: Association with maternal behavior." *Journal of Family Psychology* 10(1): 60–72.

Gordon, Jay. "Changing the sleep pattern in the family bed." Dr. Jay Gordon's Web site. http://www.drjaygordon.com/development/ap/sleep.asp (accessed February 16, 2008).

———, and Brenda Adderly. *Brighter Baby: Boost Your Child's Intelligence, Health, and Happiness through Infant Therapeutic Massage, the Mozart Effect, and More.* Washington, DC: Lifeline Press, 1999.

Gordon, Macall. 2001. "Breaking the ties that bind." *API News* 4: 1.

———. 2000. "The mommy marathon." *API News* 3(2): 8–9.

Gottman Institute. "Bringing baby home." The Gottman Institute Web site. http://www.gottman.com/parenting/baby (accessed June 8, 2008).

Gottman, John M. *The Heart of Parenting.* New York, NY: Simon and Schuster, 1997.

———, and Joan DeClaire. *Raising an Emotionally Intelligent Child.* New York, NY: Simon and Schuster, 1997.

———, and Julie Schwartz Gottman. *And Baby Makes Three: The Six-Step Plan for Preserving Marital Intimacy and Rekindling Romance After Baby Arrives.* New York, NY: Crown Publishers, 2007.

Graham, Yolanda P., Christine Heim, Sherryl H. Goodman, Andrew H. Miller, and Charles B. Nemeroff. 1999. "The effects of neonatal stress on brain development: Implications for psychopathology." *Development and Psychopathology* 11(3): 545–565.

Gray, L., L. Watt, and E. M. Blass. 2000. "Skin-to-skin contact is analgesic in healthy newborns." *Pediatrics* 105: e14.

Greven, Phillip. *Spare the Child: The Religious Roots of Punishment and the Psychological Impact of Physical Abuse.* New York, NY: Vintage Books, 1992.

Greenspan, Stanley I. *The Four-Thirds Solution: Solving the Child-Care Crisis in America Today*. Cambridge, MA: Perseus Publishing, 2001.

Grille, Robin. 2003. "Democracy begins at home." *Empathic Parenting: Journal of the Canadian Society for the Prevention of Cruelty to Children* 26(1): 11.

Hanessian, Lu. 2007. "Chaos theory." *Attachment Parenting: The Journal of API* 10(1): 10–11.

Hariri, Ahmad R., Susan Y. Bookheimer, and John C. Mazziotta. 2000. "Modulating emotional responses: Effects of a neocortical network on the limbic system." *NeuroReport* 11(1): 43–48.

Hartley, Mariette. *Breaking the Silence*. New York, NY: Signet Books, 1990.

Hartney, Christopher. "US rates of incarceration: A global perspective." National Council on Crime and Delinquency Web site. http://www.nccd-crc.org/nccd/pubs/2006nov_factsheet_incarceration.pdf (accessed May 12, 2008).

Heller, Sharon. *The Vital Touch*. New York, NY: Henry Holt and Co., 1997.

Hendrix, Harville, and Helen Hunt. *Giving the Love that Heals: A Guide for Parents*. New York, NY: Pocket Books, 1997.

Hess, R., and K. Camera. 1979. "Post-divorce family relationships as mediating factors in the consequences of divorce for children." *Journal of Social Issues* 35: 79–96.

Hunziker, Urs A., and Ronald G. Barr. 1986. "Increased carrying reduces infant crying: A randomized controlled trial." *Pediatrics* 77: 641–648.

Isabella, Russell A., and Jay Belsky. 1991. "Interactional synchrony and the origins of infant-mother attachment: A replication study." *Child Development* 62(2): 373–385.

Jackson, Christine, Donna J. Bee-Gates, and Lisa Henriksen. 1994. "Authoritative parenting, child competencies, and initiation of cigarette smoking." *Health Education Quarterly* 21(1): 103–116.

———, and Vangie A. Foshee. 1988. "Violence-related behaviors of adolescents: Relations with responsive and demanding parenting." *Journal of Adolescent Research* 13(3): 343–359.

Johnston, Janet R., M. Kline, and J. M. Tschann. 1989. "Ongoing postdivorce conflict: Effects on children of joint custody and frequent access." *American Journal of Orthopsychiatry* 59: 576–592.

Karen, Robert. *Becoming Attached*. New York, NY: Warner Books, 1994.

Karp, Harvey. *The Happiest Baby on the Block: The New Way to Calm Crying and Help Your Newborn Baby Sleep Longer*. New York, NY: Bantam Books, 2003.

Karras, Kaylene. 2005. "The ideal birth for the 'Naturally Birthing Challenged.'" *Attachment Parenting: The Journal of API* 8(2): 7.

Karr-Morse, Robin, and Meredith S. Wiley. *Ghosts from the Nursery*. New York, NY: Atlantic Monthly Press, 1997.

Kendall-Tackett, Kathleen. *Depression in New Mothers*. New York, NY: Hawthorn Press, 2003.

———. *The Hidden Feelings of Motherhood*. Oakland, CA: New Harbinger Publications, 2001.

———. 2007. "Practical steps toward achieving more balance in your life." *Attachment Parenting: The Journal of API* 10(1): 14–15.

Kimmel, Tina. 2002. "How the stats really stack up: Cosleeping is twice as safe." *Mothering* 114: 52–57.

Klaus, Marshall, John Kennell, and Phyllis Klaus. *Mothering the Mother*. Cambridge, MA: Perseus Books, 1993.

Kohn, Alfie. *Unconditional Parenting: Moving From Rewards and Punishment to Love and Reason*. New York, NY: Atria Books, 2005.

Leboyer, Frederick. *Birth without Violence*. New York, NY: Alfred A. Knopf, 1984.

Lerman, Y. 1994. "Epidemiology of acute diarrheal diseases in children in a high standard of living settlement in Israel." *Pediatric Infectious Diseases Journal* 13: 116–122.

Lester, Barry, C. F. Zachariah Boukydis, C. T. Garcia-Coll, M. Peucker, M. M. McGrath, B. R. Vohr, F. Brem, and W. Oh. 1995. "Developmental outcome as a function of the goodness of fit between the infant's cry characteristics and the mother's perception of her infant's cry." *Pediatrics* 95(4): 516–522.

Littlefield, Timothy R., Kevin M. Kelly, Jacque L. Reiff, and Jeanne K. Pomatto. 2003. "Car seats, infant carriers, and swings: Their role in deformational plagiocephaly." *Journal of Prosthetics and Orthotics* 15(3): 102–106.

Littman, Heidi, Sharon VanderBrug Medendorp, and Johanna Goldfarb. 1994. "The decision to breastfeed." *Clinical Pediatrics* 33: 214–219.

Lindgren, Astrid. "Never Violence." Alliance for Transforming the Lives of Children, http://www.atlc.org/Resources/never_violence. php.

Lockard, L. 2007. "Back to the future: How early attachments shape your relationships." *Attachment Parenting: The Journal of API* 10(3): 22.

———. 2007. "Mothering maven Martha Sears on balance." *Attachment Parenting: The Journal of API* 10(1): 1–3.

Lucas, A., R. Morley, T. J. Cole, G. Lister, and C. Leeson-Payne. 1992. "Breast milk and subsequent intelligence quotient in children born preterm." *The Lancet* 339(8788): 261–262.

Maccoby, E. E., and J. A. Martin. "Socialization in the context of the family: Parent-child interaction." In *Handbook of Child Psychology, Volume 4: Socialization, Personality, and Social Development,* edited by P. H. Mussen and E. M. Hetherington, 1–101. New York, NY: Wiley, 1983.

Magid, Ken, and Carol McKelvey. *High Risk: Children without a Conscience.* New York, NY: Bantam Books, 1987.

Mahal, Jennifer K. "Massaging baby induces bonding." *San Diego Union-Tribune.* May 3, 2008.

Mandansky, D., and C. Edelbrock. 1990. "Cosleeping in a community sample of 2- and 3-year-old children." *Pediatrics* 86: 197–203.

McCann, Donna, Angelina Barrett, Alison Cooper, Debbie Crumpler, Lindy Dalen, Kate Grimshaw, Elizabeth Kitchin, Kris Lok, Lucy Porteous, Emily Prince, Edmund Sonuga-Barke, John O. Warner, and Jim Stevenson. 2007. "Food additives and hyperactive behaviour in 3-year-old and 8/9-year-old children in the community: A randomised, double-blinded, placebo-controlled trial." *The Lancet* 370(9598): 1560–1567.

McClure, Vimala. *Infant Massage: A Handbook for Loving Parents*. New York, NY: Bantam Books, 2000.

McDonald, Timothy. "Lullabies help children's language development: study." ABCNews.com Web site. http://www.abc.net.au/news/stories/2007/12/07/2112889.htm?section=australia (accessed August 14, 2008).

McKenna, James. 1996. "Babies need their mothers beside them!" *World Health* 49: 14–16.

———. 2002. "An exclusive *Mothering* special report." *Mothering* 114: 8.

———. *Sleeping with Your Baby: A Parent's Guide to Cosleeping*. Washington, D.C.: Platypus Media, 2007.

———, E. B. Thoman, T. F. Anders, A. Sadeyh, V. L. Schechtman, and S. F. Glotzbach. 1993. "Infant-parent cosleeping in an evolutionary perspective: Implications for understanding infant sleep development and the sudden infant death syndrome." *American Sleep Disorders Association and Sleep Research Society* 16: 263–282.

"Medicating Kids." Program no. 1914K, first broadcast April 10, 2001 by PBS. Directed by Marcela Gaviria and written by Martin Smith.

Melender, Hanna-Leena. 2002. "Experiences of fears associated with pregnancy and childbirth: A study of 329 pregnant women." *Birth: Issues in Perinatal Care* 29(2): 101–111.

Mezzacappa, Elizabeth S., and Edward S. Katkin. 2002. "Breastfeeding is associated with reduced perceived stress and negative mood in mothers." *Health Psychology* 21(2): 187–191.

Midmer, D., L. Wilson, and S. Cummings. 1995. "A randomized controlled trial of the influence of prenatal parenting education on postpartum anxiety and marital adjustment." *Family Medicine* 27: 200–205.

Miller, Alice. *For Your Own Good: Hidden Cruelty in Child-Rearing and the Roots of Violence*. New York, NY: Farrar, Straus, and Giroux, 1990.

Montagu, Ashley. *Learning Non-Aggression: The Experience of Non-Literate Societies*. London, UK: Oxford University Press, 1978.

———. *Touching*. New York, NY: Harper and Row, 1986.

Mosko, Sarah, James McKenna, M. Dickel, and L. Hunt. 1993. "Parent-infant cosleeping: The appropriate context for the study of infant sleep and implications for sudden infant death syndrome (SIDS) research." *Journal of Behavioral Medicine* 16(6): 589–607.

————, Christopher Richard, and James McKenna. 1997. "Infant arousals during mother-infant bed sharing: Implications for infant sleep and sudden infant death syndrome research." *Pediatrics* 100(5): 841–850.

Mother Teresa. Quotes—Parent-Wise, http://parent-wise.org/parent/time/quotes.htm.

Nachmias, Melissa, Megan Gunnar, R. Hornik-Parritz, K. Buss, and S. Mangelsdorf. 1996. "Behavioral inhibition and stress reactivity: The moderating role of attachment security." *Child Development* 67(2): 508–522.

National Institute of Child Health and Human Development. 2003. "Does amount of time in child care predict socioemotional adjustment?" *Child Development* 74: 976–1005.

National Institute on Media and the Family. "Fact sheet: Children and advertising." National Institute on Media and the Family Web site. http://www.mediafamily.org/facts/ facts_childadv.shtml (accessed June 14, 2008).

————. "Families become MediaWise." National Institute on Media and the Family Web site. http://www.mediafamily.org/earlychild/index.shtml (accessed June 14, 2008).

————. "Tip sheet: Twelve tips to tame the tube." National Institute on Media and the Family Web site. http://www.mediafamily.org/facts/ tips_tametube.shtml (accessed June 14, 2008).

Neufeld, Gordon, and Gabor Maté. *Hold On to Your Kids: Why Parents Need to Matter More Than Peers.* New York, NY: Ballantine Books, 2006.

Newberger, Eli. *The Men They Will Become: The Nature and Nurture of Male Character.* Cambridge, MA: Perseus Books, 1999.

Newcomb, Polly A., Barry E. Storer, Matthew P. Longnecker, Robert Mittendorf, E. Robert Greenberg, Richard W. Clapp, Kenneth P. Burke, Walter C. Willett, and Brian MacMahon. 1994. "Lactation and a reduced risk of premenopausal breast cancer." *New England Journal of Medicine* 330(2): 81–87.

O'Mara, Peggy. *Having a Baby Naturally.* New York, NY: Atria Books, 2003.

Palmer, Linda F. 2004. "The chemistry of attachment." *Attachment Parenting: The Journal of API* Annual New Baby Issue: 9.

Pantley, Elizabeth. *Gentle Baby Care.* New York, NY: McGraw-Hill, 2003.

Parker, Lysa. 2005. "The greatest gifts we can give our children: An interview with Dr. Jim McKenna." *Attachment Parenting: The Journal of API* 8(1): 1–5.

———. 2006. "Happy being blue." *Attachment Parenting: The Journal of API* 9(1): 1–3.

Patterson, G. R., Barbara D. DeBaryshe, and Elizabeth Ramsey. 1989. "A developmental perspective in antisocial behavior." *American Psychologist* 44(2); 329–335.

Perry, Bruce. 2002. "Childhood experience and the expression of genetic potential: What childhood neglect tells us about nature and nurture." *Brain and Mind* 3: 79–100.

———, and Brown-O'Connor, M., Runyan, D., Walter, G., Rubenstein, J., Relationships between early experiences and long term functioning: The role of affect development in adjudicated adolescent males. (1998). 2 Feb. 2002, www.childtrauma.org/apsac_rel_between_early_exp.htm

———, and Maia Szalavitz. *The Boy Who Was Raised as a Dog.* New York, NY: Basic Books, 2006.

Pert, Candace B. *Molecules of Emotion.* New York, NY: Scribner, 1997.

Phillips, D., Professor of Psychology and Associated Faculty, Public Policy Institute, Georgetown University. Testimony before the U.S. Senate Committee on Labor and Human Resources. March 1, 1995.

Pollack, William. *Real Boys: Rescuing Our Sons from the Myths of Boyhood.* New York, NY: Owl Books, 1999.

Punger, Denise. 2005. "A physician's personal experience with a doula." *Attachment Parenting: The Journal of API* Annual New Baby Issue: 3.

Reiss, David, Jenae M. Neiderhiser, E. Mavis Hetherington, and Robert Plomin. *The Relationship Code: Deciphering Genetic and*

Social Influences on Adolescent Development. Cambridge, MA: Harvard University Press, 2000.

Rey, E., and H. Martínez. "Manejo racional del niño prematuro. [Rational management of the premature infant]." In *Curso de medicina fetal y neonatal.* Bogotá, Colombia: Universidad Nacional, 1983.

Ruiz-Peláez, Juan G., Nathalie Charpak, and Lius G. Cuervo. 2004. "Kangaroo mother care: An example to follow from developing countries." *British Medical Journal* 329(7475): 1179–1181.

Sagi, A., N. Koren-Karie, M. Gini, Y. Ziv, and T. Joels. 2002. "Shedding further light on the effects of various types and quality of early childcare on infant-mother attachment relationship: The Haifa Study of early child care." *Child Development* 73(4): 1166–1187.

Saunder, S. 1998. "Co-bathing as a gentle solution for attachment difficulties." *British Journal of Midwifery* 1(11): 716–719.

Schanberg, Saul M., and Tiffany M. Field. 1987. "Sensory deprivation stress and supplemental stimulation in the rat pup and preterm human neonate." *Child Development* 58(6): 1431–1447.

Schore, Allan N. 1996. "The experience-dependent maturation of a regulatory system in the orbital prefrontal cortex and the origin of developmental psychopathology." *Development and Psychopathology* 8: 59–87.

———, *Affect Dysregulation and Disorders of the Self.* New York: W.W. Norton & Co. 2003.

Schwartzbaum, Judith A., Stephen L. George, Charles B. Pratt, and Bertha Davis. 1991. "An exploratory study of environmental and medical factors potentially related to childhood cancer." *Medical and Pediatric Oncology* 19(2): 115–121.

Sears, William. 2004. "Bonding with your newborn." *Attachment Parenting: The Journal of API* Annual New Baby Issue: 2.

Sears, William, and Martha Sears. *The Attachment Parenting Book.* New York, NY: Little, Brown and Company, 2001.

———. "Discipline and behavior: Spanking." AskDrSears.com Web site. http://www. askdrsears.com/html/6/t062100.asp (accessed May 5, 2008).

———. *Nighttime Parenting.* Chicago, IL: La Leche League International, 1999.

Shaffer, David R. *Developmental Psychology: Childhood and Adolescence.* Pacific Grove, CA: Brookes/Cole Publishing, 1999.

Shaw, Benjamin A., Neal Krause, Linda M. Chatters, Cathleen M. Connell, and Berit Ingersoll-Dayton. 2004. "Emotional support from parents early in life, aging, and health." *Psychology and Aging* 19(1): 4–12.

Siddiqui, B., and M. E. Hagglöf. 1999. "An exploration of prenatal attachment in Swedish expectant women." *Journal of Reproductive and Infant Psychology* 17(4): 369–380.

Sidebotham, P., and the Avon Longitudinal Study of Parents and Children (ALSPAC). 2001. "Culture, stress, and the parent-child relationship: A qualitative study of parents' perceptions." *Child: Care, Health, and Development* 27(6): 469–485.

Siegel, Daniel. *The Developing Mind: How Relationships and the Brain Interact to Shape Who We Are.* New York, NY: The Guilford Press, 1999.

———, and Mary Hartzell. *Parenting from the Inside Out.* New York, NY: Tarcher, 2004.

Silver, Amy. 2004. "Interview with Reedy and P. J. Hickey." *Attachment Parenting: The Journal of API* 7(2): 1.

———. 2004. "Slings and attachment parenting." *Attachment Parenting: The Journal of API* 7(2): 2.

St. James-Roberts, Ian, Jane Hurry, J. Bowyer, and R. G. Barr. 1995. "Supplementary carrying compared with advice to increase responsive parenting as interventions to prevent persistent infant crying." *Pediatrics* 95(3): 381–388.

Stein, M. T., and J. D. Call. 2001. "Extraordinary changes in behavior in an infant after a brief separation." *Journal of Developmental and Behavioral Pediatrics* 22: 11–12.

Steinberg, Laurence, Julie D. Elmen, and Nina S. Mounts. 1989. "Authoritative parenting, psychosocial maturity, and academic success among adolescents." *Child Development* 60(6): 1424–1436.

———, Susie D. Lamborn, S. M. Dornbusch, and N. Darling. 1992. "Impact of parenting practices on adolescent achievement:

Authoritative parenting, school involvement, and encouragement to succeed." *Child Development* 63(5): 1266–1281.

Stewart, David, and Lee Stewart. 1985, "Childrearing, the roots of violence, and the principles of peace." *NAPSAC News* 10(2): 15.

Straus, Murray A. *Beating the Devil Out of Them: Corporal Punishment in American Families.* New York, NY: Lexington Books, 1994.

———, and Vera E. Mouradian. 1998. "Impulsive corporal punishment by mothers and antisocial behavior and impulsiveness of children." *Behavioral Sciences and the Law* 16(3): 353–374.

———, D. B. Sugarman, and J. Giles-Sims. 1997. "Spanking by parents and subsequent antisocial behavior of children." *Archives of Pediatric and Adolescent Medicine* 151: 761–767.

Sunderland, Margot. *The Science of Parenting.* New York, NY: DK Publishing Inc., 2006.

Tanzer, Deborah. *Why Natural Childbirth?* Garden City, NY: Doubleday, 1972.

Tarkka, Marja-Terttu. 2002. "Predictors of maternal competence by first-time mothers when the child is 8 months old: Issues and innovations in nursing practice." *Journal of Advanced Nursing* 41(3): 233–240.

———, Marita Paunonen, and Pekka Laippala. 1998. "What contributes to breastfeeding success after childbirth in a maternity ward in Finland?" *Birth: Issues in Perinatal Care* 25: 175–181.

"Ten steps of the mother-friendly childbirth initiative for mother-friendly hospitals, birth centers, and home birth services." The Coalition for Improving Maternity Services Web site. http://www.motherfriendly.org/MFCI/steps.html (accessed May 11, 2008).

"The ten steps to successful breastfeeding." Baby Friendly Hospital Initiative Web site. http://www.babyfriendlyusa.org/eng/10steps.html (accessed May 11, 2008).

"The Cornelians." *Time* magazine Web site. http://www.time.com/time/magazine/article /0,9171,855434,00.html?iid=chix-sphere (accessed May 11, 2008).

Thomas, Eleanor M. 2004. "Aggressive behaviour outcomes for young children: Change in parenting environment predicts change in behaviour." *Statistics Canada* Catalogue no. 89-599-MIE.

Available at http://www.statcan.ca/english/research/89-599-MIE/89-599-MIE2004001.pdf (accessed June 20, 2008).

U.S. Department of Labor, Bureau of Labor Statistics. *Women in the Labor Force: A Databook*. Washington, DC: U.S. Department of Labor, 2005.

Uvnäs-Moberg, Kerstin. *The Oxytocin Factor*. Translated by Roberta Francis. Cambridge, MA: Da Capo Press, 2003.

————, and M. Eriksson. 1996. "Breastfeeding: Physiological, endocrine, and behavioural adaptations caused by oxytocin and local neurogenic activity in the nipple and mammary gland." *Acta Paediatrica* 85: 525–530.

Walant, Karen B. *Creating the Capacity for Attachment: Treating Addictions and the Alienated Self.* Northvale, NJ: Jason Aronson Inc., 1995.

Wallerstein, Judith, Julia M. Lewis, and Sandra Blakeslee. *The Unexpected Legacy of Divorce: A 25 Year Landmark Study*. New York, NY: Hyperion, 2000.

Watson, John B. *Psychological Care of Infant and Child*. New York, NY: W.W. Norton, 1928.

Weisfeld, G.E., *Principles of Human Adolescence*. New York, NY: Basic Books, 1999.

Weiss, Bahr, Kenneth A. Dodge, J. E. Bates, and G. S. Pettit. 1992. "Some consequences of early harsh discipline: Child aggression and maladaptive social information processing style." *Child Development* 63(6): 1321–1335.

"What Is a Doula?" DONA International Web site. http://www.dona.org/mothers (accessed May 13, 2008).

Widström, A. M., A. B. Ransjo-Arvidson, K. Christensson, A. S. Matthiesen, J. Winberg, and K. Uvnäs-Moberg. 1987. "Gastric suction in healthy newborn infants: Effects on circulation and developing feeding behaviour." *Acta Paediatrica Scandinavica* 76: 566–572.

Witman-Flann, L. 1991. "Parent-child cosleeping: The impact on family relationships." *Dissertation Abstracts International*.

World Health Organization. "Breastfeeding." World Health Organization Web site. http://www.who.int/child_adolescent_

health/topics/prevention_care/child/nutrition/breastfeeding/en/ (accessed June 17, 2008).

———. *Global Strategy for Infant and Young Child Feeding.* Geneva, Switzerland: WHO, 2002.

Young, T. K., P. J. Martens, S. P. Taback, E. A. Sellers, H. J. Dean, M. Cheang, and B. Flette. 2002. "Type 2 diabetes mellitus in children: Prenatal and early infancy risk factors among native Canadians." *Archives of Pediatric and Adolescent Medicine* 156(7): 651–655.

Zahn-Waxler, Carolyn, Marian Radke-Yarrow, and Robert A. King. 1979. "Child rearing and children's prosocial initiations toward victims of distress." *Child Development* 50(2): 319–330.

Zhou, Qing, Nancy Eisenberg, Sandra H. Losoya, Richard A. Fabes, Mark Reiser, Ivanna K. Guthrie, Bridget C. Murphy, Amanda J. Cumberland, and Stephanie A. Shepard. 2002. "The relations of parental warmth and positive expressiveness to children's empathy-related responding and social functioning: A longitudinal study." *Child Development* 73(3): 893–915.

Index

A

abuse
  child death and, 14
  definition of, 15
  physical, 213. *See also*
    punishments
  sexual, 162
action language, positive, 225
"adaptive behavior," 207
adoption, challenges in, 114
adult relationships, 259, 296
Adventures in Tandem Nursing:
    Breastfeeding during
    Pregnancy and Beyond
    (La Leche League
    International), 75
affirmative language, 229
Ainsworth, Mary, 19–20
American Academy of Pediatrics
    (AAP), 79, 158, 161
  baby sleeping guidelines,
    174–175
  breastfeeding policy
    statement (2005), 82
  cosleeping safe practice
    guidelines, 154
amygdala, 183
And Baby Makes Three (Gottman
    and Gottman), 57–58
anger
  of parents, 211, 242
  spanking and, 242
  story about controlling,
    222–223

Anisfeld, Elizabeth, 138
API. *See* Attachment Parenting
    International (API)
apologies, offered to children,
    211, 234
appreciation. *See also* love
  maintaining positive
    marital relationship
    through, 252
  shown to partner, 254
artificial milk. *See* bottle-feeding
asking questions, 262
attachment, relationship with
    infant
  adoption and, 114
  brain and, 16–17
  bottle-feeding and, 75-77
  breastfeeding, foundation
    for. *See* breastfeeding
  categories of, 21–22
  concept of, 16
attachment behavioral system,
    158
attachment categories
  insecure-ambivalent, 21
  insecure-avoidant, 21
  insecure-disorganized/
    disoriented, 22
  secure, 21
attachment parenting
  adoption and, 114
  babywearing, importance
    of. *See* babywearing
  balancing relationship,

behavior modification, 279

behaviors

corporal punishment, 214

physical discipline and fear, 213

Being There: The Benefits of a Stay-at-Home Parent (Fox), 185

beliefs

attachment parenting practices, 216

discipline methods, 15

Bellevue Hospital, New York, 127

Belsky, Jay, 252

Bengson, Diane, 84

Bergman, Nils, 132

Better Homes and Gardens (magazine), 24

Blakeslee, Sandra, 193

bonding, and attachment, 16

books, 259, 284

bottle-feeding

bottle-propping dangers, 75–76

bottle-warming guidelines, 71

compared to breastfeeding, 74

mother's story about, 76

sensitivity to baby's cues and, 70

tips for, 75

weaning from, 84

"bottle nursing," 75–76

benefits of, 76–77

boundaries, establishing, 212–213

Bowlby, John, 19, 20, 21

"boy code," 112

boys. *See also* older children

close relationship with parents, impact on, 112–113

conventional perceptions about, 112

brain development

attachment and, 17, 100

consciousness and, 206–207

distress tantrums in, 229–230

effect of stress, 183–184

parents' role in, 101

prefrontal cortex, 206–207

REM sleep and, 153

"use it or lose it" principle, 16–17

brain imaging techniques, 182, 207

brain pathways, 229–230

brain research, child behavior, 17, 100, 207

Bradley Method, childbirth, 43

Brazelton, T. Berry, 182

Breaking the Silence (Hartley), 12

break time, 263

breastfeeding

adoptive mothers, 52

advantages of, 71–72

baby nursing and, 51–52

bottle-feeding compared

mammal species
    cache, 129
    carry, 129–130
"marasmus," 126
Maslow, Abraham, 43
massage
    advantages of, 134–137
    by fathers, 133
    by friends, 250
    as way to reconnect with baby, 190
Maté, Gabor, 84–85, 208, 220
materialism, 292
McClure, Vimala, 133
McKenna, James, 157, 163, 174
mealtime, benefits of, 84–85
memory, intrinsic, 183
Miller, Alice, 25–26
misbehavior, 221. *See also* behaviors
mistakes, learning from, 211
Moloney. James Clark, 23–24
"mommy wars," 248
Montagu, Ashley, 22, 68, 126–127, 283
mother-friendly childbirth initiative, 39–41
Mothering Multiples (Gromada), 163
Mothering the Mother (Klaus et al.), 46
mothers. *See also* mammalian mothers
    breastfeeding, decisions about, 51–52. *See also* breastfeeding
    child's emotional needs,

    meeting, 98–100
    importance of touch and, 128–129
    new, 265
    nurturing, 78
    parenting criticism, 284
    pregnancy, tips on. *See* pregnancy
    VBAC, benefiting, 50
mother's helper, 254, 263

N
naps, 264
National Institute on Media and the Family, 289
natural childbirth
    attachment parenting and, 37–38
    education classes for, 43, 44–45
    "peak experience" in, 43–44
    six care practices for, 45–46
natural consequences, 229
nature and nurture, 16–18
networking, 295
Neufeld, Gordon, 84–85, 208, 213, 220, 226
neurobiology, 182. *See also* brain development
new mothers, 265
nightmares, 170
night terrors, 170
Nighttime Parenting (Sears), 153
nighttime routines
    for infants, 165

for older children, 166–
168
night waking, 170–171
nonbiological parent, cosleeping
with, 161–162
nonmaternal care, 181
*Nonviolent Communication:
A Language of Life*
(Rosenberg), 265
Nonviolent Communication
(NVC)
components of, 225
primary goal of, 224
teaching adults to express
feelings, 109
"normative abuse," 10, 14–15
"no," saying, 211, 262
nursing
comfort, 71
as mothering tool, 71
tandem, 74–75
nutritious food, 81, 263
NVC. *See* Nonviolent
Communication (NVC)

O

observations, as components of
NVC program, 225
obstetricians, 31
offering choices, 235
Okinawan, The (film), 24
Okinawan style of parenting,
23–24
older children
finding balance with,
266–267
nighttime routines for,

166–168
transitioning out of
family bed, 168–169
O'Mara, Peggy, 37
one-on-one time, 262
oxytocin, 73, 272–273

P

parent-child relationship. *See also*
attachment parenting
in changing environment,
20
repairing damage by
parents, 211
strengthening, 4
parenting books, 184, 259
parenting classes, 252
Parenting in the Workplace
Institute in
Framingham,
Massachusetts, 188
parenting philosophy, 218–219
parenting practices
attachment, 5–6
culturally accepted,
impact of, 10–11
multicultural influences
and, 22–26
mother's story on, 117–
119
Okinawan style of, 23–24
principles of, 28–29
Watson's theory, impact
on, 11–12
parents/parenting
advice to, on sleeping
training, 174–175

advantages of, 43–44
definition of, 43
pediatricians
    advice of, 287
    baby sleeping guidelines, 174–175
    carried babies, concerned about, 139
    vaccination decision, discussing, 56
Perry, Bruce, 127–128
personal experience, of raising children, 281
physical discipline
    emotional problems, 214
    fear of punishing, 213
plagiocephaly, 75, 139
plays, imaginative, 228
positive action language, 225
positive discipline. *See* discipline
positive relationship, NVC use in, 226
postpartum depression, 55, 72, 252
postpartum psychosis, 55, 72
praise, overuse of, 236–237
prefrontal cortex, 206–207
pregnancy
    planning for baby and, 35
    breastfeeding decisions, 51–52. *See also* breastfeeding
    childbirth options, 37–38
    emotional highs and lows of, 52–53
    healthy, tips for, 50–51

parents and, 34, 54–55
Pregnancy Risk Assessment Monitoring System (PRAMS), CDC, 159
Preparing for baby
    early childbirth education and, 61
    emotional preparation and, 35–36
    healthy lifestyle, 35
    spiritual growth and, 36–37
Psychological Care of Infant and Child (Watson), 11
punishments
    connections, 222
    control, 219–220
    fear of, 213
    reasons for not working, 221
    spanking, 221

Q
"quiet sleep," periods of, 153

R
Reiss, David, 18
Relationship Code, The (Reiss), 18
Relationship Research Institute in Seattle, Washington, 248, 252
religions
    positive discipline in, 218–219
    treating fellow human beings, 218
REM (rapid eye movement)

LaVergne, TN USA
15 November 2009
164202LV00005B/89/P